COMMENTARY
ON
THE OLD TESTAMENT

THE
BOOK OF JOSHUA

by
DANIEL STEELE, D.D.

D. D. WHEDON, LL.D., EDITOR

SCHMUL PUBLISHING CO.

Published by Schmul Publishing Co.
PO Box 716
Salem, Ohio USA

Printed in the United States of America

Printed by Old Paths Tract Society
RR2, Box 43
Shoals, Indiana 47581

ISBN 0-88019-409-X

PREFACE.

THE present volume is one of a series intended to furnish a Manual Commentary on the Old Testament corresponding with Whedon's on the New. It is designed, in accordance with the plan of the entire series, to be strictly and concisely exegetical; treating the true text of Scripture as divinely inspired and authoritative, and embodying the latest results of sound biblical criticism and research.

The Notes on Joshua and the first three chapters of Judges were first prepared by Dr. Steele; but, under the pressure of numerous official duties as Professor and Vice-President of the Syracuse University, he felt unable to complete Judges and revise Joshua without greatly delaying the work. Upon his recommendation, and by approval of the general Editor, the entire volume, with Dr. Steele's manuscript, was assigned to the present writer to prepare for the press. In this final revision many changes have been made both by erasure and addition. The principal additions are inclosed in brackets [-] and braces { - }, the latter designating notes added by the general Editor. Special thanks are due to Dr. Strong, of Drew Theological Seminary, for many valuable suggestions.

All accessible works, ancient and modern, bearing on this portion of Holy Scripture, have been duly consulted.

INTRODUCTION TO THE BOOK OF JOSHUA.

General Character of the Historical Books.

IN the Hebrew Canon the Book of Joshua is the first of the *Prior Prophets*, which division comprises the Books of Joshua, Judges, Samuel, and Kings. These books were probably so named because they were written by prophets, and are so largely devoted to the history and work of the prophetical order in Israel And a deeper reason may be found in the fact that they are a history written from the prophetic or theocratic stand-point. In the arrangement of books in our English Bible they form, together with Ruth, Chronicles, Ezra, Nehemiah, and Esther, the division appropriately called the "Historical Books of the Old Testament;" but they contain THEOCRATIC HISTORY, and through them all, as through the other Scriptures, runs a unity of purpose and of general form in which we may trace the gradual unfolding of the plan of man's redemption. None but prophets could write such books as these; none but those who have communion and fellowship with the Holy Spirit can read them with proper appreciation. The inspired penmen wrote not in order to preserve great historical facts from oblivion, nor to furnish an exhaustive record of their times and people, but to show the hand of God in all the affairs of men—Jehovah in history

Very noticeable is the anonymous character of these sacred books. The writers sought not to immortalize themselves as authors, nor seem they to have once thought that their readers in after times would be curious to know their names. But, whether conscious or unconscious of the purpose they were serving, they have written books of instruction for all time. More than a hundred generations have already found them "profitable for doctrine, for reproof, for correction, for instruction in righteousness."

We are not to suppose that these writers attempted to compose an *original* history, in the modern sense: still less should we presume to test the value of these ancient records by the standard of modern historical composition, or assume that in any event the narrator has given us a full account of all he knew. The sacred writers evidently had within their reach a large number of books and documents, from which they gathered such material as suited their purpose. Old documents, such as genealogical tables, songs, public addresses, and perhaps, in some cases, narratives of particular events, were transferred entire, or with slight modification, to their pages. Sometimes the writer acknowledged his sources of information or of quotation, and sometimes not. It serves no useful purpose to attempt, with De Wette, Ewald, and other kindred spirits, to decide on purely subjective grounds the date and authorship of all the ancient sources from which the present books of Scripture were compiled. The results of such criticism are at best only a confusing mass of more or less plausible conjectures.

The biblical writers often omit the details of many interesting facts of which they evidently had abundant knowledge, and aim to give prominence to such persons and events as noticeably helped or hindered the cause of divine truth. Thus Keil truly says: "All the efforts of the people to perfect trades, arts, and sciences, also domestic, municipal, and political arrangements, are either passed over entirely, or are intimated briefly, and only in so far as they stand in connexion with the higher aims of the theocracy." Hence they are truly a sacred history, and not merely a secular history of a chosen race. But while magnifying the wonders of the Lord's hand, there is ample reason for believing that they never deviate from the strictest fidelity to fact. They seek to hide no sin of their immortal heroes, nor to cover any reproach that ever visited the chosen people. And herein lies much of the real greatness and imperishable worth of these inspired histories.

As to the general *style* of the Hebrew historians, several peculiarities in the matter of arrangement and chronology are very noticeable, and attention to them will often obviate difficulties which some critics have been prone to magnify. The exact order of events is often disregarded, and facts with their moral lessons are made prominent, as if the writer took it for granted that his readers would either know the order of events, or at least need no information on that point. The very fact that the Hebrew language has only two tenses, past and future, is evidence of a lack of precision among the Hebrews in their habits of designating time and the succession of events. In commencing a narrative the Old Testament writers sometimes announce a summary, or else the result of the whole affair, and then go on to record details in a way that might easily lead to the impression that they had passed on to narrate other events, when in fact they are only enlarging on the details of events already in substance told. At other times they anticipate events, and record them out of their proper chronological order because they are associated, in place, name, or other circumstance, with what the writer has at the time in hand. Hence the order in which a series of events is narrated is not in all cases a certain guide to the chronology of the several events.

The Historical Books, and other parts of the Old Testament Canon, contain much internal evidence to show that they were edited and arranged in their present form by a later hand. An ancient and very probable tradition assigns that work to Ezra and the Great Synagogue.

Name, Author, and Date.

The Book of Joshua takes its name from the great hero whose achievements in the conquest and settlement of the Promised Land it records. "It is not often," says Stanley, "either in sacred or common history, that we are justified in pausing on anything so outward, and usually so accidental, as a name. But if ever there be an exception, it is in the case of Joshua. His original name *Hoshea* (Salvation) is transformed into *Jehosua* or *Joshua*, (God's Salvation;) and this, according to the modification which Hebrew names underwent in their passage through the Greek language, took, in the later ages of the Jewish Church, sometimes the form of *Jason*, but more frequently that which has now become indelibly impressed upon history as the greatest of all names—JESUS. (Heb. iv, 8.) The first Joshua was to save his people from their actual foes; the second was to 'save his people from their sins.'" Among most Christian nations human reverence has long prevented its bestowal, in its New Testament form, on any human individual. (See note, Matt. i, 21.)

The distinguished chieftain of whom this history treats is already familiar to the reader of the last four books of Moses. He may be humanly styled the Conqueror of Canaan. Born about the time of Moses' flight to Midian, he must have grown up a serf in the brickyards of Egypt, and afterwards have witnessed the miracles of the Exodus. His first appearance is in the war with Amalek, (Exod. xvii, 9,) and it is noticeable that he is there introduced to us as already a valiant soldier of Jehovah. During the sublime events at Sinai he repeatedly appears as the confidential servant and companion of Moses, (Exod. xxiv, 13; xxxii, 17; xxxiii, 11;) and before the death of the great lawgiver Joshua was solemnly invested with authority, and designated as his successor. Num. xxvii, 18–23; Deut. xxxi, 23. His courage, sagacity, and faith appear conspicuously in the minority report which he and Caleb boldly urged after exploring the land of the Canaanites, (Num. xiv, 6–10,) and for their noble faith and heroism on that occasion they only, of all the thousands of Israel, twenty years old and upwards, who saw the miracles of the Exodus, were permitted to enter the Land of Promise. Num. xiv, 30. In his history of the Vandal War, Procopius relates that when the Phenicians found Joshua's invading forces irresistible, they migrated first to Egypt, and thence

westward along the northern coast of Africa, and built Tingis in Mauri-
tania, near which, in the sixth century, was found a monument bearing
in the Phenician language the inscription, "We are those who fled
from the face of Joshua the robber, the son of Nun." But modern
scholars quite generally reject the whole story.

It does not follow, because the book bears the name of Joshua, that
it was written by that great commander; but portions of it bear evidence of having been composed by an eye-witness of the events it records. Chap. v, 1, 6. The concluding portion, containing the account
of Joshua's death, must, of course, have been written by a later hand;
and Keil very plausibly supposes that the entire work was written by
one of the elders who outlived Joshua. He argues, quite conclusively,
that the conquest of Hebron by Caleb, of Debir by Othniel, and of
Leshem by the Danites, did not take place during Joshua's life-time.
Comp. chap. xv, 13–19, and xix, 47, with Judges i, 10–15, and xviii.
But the date of the book must be before the time of David, for the
Jebusites still held the citadel of Jerusalem, (chap. xv, 63;) and even
before the death of Rahab, for, according to chap. vi, 25, she was still
dwelling in Israel when our author wrote. The oft-recurring phrase,
unto this day, cannot be used to prove a date long after Joshua's time,
nor even after his death; for in chap. xxii, 3, 17, and chap. xxiii, 9, it
is used of time previous to his death, and in no instance in the book
is its use incompatible with the supposition that Joshua was still living.
The authorship cannot be authoritatively decided. There is much to
render probable the Jewish tradition that the main portion of the book
was written at various times by Joshua; but a later hand appended the
account of Joshua's death, and inserted a few other passages in different parts of the work. We may reasonably suppose that Moses' minister succeeded his master in the use of the pen, as well as in command.

Design and Value of the Book of Joshua.

The design of this book was evidently to record the leading events
in the history of Israel from the death of Moses to the death of Joshua;
to record the conquest and settlement of Canaan ; and especially to magnify the inviolable faithfulness of Jehovah as a covenant-keeping God.
The central idea on which the whole work rests is announced in Joshua's
divine commission at the very beginning of the book. Chap. i, 1–9.
Hence the importance of this book as a connecting link between the
Book of the Law and the subsequent history of Israel in Palestine
cannot be over estimated. It holds a relation to the Pentateuch
similar to that which the Acts of the Apostles holds to the four Gospels.

A large portion of the work is invaluable for the study of sacred geography. It is a complete Doomsday-book of Palestine, and all modern research and discovery tend more and more to confirm its accuracy.

The general authenticity of the narrative has not been questioned except in its supernatural events. But the *à priori* assumption that "no amount of testimony can render a miracle credible," precludes all argument so far as these records are concerned, and the discussion of the possibility of miracles is beside the purpose of this work. The alleged contradictions and discrepancies of the Book of Joshua are fully explained in our notes on the passages where they occur.

The book is readily divided into Two Parts, the first containing the History of the Conquest, the second the Allotment of the Promised Land. The following Table of Contents will serve both for an analysis and a convenient index of the whole:

Part First—The Conquest of Canaan. Chaps. i-xii.

Part Second—The Division and Settlement of Canaan.   Chaps. xiii-xxiv.

DANIEL STEELE, D.D.

THE

BOOK OF JOSHUA.

CHAPTER I.

NOW after the death of Moses the servant of the LORD it came to pass, that the LORD spake unto Joshua the son of Nun, Moses' [a]minister, saying, **2** [b]Moses my servant is dead;

a Exod. 24. 13; Deut. 1. 38.

b Deut. 34. 5.

PART FIRST.

CONQUEST OF CANAAN.

CHAPTERS I-XII.

CHAPTER I.

JOSHUA'S DIVINE COMMISSION, 1-9.

The date of these events is, according to the common chronology, 1451 years before Christ. The place was Shittim. in the plains of Moab, about seven miles east of the Jordan, and opposite Jericho. Num. xxxiii, 49. Here. in the shade of the acacia groves, Israel had been beguiled to licentiousness by the Midianites, "in the matter of Peor." (Num. xxv;) here they had been visited by the Divine judgments for their sin; and here they had witnessed the last works and received the last counsels of Moses.

1. **Now**—More properly, *and it came to pass.* Heb. וַיְהִי. With this formula most of the historical books begin. It indicates in each case an intimate connection of the narrative with what immediately precedes. Perhaps the Book of Joshua originally began with the last chapter of Deuteronomy, and, for the purpose of completing the biography of Moses, that chapter, containing the details of his death and burial, was accustomed to be read with the scroll of Deuteronomy, and finally, for convenience, was appended to it. **After the death of Moses**—These words include the thirty days of mourning in honour of the great lawgiver. Deut. xxxiv, 8. At the end of these days the succession to the leadership was revealed by the Lord. A long interregnum would have been perilous to a people so inexperienced in the art of self-government. **The Lord spake**— Whether by a direct communication through his angel, as in v, 13–15, (see vi. 2,) or by the urim of the high priest, is uncertain, but probably the latter, inasmuch as this manner of speaking is prescribed to him in Num. xxvii, 21. The urim (*lights*) and thummim (*perfections*) are always alluded to as well known, but nowhere described. They were a part of the ephod, the sacred robe of the high priest. and were either the twelve gems on the breastplate or some objects intimately connected with them. and were a divinely appointed medium of revelation. Whether the gems became luminous, or whether there was an audible voice, or whether the priest when arrayed in the ephod was endowed with a miraculous insight similar to the vision of the inspired prophet. cannot now be determined. See note on Exod. xxviii, 30. **Joshua** —Before the death of Moses this great warrior had been clothed with authority and designated as the commander-in-chief of the Israelitish armies. See Introduction. **Son of Nun**—Nothing more is known of Nun than that he was of the tribe of Ephraim. Great military genius is often cradled in obscurity. Nun lived and died undistinguished from the thousands of his brethren, who passed all their days in the Egyptian bondage; but his son, by his valour and piety, rescued his father's servile name from oblivion. So the poet Horace, by his genius, immortalized the Roman bondman who begat him. **Moses' minister**—Not his menial, but his premier in peace, his

now therefore arise, go over this Jordan, | thou, and all this people, unto the land

lieutenant in war. It was customary for great prophets to be thus attended by ministers or servants, as Elijah was ministered to by Elisha. In this relation Joshua had witnessed Moses' conversation face to face with Jehovah, (Exod. xxxiii, 11,) and had been pavilioned with his master in the cloud of Sinai. Exod. xxiv, 13. Thus had he been trained in the best possible school, and the people were prepared, by the public honour bestowed upon him, to yield him obedience when their great emancipator was taken away.

[In this verse we notice that Moses is called the *servant of Jehovah*, and Joshua *minister of Moses*. A servant is less honourable than a minister, but it is unspeakably greater to be Jehovah's servant than merely the prime minister of any earthly potentate however good and mighty. The phrase *servant of Jehovah* is applied in the Old Testament to patriarchs, prophets, kings, the whole body of the chosen people, and in some prophetical passages to Messiah. The highest type of man under the Law was a *servant* of God; it was reserved for the Gospel to develop the *son* of God, and *perfect man in Christ*.]

2. **This Jordan**—This celebrated river was in full view from the elevation on which the Israelites were encamped. Thus far in Scripture history the Jordan has acquired no special importance. But henceforth, in Jewish and Christian literature, in sacred song and figurative expression of Christian hope, this humble stream occupies a larger place in the world's thinking than the broad Amazon or the majestic Mississippi. In the poetic language of Tacitus, " The Lebanon nourishes and pours out the Jordan." It flows entire through the first and second lake, and is retained by the third. These lakes (each with a triple name) are the Merom of the Old Testament, called Samochonitis in ancient classics, and Huleh in modern geography; the second the Sea of Galilee, or Lake of Gennesaret, called also Tiberias; the third lake is the Dead Sea, called in the Old Testament the Salt Sea and the Sea of the Plain. The

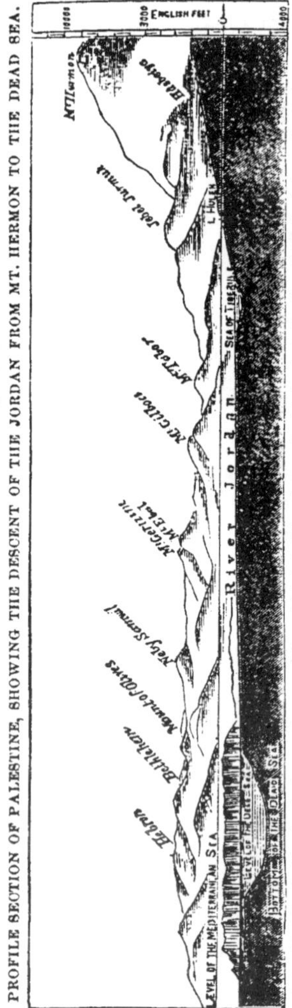

river, which in most of its course flows in a deep trench, is at the Dead Sea 1308 feet below the level of the Mediterranean. The general course of its current is to the south, but the river has a number of sharp bends, which deflect the regular flow of its waters. From the rapidity of the flow it may be styled almost a continuous cataract. From the first lake to the second, a distance of less than 9 miles, is a descent of 600 feet; and from the Lake of Tiberias to the Dead Sea are 27 great rapids, besides a great many of less magnitude. The average descent through its whole course is nearly twelve feet in a mile, justifying the name of " the Descender." Its length is about two hundred miles from the roots of Anti-Lebanon, where it bursts forth in all its purity, to the Sea of Salt, where it is lost in a briny, seething caldron. Yet the distance by a straight line between these points is less than ninety miles. There are shallows where it can be forded. It is subject to periodical overflows when the snows of Leb-

which I do give to them, *even* to the children of Israel. **3** [c] Every place that the sole of your foot shall tread upon, that have I given unto you, as I said

c Deut. 11. 24 : chap. 14. 9.

anon melt. At these times it overflows the first of the two terraces which constitute its banks. Within its lowest banks it varies in width from seventy feet, where it enters the Sea of Galilee, to one hundred and eighty yards at the Dead Sea. **All this people**—Numbering, according to the last census, 601,730, from twenty years old and upwards. See Num. xxvi. 51. Migrations on so vast a scale are not without parallel in the East. As late as the last century a whole nomadic people—400,000 Tatars—retreated under cover of a single night from the confines of Russia into their native deserts. **The land which I do give to them**—Canaan, or the Land of Promise; so called because it had been promised to the patriarchs centuries before.

3. **Every place that the sole of your foot shall tread upon**—Compare the similar language in Deut. xi, 24. The entire land was before them, and their own faith and courage were to decide how much of it they would actually possess.

4. **The wilderness** — This word is especially applied to that desert of Arabia Petræa in which the Israelites sojourned under Moses. It stretches from Mount Sinai northward between the two branches of the Red Sea to the Dead Sea, Palestine, and the Mediterranean. Its eastern boundary is Arabia Deserta and Arabia Felix; its western, Egypt and the western arm of the Red Sea. It is a rolling desert, covered generally with loose gravel and stones, and every-where furrowed and torn with torrents. Says Dr. Robinson, "A more frightful desert it had hardly been our lot to behold. Through the deep gorge on the eastern side, extending from the Gulf of Akaba to the Dead Sea, there is every indication that the Jordan once flowed before the great convulsion which depressed the Dead Sea." **This Lebanon**—A double range of mountains, with a valley called Coele (*hollow*)

unto Moses. **4** [d] From the wilderness and this Lebanon even unto the great river, the river Euphrates, all the land of the Hittites, and unto the great sea

d Gen. 15. 18 ; Exod. 23. 31 ; Num. 34 3-12.

Syria between, constituting the eastern limit of Phenicia and the northern limit of Palestine. The eastern spur, called Anti-Lebanon, terminates on the south in Mount Hermon, and was visible from Shittim. Hence the expression *this Lebanon*, like *this Jordan* in verse 2, because, though at a distance, it could be pointed out as a definite landmark. The name, which signifies *white*, is derived from the white appearance caused both by the limestone rocks and the snows. The height is about ten thousand feet. (See note on Hermon xi, 3.) **The Hittites**—Or children of Heth. A tribe of Canaanites living in Abraham's time in Hebron and its vicinity, in the southern part of the Land of Promise. As they had been an especial terror to the twelve spies, or to the craven ten, whose report disheartened the people, they are here mentioned by name, and put for the whole body of the Canaanites—Ye shall possess the land of even the dreaded Hittites. This designation of Canaan as "the land of the Hittites" occurs in the Bible only in this passage, though frequently used in the Egyptian records of Rameses II., in which Cheta or Chita appears to denote the whole country of lower and middle Syria. **The Euphrates**—"The great river" of western Asia, one thousand four hundred miles in length, is mentioned in connection with the garden of Eden, (Gen. ii, 14,) and throughout the Scripture history is often mentioned with this adjective. **Great sea**—The Mediterranean, called *great* in comparison with the small inland bodies of water, such as Genesareth and the Dead Sea. **Your coast**—Your boundaries. These included a larger territory than the Hebrews ever possessed, except for a short time during the reigns of David and Solomon. The breadth from Lebanon on the north to the desert on the south is one hundred and forty miles; the length from the Mediterranean to

toward the going down of the sun, shall be your coast. 5 *There shall not any man be able to stand before thee all the days of thy life: *as I was with Moses, so *I will be with thee: *I will not fail thee, nor forsake thee. 6 *Be strong and of a good courage: for ¹unto this people shalt thou divide for an inheritance the land, which I sware unto their fathers to give them. 7 Only be thou strong and very courageous, that thou mayest observe to do according to all the law, *which Moses my servant commanded thee: *turn not from it *to the*

e Deut. 7. 24.——*f* Exod. 3. 12.——*g* Deut. 31. 8. 23; verses 9. 17; chap. 3. 7: 6. 27; Isa. 43. 2. 5. ——*h* Deut. 31. 6. 8; Heb. 13. 5.——*i* Deut. 31. 7 23.

1 Or, *thou shalt cause this people to inherit the land*, &c.——*k* Num. 27. 23; Deut. 31. 7: chap. 11. 15.——*l* Deut. 5. 32: 28. 14.

the Euphrates is about four hundred miles, making an area of fifty-six thousand square miles, equal to the States of New York and Vermont. But Canaan proper, or Palestine, was only one hundred and forty miles by forty—an area smaller than the State of New Jersey. Jehovah devised liberal things for his people, but they failed through unbelief and cowardice to come into immediate possession of the munificent gift.

5. **Not any man be able to stand before thee**—Literally. *There shall not place himself a man before thee*, that is, for the purpose of opposition. Compare Deut. vii. 24: ix. 2: xi. 25. Divine promises often imply a condition. In this case the condition is found in the next verse—"Be strong." **I will be with thee**—He needs no other allies who is allied with the Almighty. All that He has done for Moses He pledges to do for Joshua, and all his successors who possess like precious faith. Joshua needed these strong and cheering assurances; for he appreciated the magnitude of the nation's loss in the death of Moses, and knew that a crisis had arrived in the history of the Hebrew nation. They had advanced to the borders of the Promised Land, and found it bristling with armed foes. Years of peril, warfare, and suffering were awaiting them. Although Moses had laid his hands upon him, consecrating him to the headship of his people, (Num. xxvii. 18,) he was justified in waiting for the imposition of a mightier hand.

6. **Be strong and of a good courage**—[Better, *Be strong and firm*. Michaelis remarks that the verb חזק, *to be strong*, denotes strength of hand and arm to lay hold of and retain any thing within one's grasp: while אמץ, *to be firm*, denotes rather firmness in the

knees, and ability to maintain one's position against the attack of foes. The expression occurs with increasing emphasis four times in this chapter, and is rather a command than an exhortation. Compare Isa. xxxv. 3: "Strengthen ye the weak hands, and confirm the feeble knees."] It is a command as imperative as any in the Decalogue, for strength of will and indomitable firmness must constitute the state of mind out of which all acts of obedience spring. **For unto this people shalt thou divide**—Or, *thou shalt cause this people to inherit the land*. The Lord would inspire Joshua with strength of soul by disclosing to him the grandeur of his mission. He reveals to him that his agency is the last link in the chain which unites prophecy and fulfilment, hope and fruition; that all the glorious possibilities of his nation hinge upon his own personal valor and fidelity.

7. **All the law**—The Torah, the body of moral, ceremonial, and political precepts given from Jehovah by the hand of Moses. The very conception of a moral agent involves the idea of a law. They who have not the written law are a law unto themselves. Their own conscience perceives the immutable distinction between right and wrong. In addition to this, God has added positive commands and prohibitions. These from the days of our first parents till the completion of the Torah, were of a fragmentary character; as, for example, the penalties against murder, adultery, and fornication, (Gen. ix. 6, and xxxviii. 24,) the Levirate law, (Gen. xxxviii. 8,) the distinctions of the clean and unclean beasts, (Gen. viii. 20,) and the sacredness of the Sabbath, (Exod. xvi. 23–29.) The first revelation of the law in any thing like a perfect form is found in the Book of

right hand or *to* the left, that thou mayest [2]prosper whithersoever thou goest. 8 [m]This book of the law shall not depart out of thy mouth; but [n]thou shalt meditate therein day and night, that thou mayest observe to do according to all that is written therein: for then thou shalt make thy way prosperous, and then

thou shalt [3]have good success. 9 [o]Have not I commanded thee? Be strong and of a good courage; [p]be not afraid, neither be thou dismayed: for the LORD thy God *is* with thee whithersoever thou goest.

10 Then Joshua commanded the officers of the people, saying, 11 Pass

---

2 Or, *do wisely.* Deut. 29. 9.——*m* Deut. 17. 18, 19. *n* Psa. 1. 2; 19. 14: 119. 11, 15; Prov. 2. 1, 5.

3 Or, *do wisely,* verse 7.——*o* Deut. 31. 7, 8, 23. *p* Psa. 27. 1; Jer. 1. 8.

Deuteronomy at a period when the people, educated to freedom and national responsibility, were prepared to receive it, and carry it with them to the land of promise. In this present passage we are assured that it was written in the form of a book, and appealed to as of supreme authority. When we consider the reverence with which all subsequent generations of Hebrews have regarded this "book of the law"—their jealous care lest it should be corrupted, counting the words and letters, and recording their number, indicating the middle word and the middle letter by peculiar signs—the argument amounts to a certainty that we have in our Hebrew Bibles the very Torah which Joshua is here commanded to take as his authoritative guide. Add to these considerations the respect which Jesus Christ always pays to the law, which he came not to destroy but to fulfil, and we can reasonably demand no stronger proof of the authoritative character of the Torah as a rule of life for us in all things which are not manifestly ceremonial. **To the right. . . or to the left**—Perfect obedience is represented by a straight line, and a course of sin by a crooked way. Hence the terms *right*eousness, *recti*tude, up*right*ness, and, in matters of opinion, *ortho*dox; while the word *wrong* is etymologically akin to *wrung*, twisted. **That thou mayest prosper**—Rather, *act wisely*. Sin is the highest folly, virtue is the only true wisdom.

8. **This book of the law**—Already had revelation solidified itself into a book form. The wisdom of God in selecting this form will be evident when we consider, (1) That the human race instinctively put into monumental form all the great truths, laws, discoveries, and historic events which they wish to perpetuate; (2) The untrustworthy

character of oral traditions; (3) The difficulty of corrupting documents intrusted to the guardianship of a class solemnly set apart for that purpose, and imbued with a religious awe for the very letter of the sacred manuscript, or as published to the world by the multiplication of copies scattered abroad through all lands. **Shall not depart**—The written divine law shall be a theme of constant study, thought, and conversation, the rule of both his private and official life. **Shalt meditate**—The Hebrew word הָגָה sometimes means *to mutter*, speak aloud, but "we are not to think of this meditation as a learned study, nor as a 'reading aloud,' as Bunsen explains it, but rather as a mature reflection upon the law, by which Joshua should penetrate more deeply into its meaning."—*Fay*. Happy is the nation of Bible readers ruled by one who receives the law at the mouth of God! **Have good success**—Rather, *act wisely*. Compare verse 7.

[9. **Have not I commanded thee?**—Such an emphatic interrogation is often the strongest possible form of affirmation. **Thy God is with thee**—As the soldier's valour is stimulated by the eye of his captain, so a vivid realization of the immediate presence of God is the best safeguard against unmanly terror.]

PREPARATIONS FOR THE MARCH, 10, 11.

[10. **Officers of the people**—*Shoterim;* subordinate magistrates or scribes among the Israelites, and more or less intimately associated with the administration of justice. They assisted the Egyptian taskmasters in apportioning and supervising the work of the Israelitish bondmen, (Exod. v, 10, 14, 15,) were associated with the elders (Num. xi, 16) and with the judges, (Josh.

through the host, and command the people, saying, Prepare you victuals; for *q* within three days ye shall pass over this Jordan, to go in to possess the land, which the LORD your God giveth you to possess it.

q Chap. 3. 2; see Deut. 9. 1; 11. 31.

viii, 33,) acted as overseers of levies, (Deut. xx, 5,) and from this verse, compared with chapters iii, 2, and viii, 33, it seems to have been a part of their work to notify the tribes of any public order, and prepare them for action in any emergency.]

11. **Prepare you victuals** — Provision for a journey; natural produce; not manna, for this became putrid on the second day. The manna did not cease to fall till they had entered Canaan and eaten of the corn of the land. Chap. v, 12. But it was in harmony with the divine economy that the supernatural supply should diminish as the natural supply increased in the fertile trans-Jordanic region. God never works miracles as a premium to indolence. **Within three days ye shall pass over this Jordan**—If we follow the order of the narrative, and allow that the spies were sent out after this proclamation to the officers, we shall find that the Israelites did not cross the Jordan within three days. The spies were gone three days, and the people paused on the river's bank three days more, so that the crossing could not have taken place till the seventh day. To meet this difficulty some suppose that the spies had been sent out previous to Joshua's proclamation to the officers; see note on chap. ii, 1. [But it is not necessary to understand these words of Joshua as a positive prediction that all the people would actually cross over the Jordan and be in the Promised Land within these three days. The words are literally *ye crossing*, that is, ye will be on your march to cross. He proposed within three days to break up the camp at Shittim and be on his way over the Jordan, and this is all the words can necessarily be made to mean. Keil supposes that because the two spies were detained, and obliged to hide

12 And to the Reubenites, and to the Gadites, and to half the tribe of Manasseh, spake Joshua, saying, 13 Remember *r* the word which Moses the servant of the LORD commanded you, saying, The LORD your God hath given you

r Num. 32. 20-28; chap. 22. 2, 3, 4.

three days in the mountain, (chap. ii, 22,) Joshua was thereby hindered from carrying out his purpose as he at first designed. But why is it necessary to maintain that the spies returned to Joshua at the camp at Shittim? It is not so written, (see chap. ii, 23,) and we may possibly suppose that when they returned to Joshua they found him arrived at the Jordan. But even granting that they returned to the camp at Shittim, as the history most naturally implies, the three days they hid in the mountain may have been only parts of three days. See note on chap. ii, 22.] The inspired writers directed their attention more to *facts* than to *chronological order*. In this command Joshua displays a remarkable degree of that faith and courage to which he had just been exhorted. The rapid Jordan, at its flood, is before him, and he has no boats, no bridge, no pontoon train, but he assures that vast host that they and their wives and children and flocks shall, within a few days, safely cross that angry torrent.

ADDRESS TO THE TRANS-JORDANIO TRIBES, 12–15.

Palestine, east of the Jordan, had already been conquered, and allotted, at their earnest request, to the tribes of Reuben, Gad, and the half tribe of Manasseh, in the order here enumerated, passing from the south toward the north. Num. xxxii, 23. It was a more fertile and attractive country than "the mountain," as Western Palestine is sometimes appropriately called.

13. **The Lord...hath given you rest**—He has permitted you to settle your families in fixed abodes on the express condition that you should assist in the subjugation of the land on the western side of Jordan. Num. xxxii, 16–22. The promise of these two and a half tribes, solemnly made to Moses,

rest, and hath given you this land.
14 Your wives, your little ones, and
your cattle, shall remain in the land
which Moses gave you on this side Jordan; but ye shall pass before your
brethren *armed, all the mighty men of
valour, and help them; **15** Until the
LORD have given your brethren rest, as
he hath given you, and they also have
possessed the land which the LORD your
God giveth them: *then ye shall return
unto the land of your possession, and
enjoy it, which Moses the LORD's servant gave you on this side Jordan toward
the sunrising.
16 And they answered Joshua, saying, *All that thou commandest us we
will do, and whithersoever thou sendest
us, we will go. **17** According as we
hearkened unto Moses in all things, so
will we hearken unto thee: only the
LORD thy God *be with thee, as e was
with Moses. **18** Whosoever *he be* that
doth rebel against thy commandment,

---

4 Heb. marshalled by five. See Exod. 13. 18.
s Chap. 22. 4, &c.

t Num. 32. 25; Deut. 5. 27; Rom. 13. 1, 5.
u Verse 5; 1 Sam. 20. 13; 1 Kings 1. 37.

---

must now be fulfilled. **This land**—
Like the expressions *this Jordan* and
this Lebanon, (verses 2, 4,) the land immediately around them east of Jordan,
in which all Israel was yet encamped.

14. [**This side Jordan**—An incorrect translation of בְּעֵבֶר הַיַּרְדֵּן, which
can only mean *beyond the Jordan.* Our
translators were governed, in their rendering, by the position of Joshua at the
time of this address; but the Book of
Joshua was written after the conquest
and settlement of Palestine when *beyond the Jordan* was the common term
for the country east of the Jordan, and
so the writer simply follows the *usus
loquendi* of his time. This eastern section, which in our Saviour's time was
called Perea, and was the region of
much of his ministry, (see notes on
Matt. iv, 25; Luke ix, 51,) is designated in verse 15 as (Heb.) *beyond Jordan towards the sunrising;* and in chap.
v, 1 Western Palestine is called *beyond
Jordan towards the sea.*] **Mighty men
of valour**—The more valiant of the
two and a half tribes, not their entire
military strength. From chap. iv. 13
we learn that only forty thousand of
them were required to cross to the west-
ren side; the remainder—probably about
seventy thousand, (see Num. xxvi,)—remaining on the eastern side of the river
to protect the families and substance of
the two and a half tribes from the in-
cursions of their still numerous though
defeated enemies dwelling in the wide
eastern plains. **Armed**—Scholars dif-
fer as to the meaning of this word.
Some assert that it signifies "girt about
the loins;" hence "ready, equipped,
drawn up for battle." Others, on very
good grounds, believe that it means "in
five divisions, namely, the centre, two
wings, vanguard, and rearguard," according to the usual form in which an
army marches into battle. In Exod. xiii,
18 (see note) it is rendered *harnessed.*

15. **Until the Lord have given**—
Observe how early Joshua inculcates
the idea of national unity. Perhaps
he already had forebodings of the alien-
ation of the eastern from the western tribes, in consequence of the deep
trench of the Jordanic valley, the modern Ghor. It is an historic fact that
this geographic insulation caused the
eastern tribes to cherish a national feeling far less intense than that which
animated their western brethren. Reuben, "unstable as water," (Gen. xlix, 4,)
in consequence of his separation from
the main body of the nation became a
roving Bedouin tribe.

OATH OF ALLEGIANCE TO JOSHUA, 16-18.

16. **That thou commandest we will
do**—A response not only from the eastern tribes, but also, probably, from the
entire nation, encouraging to the spirit
of the new commander. He must have
regarded it as a formal expression of
their loyalty to his authority. Like
true patriots, in their nation's extremity
they volunteer under their great captain.

17. **Only the Lord...be with thee**
—By this language they do not avow a
qualified and conditional allegiance, but
only responsively reiterate with myriads
of tongues the brief and stirring exhortation given by God, "Be strong and of
a good courage." It is because **they**
believe that Jehovah is with **Joshua**
that they bind themselves to obey **him.**

18. **Against thy commandment**—

and will not hearken unto thy words in all that thou commandest him, he shall be put to death: only *v* be strong and of a good courage.

v Ezra 10. 4; Eph. 6. 10.

Literally, *Every man who rebels against thy mouth;* that is, who shows contempt for thy commands. **Shall be put to death**—A righteous verdict against the rebel, and in accordance with the law of the Most High. Deut. xvii, 12. Resistance to His chosen representative is a crime no less heinous than avowed rebellion against His sovereignty. So long as a government is subserving its ends in administering justice and conserving human society, the attempt to subvert it by violence is a crime of the greatest enormity, striking at the very foundation of all the earthly interests of mankind, and opening wide the floodgates of civil war. Notes Rom. xiii, 1–7.

CHAPTER II.
THE ADVENTURES OF THE TWO SPIES, 1–24.

[Some forty years before this date Moses had sent out from the wilderness of Paran twelve spies, and among them Joshua, to search the Land of Promise. It was not a secret movement then, but the chosen twelve were prominent chiefs, "heads of the children of Israel." Num. xiii, 3. Only two of the twelve brought back an encouraging report, and it is noticeable that Joshua, one of the old spies, and now Moses' successor. sends only two to spy out Jericho. For so dangerous a mission two were better than twelve.

1. **Sent out**—Some render *had sent,* as in the margin, and suppose that the spies had been sent out some days before the events of the last chapter. But the *vav consecutive* with which this verse begins (וַיִּשְׁלַח) is properly rendered *Then sent* Joshua, etc., and a pluperfect rendering will not materially relieve the difficulty stated in chap. i, 11. "Even if the spies had been despatched before the events narrated in chap. i, 10–18, it would not be grammatically correct to render וַיִּשְׁלַח as a pluper-

CHAPTER II.

AND Joshua the son of Nun [1] sent [a] out of Shittim two men to spy secretly, saying, Go view the land, even

1 Or, *had sent.*——*a* Num. 25. 1.

fect; and much less is this allowable if such a supposition be unfounded."—*Keil.*] **Shittim**—The plain of acacia shrubs at the foot of the mountains on the eastern side of the Jordan, directly opposite Jericho, in which Moses had last pitched the Israelitish camp. Num. xxv, 1; xxxiii, 49. **Secretly**—The Masoretic conjunctive accent connects this word with *saying,* rather than with *to spy,* as is done in the English version; but the word is best understood as qualifying Joshua's whole procedure. He communicated his orders to the two men, and also **sent** them out **secretly** in order to avoid betrayal by any evil-minded person in his own camp. All spying necessarily involves secrecy, and in this case the perilous business was a military necessity. An unexplored land was before them, and the number and spirit of the enemy, and his military preparations and plans, were utterly unknown to Joshua. Faith always uses means. **Even Jericho**—The command may be better rendered. *Go view the land, and particularly Jericho.* This ancient town, (called also the "City of Palm Trees,") was situated in a plain of the same name about six miles west of the Jordan, near where it enters into the Dead Sea, and about nineteen miles northeast of Jerusalem. It was a walled city, rich and populous, having commerce with Babylon and the far East. According to Stanley it was the only important town in the Jordan valley, and its situation must always have rendered its occupation necessary to any invader from the east. "It was the key of western Palestine, as standing at the entrance of the two main passes into the central mountains. From the issues of the torrent Kelt, on the south, to the copious spring, afterwards called the 'Fountain of Elisha,' on the north, the ancient city ran along the base of the mountains, and thus commanded the oasis of the desert valley, the garden of verdure, which

Jericho. And they went, and [b] came into a harlot's house, named [c] Rahab, and [2] lodged there. 2 And [d] it was told the king of Jericho, saying, Behold, there came men in hither to night of the children of Israel to search out the country.

3 And the king of Jericho sent unto Rahab, saying, Bring forth the men that are come to thee, which are entered into thine house: for they be come to search out all the country. 4 [e] And the woman took the two men, and hid them, and

---

[b] Heb. 11. 31; James 2. 25.——[c] Matt. 1. 5.
[2] Heb. *lay*.

[d] Psa. 127. 1; Prov. 21. 30.——[e] See 2 Sam. 17. 19, 20.

---

clustering around these waters has, through the various stages of its long existence, secured its prosperity and grandeur." The modern village Rihah is, by some travellers, identified with ancient Jericho, and is described by Dr. Olin as one of the meanest and foulest of Palestine, containing about forty houses, with a sickly, indolent, and vicious population. **Came into a harlot's house**—[Literally, *into the house of a woman, a harlot*. Their entrance into such a house would excite less suspicion, and, her house being upon the wall, (ver. 15,) their escape from the city in case of necessity would be more easy. Knobel supposes that, as it was evening twilight when the spies reached Jericho, the time when harlots were wont to walk the streets, (Job xxiv, 15; Prov. vii, 9; Isa. xxiii, 16,) they met with Rahab at some corner and followed her to her house.] Josephus and other Jewish writers, and also some Christian commentators, unwilling to believe that these spies, intrusted with such a responsible mission, would have gone to a harlot's house, or that Rahab, who married Salmon and became an ancestress of our Lord, and is commended by an apostle, could have been a woman of ill-fame, maintain that she was not a harlot, but a *hostess* or inn-keeper. But the Hebrew word זוֹנָה means always, elsewhere, a *harlot*, and is so rendered in the Septuagint and Vulgate. Also in the New Testament she is called emphatically *the harlot*, ἡ πόρνη, (Heb. xi, 31; James ii, 25.) And not only on philological grounds is the rendering *hostess* untenable, but oriental customs are against such an interpretation. In the east there are no proper inns, but as a kind of substitute there are khans or caravansaries (See note and cut at Luke ii, 7.) It would have been a thing without parallel in

that land for a single woman, or even a man, to be found keeping a public house. Rahab was probably unmarried; for though she had father and mother, brothers and sisters, (verse 13,) there is no hint that she had husband or child, and it is notorious that in the east rarely any but disreputable women remain single. On her falsehoods and her faith see note on verse 5. **Lodged there**—Rather, *they lay down there*. Verse 8 shows that they ascended the house top to pass the night there.

2. **It was told the king**—The chief of each great city, and even of each petty clan, is in the Old Testament dignified by the appellation of *king*. At this time of alarm, when the invading foe was only a few miles off, a shrewd king would naturally give orders to watch closely every suspicious-looking stranger. **There came men ...to search out the country**—The peculiar Hebrew physiognomy of the two spies, and perhaps, also, their entering the eastern gate, were strong grounds of suspicion.

3. **Sent unto Rahab**—The spies had been traced to the harlot's house, and possibly Rahab had also, by open avowal of her belief in the approaching triumph of the Hebrews, already drawn suspicion on herself.

4. **Hid them**—Literally, *hid him*. Hebrew usage shows many such sudden transitions from plural to singular. Perhaps we may see in this instance an intimation of the haste with which she concealed the men, hiding one of them herself with the flax (verse 6) and leaving the other to cover himself. Some think she had taken the precaution to conceal the men before the king's messengers arrived, and verse 6 seems to favor the supposition. **I wist not whence they were**—Better, *I knew not*, for the verb *wist* is obso-

said thus, There came men unto me, but I wist not whence they *were:* **5** And it came to pass *about the time* of shutting of the gate, when it was dark, that the men went out; whither the men went, I wot not: pursue after them quickly; for ye shall overtake them. **6** But *she* had brought them up to the roof of the house, and hid them with the stalks of flax, which she had laid in order upon

---

f See Exod. 1. 17; 2 Sam. 17. 19.

---

lete. Rahab could not safely deny that the men had entered her house, for other eyes than hers had seen them; but it is difficult to believe that she knew not whence they were. She may not, however, have had positive knowledge that they were spies.

5. [**The men went out**—This statement was a wilful falsehood, and cannot be justified by saying that oriental hospitality required a person to utter falsehood if necessary to defend a guest. It may, indeed, relieve the case somewhat to urge that before the Gospel strict truth, in Jew or heathen, was a virtue utterly unknown; but it is altogether superfluous to attempt either to apologize for Rahab's previous harlotry or to justify her falsehoods. We must distinguish, however, between her vices and her virtues. The sacred writers record her vices without a word of comment or apology. Even with this alloy, however, they attest the justifying power of her faith. The epistle to the Hebrews (xi, 31) extols her faith in Israel's God, and James (ii, 25) makes mention of her praise-worthy works of hospi-tality. The one declares that her faith saved her from perishing with the unbēlieving inhabitants of Jericho; the other shows that her faith was not without its appropri-ate fruits.] { Verse 11, however, shows that Ra-hab had long entertained a sincere faith in Jehovah as the true God, and her conduct toward the spies was the imperfect manifestation of that faith which resulted in her true incor-poration into Israel, and obtaining a place in the genealogy of the Messiah. Matt. i, 5. Her falsehood on the pres-

ent occasion was far less condemning than that of Abraham on two occasions. Gen. xii. 13; xx. 2. It was also a strat-agem of war, which even our Christian civilization has hardly attained the vir-tue of disusing. }

6. **She had brought them up to the roof of the house**—This verse more fully explains verse 4, by detail-ing the place and manner of her con-cealing the spies. Eastern houses have flat roofs, surrounded with a para-pet to prevent falling off. Deut. xxviii. 8. Here the family often sleep, sit, walk. and store such articles as will not be damaged by the exposure. Sometimes the roof is shaded by means of an awning supported by posts. See note on Acts x. 9. **Stalks of flax**—Heb. *flax of the tree;* that is, flax in the tree or stalk. Some render these words stalks or pods of *cotton*, but without sufficient authority. Flax is said to grow in Egypt to a great size, and its stalks attain the thickness of a

Flax. (*Linum usitatissimum.*)

cane, and so it doubtless did in the rich plain of Jericho. To dry stalks of such thickness much exposure to the sun would be necessary, and they were laid out in such abundance on the roof. **7** And the men pursued after them the way to Jordan unto the fords: and as soon as they which pursued after them were gone out, they shut the gate. **8** And before they were laid down, she came up unto them upon the roof; **9** And she said unto the men, I know that the Lord hath given you the land, and that ͛ your terror is fallen upon us, and that all the inhabitants of the land ˢ faint because of you. **10** For we have heard how the Lord ʰ dried up the water of the Red Sea for you, when ye came out of Egypt; and ⁱ what ye did unto the two kings of the Amorites, that *were* on the other side Jordan, Sihon

---

g Gen. 35. 5; Exod. 23. 27; Deut. 2. 25; 11 25.
3 Heb. *melt*; Exod. 15. 15.

h Exod. 14. 21; chap. 4. 23.
i Num. 21. 24. 34, 35.

Rahab's house that the two men could be easily concealed among them.

7. The men pursued after them—That is, the men of Jericho pursued, as they thought, after the spies. **The way to Jordan**—The most direct way to the Jordan, the way which they naturally thought the spies, in their hasty flight, would take. **Unto the fords**—Heb., *the crossing places;* certain well-known places of shallow water where the Jordan might be waded. There is no intimation that the pursuers crossed the fords. As the plural is used, we infer that there were several places of this kind near Jericho, and that the pursuers took different routes to insure the capture of the fugitives. **They shut the gate**—To prevent the escape of the spies should they still be in the city, and to secure the city against the ingress of foes by night.

8. Before they were laid down—That is, to sleep. They had been hidden where it was uncomfortable to sleep; but now that their pursuers are put upon the wrong track, they come forth from their hiding places.

9. I know that the Lord hath given you the land—Mark the strength of her affirmation: not *I believe,* but *I know.* Rahab now discloses unto them the cause of her hospitality, her firm conviction that the Hebrews were destined to overthrow her people. This belief arose from the miraculous passage of the Red Sea, and the easy conquest of Eastern Palestine. With characteristic womanly penetration she had read the secret fears of her countrymen, and had interpreted them as tokens of coming defeat to her people. Thus the very knowledge which Joshua was most desirous of attaining, namely, the state of feeling among the Canaanites, is freely communicated to the spies. To dis-

hearten a nation is to conquer it. **Your terror**—Fear of you has paralyzed us. Moses, in his last discourse, had predicted this result. Deut. ii, 25; xi, 25. **All the inhabitants of the land faint** —For **faint,** the Hebrew reads, *are melted;* an expression showing the utter prostration of their confidence and resolution. This despair of the people, whether natural or supernatural, prevented them from making any combination to resist the invading host at the best place for such resistance— the passage of the Jordan.

10. We have heard—An event so wonderful filled the world with amazement. Traders and caravans passing from Egypt through the deserts would frequently pass through Jericho, and spread the tidings of the Hebrews' triumphs. Of all the miracles which attended the exodus from Egypt, none was capable of producing so profound an impression upon all surrounding nations as the drying up of the Red Sea, the safe passage of the Israelites, and the destruction of the Egyptian host by the rolling back of the parted surges. Exod. xiv, 15–31. The lapse of forty years had not effaced that deep impression—an incidental proof of the magnitude of the miracle. Events more recent and nearer to them had increased their alarm. **The Amorites** east of the Jordan, who had evinced their martial prowess by conquering the king of Moab and seizing his land, were in turn subdued by the resistless arms of the Israelites. The Amorites were the most powerful and distinguished of the Canaanitish nations, and occupied a tract on both sides of the Jordan. Those on the east side were under **two kings, Sihon and Og.** The former refused passage to the Hebrews through his territory, came to Jahaz, fought, and was

and Og, whom ye utterly destroyed.
11 And as soon as we had *k* heard *these things,* *l* our hearts did melt, neither *4* did there remain any more courage in any man, because of you: for *m* the LORD your God, he *is* God in heaven above, and in earth beneath. **12** Now therefore, I pray you, *n* swear unto me by the LORD, since I have showed you kindness, that ye will also show kindness unto *o* my father's house, and *p* give me

---

k Exod. 15. 14, 15.——*l* Chap. 5. 1; 7. 5; Isa. 13. 7.——*4* Heb. *rose up.*——*m* Deut. 4. 39.——*n* See 1 Sam. 20. 14, 15, 17.

---

defeated. Og also gave battle at Edrei, and was totally routed. See on Num. xxi, 21–35.

11. **For the Lord your God, he is God in heaven above, and in earth beneath** — This is the full profession of Rahab's faith in the God of Israel. It was a complete renunciation of her idolatry and harlotry. It was a change in belief, feeling, will, and action, which brought her to the worship of the true God, and to a maternity of the Messiah in David's royal line. However alloyed by one imperfection, it was a true faith working out its true results. And the wide-spread terror of these nations, as described in the last verse, and Rahab's faith, were in accordance with God's purpose in raising up Pharaoh and diffusing his " name." Note on Rom. ix, 17.

12. **Swear unto me**—She gives still stronger proof of her confidence in the success of the Israelites by wishing to enter into covenant with the spies for the salvation of herself and her father's family. She feels that if they swear by Israel's mighty God they will not dare prove false. Her faith assumes a practical character, and shows itself by works. It impels her to bargain for her deliverance from the destruction which she sees impending over the city. **Since I have showed you kindness**—Rahab here makes a good application of the Golden Rule. **Give me a true token**—Some visible, material proof of the oath; some object which she may keep and produce as evidence that such a solemn compact has been entered into by the parties. This token was a substitute for a written covenant bearing their signatures.

a true token: **13** And *that* ye will save alive my father, and my mother, and my brethren, and my sisters, and all that they have, and deliver our lives from death. **14** And the men answered her, Our life *5* for yours, if ye utter not this our business. And it shall be, when the LORD hath given us the land, that *q* we will deal kindly and truly with thee. **15** Then she *r* let them down by a cord through the window: for her

---

o See 1 Tim. 5. 8.——*p* Verse 18.——*5* Heb. *instead of you to die.*——*q* Judg. 1. 24; Matt. 5. 7.——*r* Acts 9. 25.

---

13. **And that ye will save alive my father**—The English version wrongly supplies *that.* Read, *And ye shall save alive,* etc. She was by no means destitute of natural affection. That she does not stipulate for the salvation of the entire state of Jericho is no evidence of her want of patriotism. She was too deeply impressed with the belief of the coming overthrow to ask so much. Our ties of consanguinity should induce us to make extraordinary efforts for the conversion of our kindred to God. This is the highest purpose of the creation of such ties in the human soul. **All that they have**—It is not necessary to limit this clause to persons only; it may include portable possessions also. Comp. chap. vi, 23, note.

14. **Our life for yours**—According to Osiander, this form of oath may be thus paraphrased: " We place our life and soul in the hand of God as a pledge for thee, in order that he may destroy us if any one injures thee or thine." **If ye utter not this our business**—This is the indispensable condition on which their oath and her deliverance depend.

15. **Then she let them down by a cord**—[Many interpreters are of opinion that there is a confusion in the order of verses here, and that this verse should follow the first sentence of verse 21. For it is improbable, they urge, that Rahab and the spies continued to converse after the latter were let down from the window, inasmuch as such conversation would have led to their detection and exposure. But against such an opinion are the words, *Thou didst let us down,* (verse 18;) and as for the confusion of verses, Keil well re-

..ouse *was* upon the town wall, and she dwelt upon the wall. **16** And she said unto them, *"Get you to the mountain, lest the pursuers meet you; and hide yourselves there three days, until the pursuers be returned: and afterward may ye go your way. **17** And the men

s 1 Sam. 23. 14, 29.——*t* Exod. 20. 7

marks that "the Hebrews often connect together the principal circumstances attending any particular event, and, after fully describing these, proceed to fill up the details of minor importance. This, however, is not a confusion in the order of events, but an anticipation of the result consequent upon a well-arranged division of the subject-matter."] Some have thought that it was impossible that she could let them down alone, and they have furnished her with "friends or domestics" to assist her. But there is no need of this assistance. By fastening the cord to something within the room they could descend, sailor-like, even without aid from within. Paul was

said unto her, We *will be* 'blameless of this thine oath which thou hast made us swear. **18** "Behold, *when* we come into the land, thou shalt bind this line of scarlet thread in the window which thou didst let us down by: *'and thou shalt* *b* bring thy father, and thy mother, and

u Verse 12.——*v* Chap. 6 23.——*6* Heb. *gather.*

let down in a basket. (2 Cor. xi, 33.) **Her house was upon the town wall** בְּקִיר הַחוֹמָה, *in the depth of the wall.* Her house was so constructed that the city wall formed also the back wall of the house. **She dwelt upon the wall**—For her house was built on the wall, and projected beyond its outer edge, so that from one of its outer windows the men could be let down beyond the walls of the city. (See note on Acts ix, 25.)

16. **Get you to the mountain**—Heb. *Mountainwards go ye.* By the device of going westward to the mountains behind the city, instead of eastward toward the Jordan, they would avoid pursuit, and secure a hiding place in some of their caverns till the pursuers had returned.

17. **We will be blameless of this thine oath**—That is, released from the oath which we have taken, provided you do not fulfil the following conditions.

18. **Thou shalt bind this line of scarlet thread in the window**—A small rope or cord composed of crimson threads. The English version conveys the idea that this cord was used in letting down the spies. But the Hebrew, Septuagint, and Vulgate make the window the antecedent of *which*, thus—*the window through which* thou didst let us down. The scarlet cord was probably the *token* (ver. 12) given to Rahab in proof of their oath. But the **scarlet** of the thread by which she and her house were to be saved, though a suggestive emblem of the blood of the atonement, (as advanced by St. Clement,) can hardly be considered, like the blood of the paschal lamb on the door post, an appointed type. **And thou shalt bring thy father**—The persons to whom deliverance is pledged must be separated from the mass of the poo-

thy brethren, and all thy father's household, home unto thee. **19** And it shall be, *that* [w] whosoever shall go out of the doors of thy house into the street, his blood *shall be* upon his head, and we *will be* guiltless : and whosoever shall be with thee in the house, [x] his blood *shall be* on our head, if *any* hand be upon him. **20** And [y] if thou utter this our business, then we will be quit of thine oath which thou hast made us to swear. **21** And she said, According unto your words, so *be* it. And she sent them away, and they departed : and she

bound the scarlet line in the window. **22** And they went, and came unto the mountain, and abode there three days, until the pursuers were returned : and the pursuers sought *them* throughout all the way, but [z] found *them* not. **23** So the two men returned, and descended from the mountain, and passed over, and came to Joshua the son of Nun, and told him all *things* that befell them : **24** And they said unto Joshua, Truly [a] the LORD hath delivered into our hands all the land ; for even all the inhabitants of the country do [7] faint because of us.

w Exod. 12. 13, 23 ; 1 Kings 2. 36, 42.——x Matt. 27. 25.——y Prov. 11. 13.——z 1 Sam. 19. 10, 12 ; 2 Sam. 17. 20 ; Psa. 32. 7.——a Exod. 23. 31 ; chap. 6. 2 ; 21. 44.——7 Heb. *melt*, verse 9.

ple and gathered within the house of Rahab, otherwise they must perish in the impending universal destruction. So must those who hope to escape the general doom of this sinful world be gathered into the house of God, the Church of Jesus Christ.

19. [**His blood shall be upon his head**—A technical formula of retribution indicating the punishment of death when justly brought upon one's self, and equivalent to, Let the guilt of his death fall back upon himself. See note on Acts xviii, 6.] **If any hand be upon him**—That is, to injure or to slay.

20. **Quit of thine oath**—Released from its obligation. The condition mentioned in verse 14 is here repeated as if to give it emphasis.

21. **And she bound the scarlet line in the window**—This statement is here made to complete the account, not to indicate that she bound the line in the window as soon as the spies were gone. She did this on the approach of the Hebrew host, in season to secure the deliverance of which this was the token. To have displayed it immediately would have been unnecessary, and would have incurred the suspicions of her watchful countrymen.

22. **Abode there three days**—In reckoning time, the Jews count as whole days the parts of days which may be included in a given period. Hence the body of Jesus was said to be in the tomb three days, though it was laid there on Friday evening and he came forth on Sunday morning—a space of thirty-six hours. See note on Matt. xii, 40. [So these spies may have re-

mained in the caverns of the mountains only parts of three days, and the entire time of their absence from the camp at Shittim fell within the three days at the end of which, if not before, Joshua intended to be on his march across the Jordan. See note on chap. i, 11.]

23. **Passed over**—That is, Jordan. These scouts were probably expert in swimming, for the Jordan was then at its flood. **Came to Joshua**—It is not necessary to suppose that they returned to the camp at Shittim. But the history most naturally implies this.

24. **Truly the Lord hath delivered into our hands all the land**—A nation palsied with despair is already conquered. The result of the mission of the spies was very encouraging to Joshua. The principal thing they reported, and probably that which it had been their chief object to ascertain, was the fear and trembling which prevailed among the idolatrous inhabitants of the land.

CHAPTER III.

THE PASSAGE OF THE JORDAN. 1–17.

Immediately after the return of the spies, or possibly before this event, the Israelites leave their long occupied camp at Shittim, and move to the banks of the Jordan. A nation moving toward a swollen and angry river with perfect confidence that they should cross it, and yet in perfect ignorance of the manner of such an achievement, is a spectacle of thrilling moral sublimity. Thus marched Moses with the Hebrew people to the Red Sea.

CHAPTER III.

AND Joshua rose early in the morning; and they removed [a] from Shittim, and came to Jordan, he and all the children of Israel, and lodged there before they passed over. **2** And it came to pass [b] after three days, that the officers went through the host; **3** And they commanded the people, saying, [c] When ye see the ark of the covenant of the LORD your God, [d] and the priests the Levites bearing it, then ye shall remove from your place, and go after it. **4** [e] Yet there shall be a space between you and it, about two thousand cubits by measure: come not near unto it, that ye may

---

a Chap. 2. 1. —— *b* Chap. 1. 10, 11. —— *c* See Num. 10. 33. —— *d* Deut. 31. 9, 25. —— *e* Exod. 19. 12.

---

1. Rose early in the morning—According to a necessary custom in hot countries to work by night or early dawn and rest at noonday. Compare Gen. xix, 2, 27; xx, 3; xxviii, 18. **Came to Jordan**—Not close up to the brink of the river, but within some two thousand cubits of it. Ver. 4. **Lodged there**—Not merely *spent one night there*, as some understand, but *abode there* (for לון often has this sense) three days, as the next verse most naturally explains.

2. [**After three days** —Obviously three days after they came to the Jordan, near whose banks they lodged for this length of time, probably to make preparations for crossing. Their camp consisted not merely of armed men, but of the entire population, including women and children, with all their possessions, and a delay of three days before crossing into the enemy's country might have been useful for many reasons now unknown to us. To identify these three days with those mentioned chap. i, 11, is altogether unnecessary, and never would have been attempted but for the supposition, wholly untenable, that Joshua completed the passage of the Jordan within three days from his giving the order to prepare to cross. See notes on chaps. i, 11, and ii, 22. Strangely have some rationalistic critics argued that because the historian records in one place an order for the people to prepare to cross the Jordan in three days, and afterwards states that they stopped at the river three days, therefore his narrative was compiled from two different and contradictory documents, and these two periods of three days each were confounded by him!] **Officers**—See note chap. i, 10.

3. **When ye see the ark of the covenant**—This was a chest made of shittim or acacia wood, four feet in length, and two and one third feet in breadth and depth. It was overlaid with gold within and without. The cover, which was edged with gold, was called the mercy-seat. Standing on this lid were the cherubim with outstretched wings. The ark was borne upon the shoulders by means of rods passing through two rings on each of the two sides. When transported, it was enveloped in the veil of the dismantled tabernacle, the curtain of badger skins, and the blue cloth, (Num. iv, 5, 6,) and was therefore not seen. Its name is derived from its chief contents, the "covenant of Sinai"—the two tables of stone, on which was the Decalogue, written by the finger of God. From Heb. ix, 4, we learn that it contained also "the pot of manna," and "Aaron's rod that budded." It was never seen save by the high priest, thus symbolizing the invisible Jehovah. See on Exod. xxv, 10–22. **And the priests the Levites**—The *Levite-priests*, as distinguished from all irregular priests who are not Levitical. Such occasionally arose in times of apostasy from the law. On ordinary occasions the Levites of the house of Kohath, by special command, bore the ark. But when removed from within the veil, or when borne on festive occasions of extraordinary interest, the priests, the offspring of Aaron, were the bearers. Chap. vi, 6 and 1 Kings viii, 3, 6. **Go after it**—Let the ark of God be your leader, and move ye as the ark moves. Heretofore it stood at the centre when Israel was encamped, and in mid army when they marched. The ark now led them, as heretofore the pillar of fire.

4. **Space . . . two thousand cubits**—The design of this space of a thousand yards—more than half a mile—was that the people might see the way to

know the way by which ye must go: for ye have not passed *this* way ¹ heretofore. **5** And Joshua said unto the people, *f* Sanctify yourselves: for to morrow the LORD will do wonders among you. **6** And Joshua spake unto the priests, saying, *g* Take up the ark of the covenant, and pass over before the people. And they took up the ark of the covenant, and went before the people.

---

1 Heb. *since yesterday, and the third day.* ——*f* Exod. 19. 10, 14, 15; Lev. 20. 7; Num. 11. 18; chap. 7. 13; 1 Sam. 16. 5; Joel 2. 16.

---

the opened passage through the Jordan. Some have supposed that this space was required on account of the sacredness of the ark. But it is not stated in the text, nor was such a space ever required during all their journeyings in the wilderness, nor ever afterwards. In this case the miraculous division of waters would be more impressive because the required space would render it visible to all. **For ye have not passed this way heretofore**—The Heb. *yesterday and the day before* is equivalent to *previously.* The Greeks have a similar expression: χϑιζά τε καὶ πρωΐζα. *Homer's Iliad.* ii, 303.

5. **Sanctify yourselves**—By sacred ablutions and observances, and by a change of raiment where the washing of the raiment was impracticable. Compare the marginal references. **The Lord will do wonders among you**—He will open a passage through the Jordan as he did through the Red Sea, and lead his people through dry-shod. The miracle of the Red Sea was a **wonder** whose name had been noised abroad for forty years, (chap. ii, 10,) and this at the Jordan was to be like it.

6. **Take up the ark**—This command was among the announcements relating to the order of crossing, and not to the crossing itself, which took place on the next day. **And they took up the ark**—A statement which is, according to the rules of modern composition, brought in before its proper place, which would naturally be between verses 13 and 14. For the message from God to Joshua, and the address of the latter, must have been given before the priests moved. But this is the manner of the Hebrew historians,

7 And the LORD said unto Joshua, This day will I begin to *h* magnify thee in the sight of all Israel, that they may know that, *i* as I was with Moses, *so* I will be with thee. **8** And thou shalt command *k* the priests that bear the ark of the covenant, saying, When ye are come to the brink of the water of Jordan, *l* ye shall stand still in Jordan. **9** And Joshua said unto the children of Israel, Come

---

g Num. 4. 15.——*h* Chap. 4. 14; 1 Chron. 29. 25; 2 Chron. 1. 1.——*i* Chap. 1. 5.——*k* Verse 3.—— *l* Verse 17.

---

who often thus mention the fulfilment of a prophecy or the execution of a command in the immediate connection.

·7. **This day will I begin to magnify thee**—This was only the *beginning* of a glorious succession of miracles attesting the divine commission of Joshua. Jehovah pledges to make Joshua great in the estimation of the people, and thus secure to him their promised loyalty and obedience. Compare chap. i, 17. **As I was with Moses**—As I crowned Moses with divine honour when, at the outstretching of his rod, I divided the waters of the Red Sea, so will I honour thee by rolling back the Jordan, when, at thy command, the symbol of my presence shall be borne to the river's brink. Special honour had been put upon Joshua when he was permitted to accompany Moses up the Mount, but it was eclipsed by the greater honour of his master, who alone was permitted to enter the cloud of the glory of the Lord. Exod. xxiv, 13–16. Moses on a former occasion (Deut. xxxi, 7) had magnified Joshua in the sight of all Israel, but now a Greater than Moses is about to magnify him in the sight of all mankind.

8. **The brink of the water**—Heb. *end of the water*, that is, the eastern margin of the river. It is evident from Joshua's address to the people, which immediately follows, that all the Lord s words to Joshua are not reported here. The abbreviation is to prevent repetition. The main point is to show that the whole order of the crossing was arranged by the Lord and not by Joshua. **Stand still in Jordan**—As a solemn and impressive indication to the passing host that the miracle is wrought

hither, and hear the words of the LORD your God. **10** And Joshua said, Hereby ye shall know that *m* the living God is among you, and *that* he will without fail *n* drive out from before you the Canaanites, and the Hittites, and the

m Deut. 5. 26; 1 Sam. 17. 26; 2 Kings 19. 4; Hos. 1. 10; Matt. 16. 16; 1 Thess. 1. 9.

n Exod. 33. 2; Deut. 7. 1; Psa. 44. 2.

by Jehovah, whose chosen ministers are the priests, and the symbol of whose presence is the ark.

9. **Unto the children of Israel**—The objection that Colenso urges against these addresses to the children of Israel by Moses and by Joshua, that it was a physical impossibility for so vast an encampment to hear the words of one speaker, falls to the ground when we reflect that all the people were addressed, not personally *en masse*, but representatively. as specified verse 2 and chap. i, 10. 16, through the heads and officers of their tribes.

10. **The living God is among you** —The adjective *living* is here and elsewhere applied to God in the sense of *true*, in opposition to the *false* pagan gods; and also in the sense of *efficient*, in opposition to the *dead* idols of the heathen world. In Psa. cvi, 28, the heathen are spoken of as eating the sacrifices of the dead—that is, dead idol gods. Jeremiah (x, 3–10) gives a detailed account of the process of manufacturing an idol, and then, in striking contrast, sets forth Jehovah as the *living* God. We may also with equal truth affirm that the attribute *living* signifies the *providential* care of the *personal* God, instead of the blind, impersonal force, the nondescript agency, which, entombed in matter, is indifferent to the wants and progress of men. The design of Joshua is to inspire faith and courage in the hearts of his people. Hence he represents to them that God will demonstrate by a series of astonishing miracles that he dwells not in serene repose, careless of their good, but that he is *alive* to their interests, and will overrule the laws of nature to secure their triumph. **Without fail drive out**—A strong promise, yet not unconditional. When man fails, God refuses. See notes on chap. i, 4, 5, 6.

Seven tribes are now enumerated, who shall, by the faithful co-operation of Israel with Jehovah, be driven from the Land of Promise. All of these tribes are of the same stock as the Phenicians. "It is startling to be reminded that the detested and accursed race, as it appears in the books of Joshua and Judges, is the same as that to which from Greece we look back as the parent of letters, of commerce, of civilization."—*Stanley*. See note on Acts viii, 40. Their character, as portrayed by Gentile writers, coincides substantially with that delineated by the Scriptures—their dusky complexion, their southern origin, their preservation of monarchical, federal, and aristocratic institutions, their superiority to surrounding nations in social arts, and their human sacrifices, licentious orgies, and multitudes of gods. In Gen. xv, 19–21, *ten* nations are mentioned, whose land was promised to the seed of Abraham. It is impossible at present to tell the exact location of all these tribes. Some of them seem to have become divided, and, like the tribes of Dan and Manasseh in Israel, become settled in different parts of the land. The **Canaanites** were, strictly speaking, the *lowlanders*, who inhabited the lower tracts of Palestine, on the sea-coast and western bank of the Jordan. Num. xiii, 29. But this term is often used in a wider sense, including all the tribes west of the Jordan and in Phenicia deriving their descent from Canaan. Gen. x, 15–18. **Hittites**—Or, *Chittites*. Of these Abraham purchased Machpelah, (Gen. xxiii, 10,) and among them Esau married two wives. Gen. xxvi, 34. See note on chap. i, 4. **Hivites**—Or, the *Chivite*. The Hebrew name is always in the singular. This tribe dwelt at the foot of Hermon, (chap. xi, 3,) and "in mount Lebanon, from mount Baalhermon unto the entering in of Hamath," (Judg. iii, 3;) also at Gibeon (chap. ix, 7; xi, 19) and at Shechem. Gen. xxxiv, 2. Gesenius and Fürst

Hivites, and the Perizzites, and the Gir- | gashites, and the Amorites, and the

explain the name as *villagers.* Ewald explains it as *mid-landers,* and supposes that " they loved peaceful occu-pations and trading pursuits in well-ordered communities and fortified cities, and loca-ed themselves principally in districts the most suitable for peaceful civil life, and such as have from the ear-nest times possessed the most flourishing inland cit-es."] **Perizzites** — Heb., *rustics* or *countrymen.* They inhabited the mountainous regions subsequently allot-ed to Judah and Ephraim, a part of which was after-wards called Samaria. Chap. xi, 13; xvii, 15. They were engaged in agricultural pur-suits. Hence in a wider sense the term **Perizzites** some-times includes all the agri-cultural Canaanites, in dis-tinction from those engaged in trade and commerce.— **Girgashites** — The resi-dence of this tribe is not distinctly specified in the Old Testament. Eusebius affirms that they dwelt east of the Jordan, and many writers incline to locate them east of lake Gennesa-ret. For here, according to Matt. viii, 28, lay " the coun-try of the *Gergesenes,*" iden-tical with the name of this tribe, as given in the Septu-agint and Vulgate versions.] **Amorites**—The *mountain-eers;* the largest, most pow-erful, and wide-spread tribe of all. Therefore their name is sometimes taken in a wide sense, to include all the Canaanitish tribes, as in chap. xxiv, 18. A part of them dwelt in the mountainous tract after-wards allotted to Judah, and were sub-ject to five kings. Chap. x, 5. An-other part had possession of the region

east of the Jordan, between the Arnon and the Jabbok. See note on chap. ii, 10. **The Jebusites** inhabited the city and neighbouring mountains of *Jebus*—ancient Jerusalem. They were not expelled from the city till the time of David. 2 Sam. v, 6, 8.

Jebusites. **11** Behold, the ark of the covenant of °the Lord of all the earth passeth over before you into Jordan. **12** Now therefore ᴾtake you twelve men out of the tribes of Israel, out of every tribe a man. **13** And it shall come to pass, q as soon as the soles of the feet of the priests that bear the ark of the LORD, ʳ the Lord of all the earth, shall rest in the waters of Jordan, *that* the waters of Jordan shall be cut off *from* the waters that come down from above; and they

---

o Verse 13; Micah 4. 13; Zech. 4. 14; 6. 5.   *p* Chap. 4. 2.——*q* Verses 15, 16.——*r* Verse 11.

---

11. **The ark of the covenant of the Lord of all the earth**—Here are four words grammatically dependent on one another, though slightly separated by the disjunctive accent. But this Hebrew accent by no means requires so strange a translation as that adopted by some scholars, which makes *Lord of all the earth* in apposition with *ark of the covenant.* ⎰ This would be to make the ark of Jehovah identical with Jehovah. ⎱ This claim of universal dominion for Jehovah, in contrast with the limited sway of the local gods of the pagans, not only enthrones Jehovah over all nations, but also over the forces of the material world. Perhaps no miracle of Jesus inspired such overwhelming awe in his disciples as his control of the winds and the waves.

12. [**Now therefore take you twelve men**—Emphasis is put on **now.** The election of these twelve men is to take place immediately, not after they cross the Jordan. The purpose for which they are selected is shown in chap. iv, 4, 5, where it will be seen that a visible memorial of this miracle is provided for before it takes place. The men were designated at this time because they could not be elected while the people were crossing, and afterwards there would be too little time. Hence the assumption of some that this verse is brought in by mistake, being disconnected from the succeeding chapter, is utterly groundless. The men are mentioned before the moving of the ark because they were chosen then.] **Out of every tribe a man**—This was done that every tribe might be represented in the memorial, and have its accredited witness of the great event.

13. **The Lord**—Heb., *Jehovah.* **The Lord of all the earth**—The efficient cause of the miracle. **Shall rest in**

the waters—The Jordan had two, and in some places three, banks. See cut and note Matt. iii, 6. At its flood it overflowed the first and second banks, and covered the whole space between the terraces formed by the second and third banks. The waters on each side would be comparatively shallow. Here the priests were to stand or rest in the shoal water on the eastern bank until the waves receded, and the river's channel was made bare; then they advanced into the midst of the channel of the Jordan, and there stood until all the people had crossed. Verse 17. **The waters of Jordan shall be cut off from the waters that come down**—Grammatically, **waters that come down** is in apposition with **waters of Jordan,** and the word **from,** supplied in our English version, is incorrect and misleading. It is better to omit **from,** and substitute *namely,* and render, *The waters of Jordan shall be cut off,* namely, *the waters that come down from above.* **And they shall stand upon a heap**—Or, *stand up, one mass.* The word for **heap** is best understood by referring to its use in the description of the division of the Red Sea in Exod. xv, 8, and in Psa. lxxviii, 13. By comparing these passages with Exod. xiv, 22, where it is said, " The waters were a wall unto them on their right hand and on their left," we arrive at the conclusion that the phenomenon presented by the word **heap** was that of an upright mass of water held back by Omnipotence. ⎰ We take the meaning to be that just above the crossing the waters were " congealed," or solidified, as if dammed up by an invisible perpendicular wall across the channel, causing the waters above to overflow all the banks. Below the miraculous dam the channel ran dry to the Dead Sea. ⎱ Compare note on verse 16. No natural agent was employed in the working of this miracle.

*shall stand upon a heap. **14** And it came to pass, when the people removed from their tents, to pass over Jordan, and the priests bearing the ᵗark of the covenant before the people; **15** And as

they that bare the ark were come unto Jordan, and ᵘthe feet of the priests that bare the ark were dipped in the brim of the water, (for ᵛJordan overfloweth all his banks ᵂall the time of harvest,)

---

s Psa. 78. 13; 114. 3.——*t* Acts 7. 45.
u Verse 13.

v 1 Chron. 12. 15; Jer. 12. 5; 49. 19.
w Chap. 4. 18; 5. 10. 12.

In the division of the Red Sea the Lord caused a strong east wind to blow all night, when Moses stretched out his hand over the sea. Exod. xiv, 21. But in the passage of the Jordan "there was neither wind nor tide, to the agency of which the effect could be attributed; and if the river was actually passed, at a high stage of its waters, without boats or bridges. the evidence of the miracle was irresistible—the current must have been suspended by supernatural power." In the most degenerate periods of Jewish history this great miracle was never once questioned. So far as we know even the skeptical and materialistic Sadducees, who sifted the traditions of the elders with a destructiveness rivaling the German rationalists, never assailed this manifest token of supernatural power in their nation's induction into the Land of Promise.

14. And the priests bearing the ark—The word **priests** is the grammatical subject of the implied verb, *were.* [Verses 14–16 should be rendered thus: And it came to pass while the people were removing from their tents to cross the Jordan, and the priests bearing the ark of the covenant were before the people, and as those bearing the ark came to the Jordan, and the feet of the priests bearing the ark were dipped in the edge of the waters, (and the Jordan was full over all its banks all the days of harvest,) then stood the waters which came down from above; they rose up, one mass, very far away, in Adam, the city which is beside Zarthan, and those [waters] which came down upon the Sea of the Wilderness, the Salt Sea, were entirely cut off, and the people crossed in front of Jericho.]

15. Overfloweth all his banks—The Jordan flows in a deep valley about three quarters of a mile wide, and about fifty feet deeper than the

wide plain (the Ghor) in which it lies. In this lower valley a narrow fringe of canes, intermingled with trees, runs along the edge of the river. In the ordinary swellings of Jordan the water overflows this strip of vegetation. driving the beasts of prey from their dens to ravage the surrounding country. Jer. xii, 5. Ordinarily the lower terrace of the river was dry, and the people went unto the Jordan for wood. 2 Kings vi, 2: also see note on Matt. iii. 6. Dr. Robinson visited the Jordan on the 12th of May, and found the stream so swollen that the water reached to the very top of the banks, and in some places flowed a little over and covered the roots of the bushes. The river was then about forty yards wide, and from ten to twelve feet deep. But when the Israelites crossed the waters must have been higher, as it is distinctly said that they overflowed all the banks. The idea that the river was forded by this multitude is inadmissible. The fact that the spies swam the river, and that the Arabs of modern times pass over in the rainy season in a few places known only to themselves, can by no means disprove this striking and well-attested miracle. **All the time of harvest**—The Hebrew word for **harvest,** according to Gesenius, here designates the grain harvest, in distinction from the fruit harvest. We are informed by Robinson that the barley harvest precedes the wheat harvest about two weeks. At Jericho, in the depressed valley of the Jordan, the barley was cut in the last half of April, and the wheat in the first half of May, about three weeks earlier than on the mountains of Hebron and Carmel. The reason for the overflow at this time instead of the winter—which, in that latitude, is the rainy season—is because the snow on the Lebanon, "which nourishes and pours out the

16 That the waters which came down from above stood *and* rose up upon a heap very far from the city Adam, that *is* beside [x] Zaretan; and those that came down [y] toward the sea of the plain, *even* [z] the salt sea, failed, *and* were cut off: and the people passed over right against Jericho. **17** And the priests that bare the ark of the covenant of the LORD stood firm on dry ground in the midst

---

x 1 Kings 4. 12; 7. 46.——*y* Deut. 3. 17.   *z* Gen. 14. 3: Num. 34. 3.

Jordan," melts at that time with the increasing heat of the summer.

Blunt observes here some undesigned coincidences with the books of Moses, which clearly demonstrate the reality and truth of this narration. In Exod. ix. 31–32, we read that the hail, which fell a few days before the first passover in Egypt, smote the *flax* and the *barley;* " for the barley was in the ear, and the flax was bolled. But the wheat and the rye were not smitten, for they were not grown up." Now the Jordan was passed on the 10th of Abib, four days before the passover, when we find the *barley* harvesting going on in the Jordan valley. This small circumstance, trifling though it be, confirms the truth of the account. So minute a coincidence between two histories would not have been designed by those perpetrating literary forgeries. Again, flax is cut or pulled when in the boll, as it was in Egypt when the hail cut it down. Forty years afterwards, in about the same latitude, at the same time of the year, Rahab covers the two spies to Jericho with *stalks of flax* which she had spread to cure on the roof. " How very minute is this incident! Could the historian have contemplated for one moment the effect which a trifle about a flax stalk might have in corroboration of his account of the passage of the Jordan? Is it possible for the most jealous examiner of human testimony to imagine that these flax stalks were fixed upon above all things in the world for the covering of the spies, because they were known to be ripe with the barley, and the barley was known to be ripe at the passover, and the passover was known to be the season when the Israelites set foot in Canaan?"

16. **The city Adam, that is beside Zaretan**—It is impossible to locate these cities; no traces of them remain. The latter city is elsewhere more correctly spelled *Zarthan.* There is in the Hebrew a marginal reading which is generally preferred by the critics: " The waters stood and rose up upon one heap very far off—by Adam, the city that is by the side of Zarthan." In accordance with this reading many commentators suppose that the entire channel of the Jordan was dry for many miles above the place of crossing, and that the waters were rolled back and piled up in a place many miles distant towards, or near, the Sea of Tiberias. The following is Stanley's graphic description: " On the broken edge of the swollen stream the band of priests stood, with the ark on their shoulders. Suddenly the full bed of the Jordan was dried before them. High up the river, far, far away, in Adam, (that is, at a distance of thirty miles from the encampment,) the waters stood which ' descended ' from the heights above; stood, and rose up as if gathered into a waterskin, as if in a barrier or heap, as if congealed, (LXX;) and those that descended toward the Sea of the Desert, the Salt Sea, failed, and were cut off. Thus the scene presented is of the ' descending stream,' (Jordan, etymologically, means the *Descender*,) not parted asunder, as we generally fancy, but, as the Psalm expresses it, (cxiv, 3,) ' turned backwards; ' the whole bed of the river left dry from north to south, through its long windings; the huge stones lying bare here and there, embedded in the soft bottom; or the shingly pebbles drifted along the course of the channel." To this theory of the miracle, which is also that of Dr. A. Clarke, we object. We see no reason for heaping up the waters in a far-distant place where there were no Hebrew witnesses.

17. **The priests : . . stood firm on dry ground**—The priests stood above, near the wall of waters, and the people passed below. The ark,

of Jordan, [n] and all the Israelites passed over on dry ground, until all the people were passed clean over Jordan.

CHAPTER IV.

AND it came to pass, when all the people were clean passed [a] over Jordan, that the LORD spake unto Joshua, saying, **2** [b] Take you twelve men out of the people, out of every tribe a man, **3** And command ye them, saying,

---

[n] See Exod. 14. 29.——[a] Deut. 27. 2; chap. 3. 17.
[b] Chap. 3. 12.

---

the symbol of the presence of Jehovah, was the instrument of the miracle, as the rod of Moses had been in the division of the Red Sea. Thus God honours his own ordinances. **Dry ground**—Not hard and dusty ground, but dry only in the sense of being drained of water. See note on chap. iv, 18. ⎰ **All the Israelites passed ...clean over Jordan**—The Jordan is now passed, and *Canaan is attained!* The forty years' sojourn is closed, and for the first ecstatic moment the feet of the tribes are standing on the Promised Land! Their departure from Egypt and their arrival in Canaan are signalized by parallel miracles of sea and river. Both at their exit and at their entrance Jehovah leads them through a watery gate, by cleaving the waves asunder. Through all ages the Church has seen in the desert sojourn the symbol of our probationary life, and in the crossing the Jordan the symbol of death. Yet is there this memorable difference: the crossing the Jordan was to Israel the commencement of a new warfare; the transit of Christian death is into eternal repose. ⎱

CHAPTER IV.

BUILDING MONUMENTS.—1-24.

[This chapter, more than many others, affords us a noticeable example of the style of the Hebrew historian. While the central theme of the whole chapter is the building of the stone monument in Gilgal, observe how further particulars of the passage of the Jordan are recorded, which the writer did not wish to interrupt the order of his narrative, in chapter iii, to tell. Strict chronological order is not sought after by him, but rather a record of the facts, leaving the reader's common sense to infer the order; or rather, treating the order of events as of little moment. See Introduction.]

1. **All the people**—All the people of the nine and a half tribes which afterwards permanently occupied Western Palestine, and the forty thousand picked soldiers of the Eastern tribes.

[2. **Take you twelve men**—These men were surely not elected after the people had crossed the Jordan and while the priests were standing in the river bed, but previously, as chapter iii. 12 clearly implies. See note there. The command there given to Joshua was to elect the twelve men *now*—that is, before crossing—and the exact repetition of the command in this place is only in keeping with the simple style of the Hebrew historian. The choosing of the twelve men, which was, perhaps, done by a popular election, took place before they crossed over; the orders to take each man a stone from the midst of the Jordan were given after all the people had crossed.]

3. **The place where the priests' feet stood firm**—After the waters had rolled away at the touch of the priests' feet, they bore the ark into the middle and deepest part of the channel. See note on chap. iii, 13. This is also implied in the command, "Come ye up out of Jordan." Verse 17. **Lodging place**—Gilgal, six miles west of the Jordan. See verses 19, 20. They lodged at Gilgal not one night only, but many days.

5. **Pass over before the ark**—Advance to a position immediately in

---

Take you hence out of the midst of Jordan, out of the place where [c] the priests' feet stood firm, twelve stones, and ye shall carry them over with you, and leave them in [d] the lodging place, where ye shall lodge this night. **4** Then Joshua called the twelve men, whom he [e] had prepared of the children of Israel, out of every tribe a man: **5** And Joshua said unto them, Pass over before the ark of the LORD your God into the midst of

---

[c] Chap. 3. 13.——[d] Verses 19, 20.
[e] Mark 3. 14-19.

Jordan, and take you up every man of you a stone upon his shoulder, according unto the number of the tribes of the children of Israel: **6** That this may be a sign among you, *that* [f] when your children ask *their fathers* [1] in time to come, saying. What *mean* ye by these stones? **7** Then ye shall answer them, That [g] the waters of Jordan were cut off before the ark of the covenant of the LORD; when it passed over Jordan, the

waters of Jordan were cut off: and these stones shall be for [h] a memorial unto the children of Israel for ever. **8** And the children of Israel did so as Joshua commanded, and took up twelve stones out of the midst of Jordan, as the LORD spake unto Joshua, according to the number of the tribes of the children of Israel, and carried them over with them unto the place where they lodged, and laid them down there. **9** And Joshua

---

f Verse 21; Exod. 12. 26; 13. 14; Deut. 6. 20; Psa. 44. 1; 78. 3-6.

1 Heb. *to morrow.*——*g* Chap. 3. 13, 16. *h* Exod. 12. 14; Num. 16. 40.

---

front of the ark, and take up the stones. As this order seems to have been given after the people had crossed, we naturally understand that the twelve men passed back again to the place where the ark rested, and thence transported the stones, while all Israel stood beholding them. **According unto the number of the tribes**—A memorial not only of the wonderful interposition of Jehovah, but of the federal unity of the nation—one composed of twelve.

6. **That this may be a sign among you**—By this simple device two grand purposes are subserved: (1.) The preservation of national history and religious knowledge; (2.) The religious education of the young. The inquisitiveness of the children is not to be repressed, but rather stimulated by impressive monuments of historical events, and by symbols of religious truths. "Object teaching," which has recently been brought forward in the art of education, is here introduced as a method of instruction by God himself. By the presentation of visible objects to the eye, divine truth may be most vividly photographed upon the soul. Hence the value of travel in historic lands as an educator. Renan says: "Seeing Palestine is the fifth gospel."

7. **Memorial . . . for ever**—The Hebrew word here used is the strongest one in the language to express *eternity*. But it is often used in a popular way to indicate not absolute eternity, but a period indefinitely long, especially when the "speaker is led by his strong desire to overlook the fact that what he is speaking of must have an end."—*Keil.* The importance of this memorial

as a proof of the miraculous passage of the Jordan is thus set forth by Mr. Leslie: "Let us suppose that there never was any such thing as that passage over Jordan; that these stones at Gilgal were set up on some other occasion; and that some designing man in an after age invented this book of Joshua, affirmed that it was written at the time of that imaginary event by Joshua himself, and adduced this pile of stones as a testimony of the truth of it; would not every body say to him, 'We know this pile very well; but we never before heard of this reason for it, nor of this book of Joshua; where has it lain concealed all this while, and where and how came you, after so many ages, to find it? Besides, this book tells us that this passage over Jordan was ordained to be taught our children from age to age, and therefore that they were always to be instructed in the meaning of this particular monument as a memorial of it; but we were never so taught when we were children, nor did we ever teach our children any such thing; and it is in the highest degree improbable that such an emphatic ordinance should have been forgotten, during the continuance of so remarkable a pile, set up for the express purpose of perpetuating its remembrance.'"

8. **Israel did so**—They did so by their twelve representatives, according to the old law-maxim: *Qui facit per alium, facit per se*—"He who acts through another acts through himself." **And laid them down**—They did **not** construct them into a monument. This Joshua did afterwards. Verse 20.

9. **And Joshua set up twelve**

set up *twelve stones in the midst of Jordan, in the place where the feet of the priests which bare the ark of the covenant stood: and they are there unto this day. **10** For the priests which

bare the ark stood in the midst of Jordan, until every thing was finished that the LORD commanded Joshua to speak unto the people, according to all that Moses commanded Joshua: and the

---

i Exod. 2S. 21;   1 Kings 16. 31.

---

stones in the midst of Jordan—[The **and** at the beginning of this verse, and **twelve stones,** without the article, indicate with sufficient clearness that these twelve stones were different from those just mentioned in verse 8. This is still more evident from the fact that these were set up **in the midst of Jordan,** those *in Gilgal.* Verse 20. The fact that we find no record of any command from God to Joshua to erect this monument in the river does not disprove the existence of such a command, which a concise writer may omit, and yet describe its execution. See note on chap. iii. 6. Or we may suppose that Joshua and the elders erected this river monument for their own satisfaction, and not by divine command.] But if these stones were set up in the midst of the river they must have been covered by the returning waters and probably swept away: how, then, could our author have known that they were there in his day? We reply that even if the pile was always below the surface of the water it might be seen or felt by careful examination, and be a thing of deep interest, especially to the men of that generation. But it is probable that these stones were not limited in size to the carrying capacity of one man: and they may have been placed upon an elevated base of rocks, so that they would ordinarily rise above the top of the water. It is very certain that our author, perhaps himself an eye-witness of the crossing of the Jordan, had more means of ascertaining the truth of his statements than we of the present day can possibly have to contradict his testimony. The word for **set up** signifies *rear up, erect,* and implies that the monument was of considerable height. As the memorial at Gilgal indicated very definitely the place of the passage, the monument to show the spot where the priests stood with the

ark on their shoulders needed not to be very conspicuous. **And they are there unto this day**—This implies that the stones were for years visible either beneath or above the waters; otherwise the presence of the monument at a later day could not be asserted. On the theory that Joshua is the author of this book in its present form, having written it in his last years, it was about twenty years after these events that this memorial was existing. But if these words were added by a later hand they show the still longer continuance of the monument.

10. **The priests ... stood ... until every thing was finished**—It is not necessary to suppose that the building of the river monument took place *after* the people had passed, but it could have been built *while* they were hastening across the dry channel. This would abbreviate the time of the priests standing still and supporting the ark. **According to all that Moses commanded Joshua**—We do not find in the books of Moses any directions respecting the manner of passing over the Jordan, and of perpetuating the remembrance of that event. The meaning of this passage must be that Joshua obeyed Jehovah as Moses had commanded him, without being enjoined any special duty in this case. Num. xxvii, 23; Deut iii, 28, and xxxi. 23. In accordance with the precept of his illustrious predecessor, he had been very attentive to the words of God. **And the people hasted**—There were obvious reasons for their haste. The priests were in a painful attitude, bearing the ark with the tables of stone within. The waters, rising up above, with no visible barrier to keep them from dashing suddenly down upon the people in the channel, would produce a trepidation in the beholders, and quicken their pace. Haste was also necessary in order that the entire na-

people [k] hasted and passed over. **11** And it came to pass, when all the people were clean passed over, that the ark of the LORD passed over, and the priests, in the presence of the people. **12** And [l] the children of Reuben, and the children of Gad, and half the tribe of Manasseh, passed over armed before the children of Israel, as Moses spake unto them: **13** About forty thousand [2] prepared for war passed over before the LORD unto battle, to the plains of Jericho. **14** On that day the LORD [m] magnified Joshua in the sight of all Israel;

and they feared him, as they feared Moses, all the days of his life. **15** And the LORD spake unto Joshua, saying, **16** Command the priests that bear [n] the ark of the testimony, that they come up out of Jordan. **17** Joshua therefore commanded the priests, saying, Come ye up out of Jordan. **18** And it came to pass, when the priests that bare the ark of the covenant of the LORD were come up out of the midst of Jordan, *and* the soles of the priests' feet were [3] lifted up unto the dry land, that the waters of Jordan returned unto their place, [o] and

k Exod. 12. 39; Psa. 119. 60; Eccles. 9. 10.——
l Num. 32. 20, 27, 28.——2 Or, *ready armed.*

m Chap. 3. 7.——*n* Exod. 25. 16, 22.——3 Heb.
plucked up.——*o* Chap. 3. 15.

tion. with all their possessions, might cross in one day. The supernatural never supersedes the fullest exercise of our natural abilities.

11. **The ark of the Lord passed over**—Great prominence is given to the ark as the visible instrument of the miracle, the first to enter and the last to leave the bed of the Jordan. **In the presence of the people**—Who, after their own hasty passage, were now standing on the western bank. contemplating the wonderful spectacle. This greatest miracle of the Old Testament had at least a million eye-witnesses.

12. **And the children of Reuben**—The conjunction **and** does not indicate the order of events, but the historian wishes by repetition to give emphasis to the statement that the eastern tribes had already passed over to assist their brethren in the conquest of the land. **Armed**—See chap. i, 14, note. **Before**—That is. in sight of. They were. perhaps, placed in the van to ensure the fulfilling of their promise, or because they were unencumbered with their families and flocks, which they had left on the eastern side of the river.

13. **Forty thousand**—For their entire military strength see chap. i, 14, note. **Plains of Jericho**—A part of the Ghor or Arabah near Jericho. The mountains on the west fall back considerably to the south of the entrance into the Wady Kelt, and sweep toward the southwest, and then turn again toward the Dead Sea. The valley on the west of the Jordan is at this point seven miles wide.

14. **The Lord magnified Joshua** —This is the fulfilment of the promise in chap. iii. 7. See the note. **And they feared him, as they feared Moses**—"This was not, indeed, the chief design of the miracle. to exalt the power and authority of Joshua. But as it was of the greatest importance to the people generally that the government of Joshua should be firmly established, it is very properly mentioned as the crowning advantage resulting from it, that he was. as it were. invested with sacred insignia. which produced such veneration among the people that no one dared to despise him."—*Calvin*. **All the days of his life**—Joshua's life.

15. **The Lord spake unto Joshua** —The Hebrew having no pluperfect, this may be rendered *had spoken*. This repetition of what has been previously described is for the purpose of showing how Joshua was magnified. by connecting his agency with the miracle. "The priests did not quit their station till Joshua, who had ordered them thither, ordered them thence; nor did he thus order them until the Lord commanded him: so obedient were all parties to the word of God."—*Scott*.

16. **Ark of the testimony**—This was so called because it contained the two tables of testimony. Deut. xxxi, 18; see note on chap. iii, 3. Gesenius renders, *ark of the law.*

18. **The soles of the priests' feet were lifted up unto the dry land**— Hebrew, *plucked up*, that is, from the miry bed of the river, which was **dry** only in the sense of being drained of water. **The waters of Jordan**

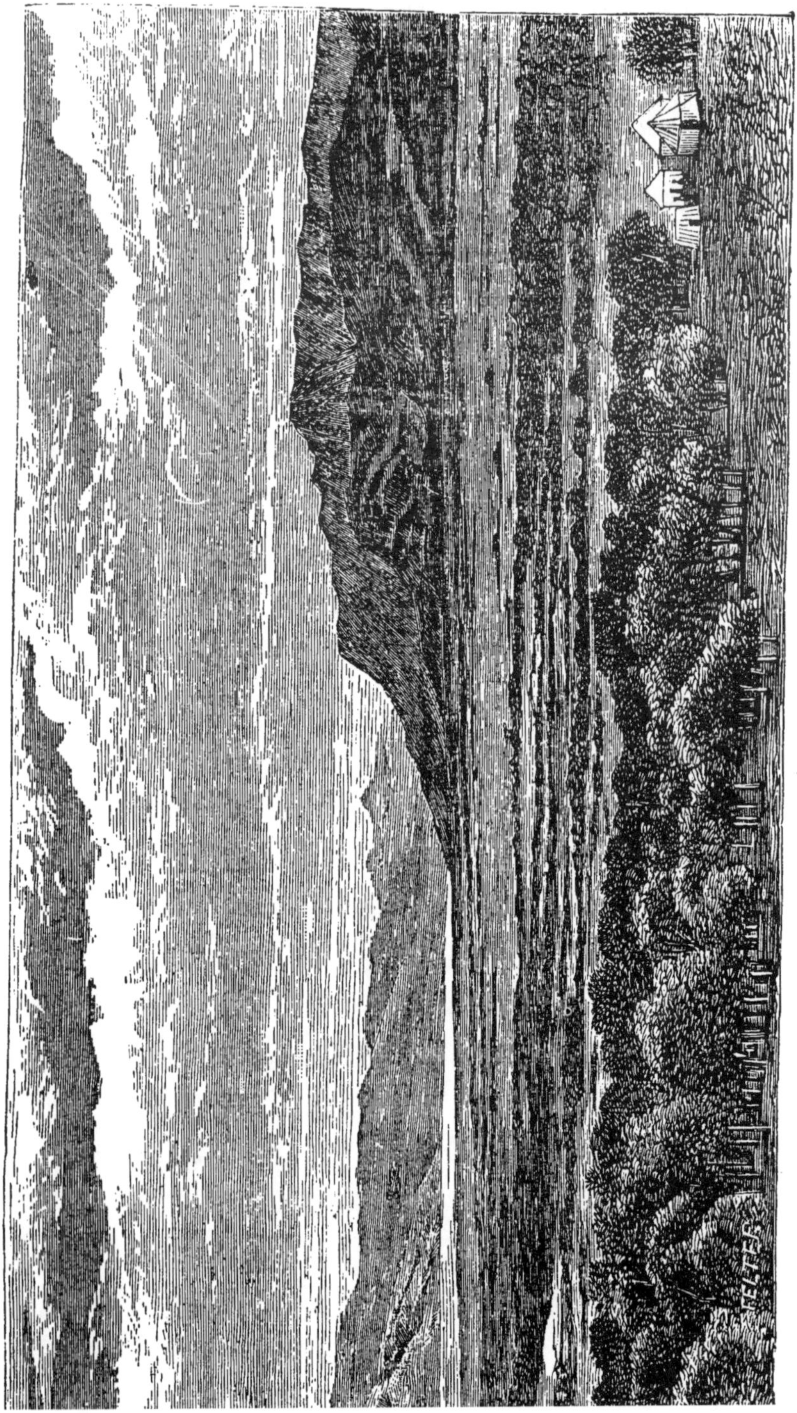

PLAINS OF JERICHO.

[4] flowed over all his banks, as *they did*
before. **19** And the people came up
out of Jordan on the tenth *day* of the
first month, and encamped [p] in Gilgal,
in the east border of Jericho. **20** And
[q] those twelve stones, which they took
out of Jordan, did Joshua pitch in Gilgal. **21** And he spake unto the children of Israel, saying, [r] When your children shall ask their fathers [5] in time to
come, saying, What *mean* these stones?
22 Then ye shall let your children know,
saying, [s] Israel came over this Jordan on
dry land. **23** For the LORD your God
dried up the waters of Jordan from before you, until ye were passed over, as
the LORD your God did to the Red Sea,
[t] which he dried up from before us, until we were gone over: **24** [u] That all the
people of the earth might know the
hand of the LORD, that it *is* [v] mighty:
that ye might [w] fear the LORD your God
[6] for ever.

CHAPTER V.

AND it came to pass, when all the kings of the Amorites, which *were* on the side of Jordan westward,

4 Heb. *went*.——*p* Chap. 5. 9.——*q* Verse 3.——*r* Verse 6.——5 Heb. *to morrow*.——*s* Chap. 3. 17.——*t* Exod. 14. 21.——*u* 1 Kings 8. 42, 43; 2 Kings 19. 19; Psa. 106. 8.——*v* Exod. 15. 16; 1 Chron. 29. 12; Psa. 89. 13.——*w* Exod. 49. 31; Deut. 6. 2; Psa. 89. 7; Jer. 10. 7.——6 Heb. *all days*.

returned—As the waters suddenly stopped when the ark was borne into them, and flowed onward again when the ark left the bed of the river, the wonderful miracle must be ascribed to the ark as the instrument, and to God as the efficient cause.

19. **The tenth day of the first month**—In chap. v, 10, we learn that the passover, the anniversary of the Exodus, occurred on the fourteenth of the same month, so that there were forty years, wanting four days, between the departure from Egypt and the entrance into Canaan. They did not enter earlier because of their unbelief. Heb. iii, 19. **Gilgal**—On the significance which the Israelites afterwards attached to this name, see note on chap. v, 9. According to Josephus, Gilgal was fifty stadia, about six miles, from the Jordan, and ten stadia, exceeding a mile, from Jericho. No trace of the name or site now remains. This Gilgal must be carefully distinguished from another Gilgal in Central Palestine, known by the modern name *Jiljilia*. See note on chap. ix, 6. Gilgal is noted as the first encampment of Israel in Canaan. Here was the scene of the circumcision, here the first passover was celebrated in the land, and here the manna ceased to fall.

20. **Did Joshua pitch in Gilgal**—The Hebrew word here rendered **pitch** is precisely the same as that rendered *set up* in verse 9, where see note. These twelve memorial stones were here built up by Joshua into a perpetual monument, resting, doubtless, upon a pedestal, to render it more conspicuous. More than six hundred years afterwards the Minor Prophets, Hosea (iv, 15; ix, 15; xii, 11) and Amos, (iv, 4; v, 5,) repeatedly reprove the Jews for going to Gilgal "to multiply transgression;" and Stanley, in his History of the Jewish Church, suggests that this monument came to be regarded with idolatrous veneration, like the worship of the cross among the Papists.

24. **All the people of the earth**—We need not limit this expression to mean merely the nations of the land of Canaan, for this amazing miracle was doubtless designed to teach impressive lessons of divine power to the nations of all coming ages.

CHAPTER V.

CONSTERNATION OF THE CANAANITES, 1.

1. **It came to pass**—Immediately after the Israelites had crossed, the miracle was heralded to all the kings of the land. This verse is closely related to the last verse of the preceding chapter, showing how the miracle of the Jordan at once made the neighbouring nations know the power of Jehovah's hand. It also serves to show why Joshua might, without fear of attack, embrace this opportunity to circumcise the people. **Amorites**—See note on chap. ii, 10. **On the side of Jordan westward**—Literally, *beyond Jordan seaward*. The Amorites east of the Jordan, ruled by Sihon and Og, had been already defeated. **The**

and all the kings of the Canaanites, *a* which *were* by the sea, *b* heard that the Lord had dried up the waters of Jordan from before the children of Israel, until we were passed over, that their heart melted, *c* neither was there spirit in them any more, because of the children of Israel.

2 At that time the Lord said unto Joshua, Make thee [1] *d* sharp knives, and circumcise again the children of Israel the second time. **3** And Joshua made

a Num. 13. 29.——*b* Exod. 15. 14, 15; Chap. 2, 9, 10, 11; Psa. 48. 6; Ezek. 21. 7.

c 1 Kings 10. 5.——1 Or. *knives of flints.* *d* Exod. 4. 25.

Canaanites, which were by the sea —The various heathen tribes and nations along the Mediterranean Sea. A narrow plain extends along this sea from Gaza in the south to the northern limits of Phenicia. The Amorites and Canaanites, because of their superiority in numbers and political power, are put here apparently for all the nations of the land. **We were passed over**—This expression naturally implies that the writer was an eye-witness of the scene described. **Their heart melted**—Their hope and courage died within them, for they despaired of conquering an almighty foe.

CIRCUMCISION RESTORED, 2–9.

[It seems at first sight strange that the chosen people for forty years neglected circumcision. The clue to a proper explanation of this neglect is furnished in the following verses, especially in verse 9, where allusion is made to *the reproach of Egypt.* This reproach is explained, in Exod. xxxii, 12; Num. xiv, 13–16: Deut. ix, 28, as the scoffing words and ridicule which the Egyptians would so naturally utter against the Hebrews when the latter suffered from God's anger. After the rebellion and murmuring at Kadesh, Jehovah condemned that generation to perish in the wilderness. Num. xiv, 29–34. During the forty years that followed they were under the ban of that sweeping curse, and observed neither circumcision nor the passover. These sacraments were sacred seals of their covenant with Jehovah, and, the covenant being broken by their rebellion, that cursed generation could not renew it. See further on verses 5 and 6. But the mighty miracle of the Jordan, which now spread terror among the nations, silenced this reproach, and hence the propriety of renewing the covenant in Gilgal.]

2. **At that time**—That is, during the interval of four days between the passage of Jordan and the passover, (see chap. iv, 19, note,) and while their foes are dismayed and panic-stricken. This was a very opportune occasion to perform the rite of circumcision, which for a season unfitted its subjects for military duty. **Circumcise again . . . the second time**—This does not imply that there had been a previous *time* of general circumcising, as some say, at Sinai, but a previous *state* of circumcision. See verse 5. The rite was not performed twice on the same individual, but the sense is, Resume again the rite of circumcision as it was practiced forty years ago. **The children of Israel**—All the males who were born after the Hebrews left Egypt. **Sharp knives** — Hebrew. *knives of rocks, stones, or flints.* Such an instrument was used by Zipporah in circumcising the son of Moses. Exod. iv, 25. Knives among rude barbarians are first made of flint. It is probable that this was used in the first circumcision by the patriarchs, and the same instrument was used by Joshua not from necessity —for he had iron tools—but from deference to ancient custom. It is said also that the wound made with a sharp stone is less liable to inflammation than one made with metal. These knives were to be made for the occasion, as it would not be proper to use in a religious rite instruments employed in common uses. Knives that had been used for other purposes might inoculate the circumcised person with the virus of some disease. Hiob Ludolph, in his history of the Ethiopians, speaks of a tribe of the Alnæi who performed the rite with stone knives as recently as one hundred and sixty years ago. According to the Septuagint version of Joshua xxiv, 30, the stone knives used on this occasion were deposited in the

him sharp knives, and circumcised the children of Israel at [2]the hill of the foreskins. **4** And this *is* the cause why Joshua did circumcise : *e* All the people that came out of Egypt, *that were* males, *even* all the men of war, died in the wilderness by the way, after they came out of Egypt. **5** Now all the people that came out were circumcised ; but all the people *that were* born in the wilderness by the way as they came forth out of Egypt, *them* [f] they had not circumcised. **6** For the children of Israel walked [g] forty years in the wilderness, till all the people *that were* men of war, which came out of Egypt, were consumed, because they obeyed not the voice of the LORD : unto whom the LORD sware that [h] he would not show them the land, which the LORD sware unto their fathers that he would give us, [i] a land that floweth with milk and honey. **7** And [k] their children *whom* he raised up in their stead, them Joshua circumcised : for they were uncircumcised, because they had not circumcised them by the

---

2 Or, *Gibeah-haaraloth.*——*e* Num. 14. 29; 26. 64, 65; Deut. 2. 16.——*f* Deut. 12. 8, 9; Hosea 6. 6, 7.

g Num. 14. 33; Deut. 1. 3; 2. 7, 14; Psa. 95. 10. ——*h* Num. 14. 23; Psa. 95. 11; Heb. 3. 11.—— *i* Exod. 3. 8.——*k* Num. 14. 31; Deut. 1. 39.

---

tomb of Joshua as sacred relics. Perhaps some modern geologists would consider them relics of a " stone age."

3. **Hill of the foreskins**—The hill on which this rite occurred, one of the many argillaceous hills on the terrace of the valley, receives its name from the prepuces buried in it, and not, as the Rabbins say, from the quantity piled up there.

4. **And this is the cause**—As this book contains not only a record of events, but also ascribes a rational cause to each, it may be classed among philosophical histories. **All the people**—This expression is limited first to the males, and then to those of military age, from twenty years old and upwards. Num. xiv, 29–32. **Died in the wilderness**—Because of their rebellion against Jehovah, and the cowardice displayed when the panic-stricken spies made their exaggerated report. Num. xiv, 21–35. Caleb and Joshua were the only exceptions to this sweeping sentence. Num. xxvi, 64, 65.

5. **All the people that came out were circumcised**—That is, had been circumcised in infancy. Lev. xii, 3. **The people…born in the wilderness…they had not circumcised**—Various reasons have been assigned for the neglect in the wilderness of this rite, which was so scrupulously performed in Egypt. The fact that they were in an unsettled condition is not a sufficient reason, for they dwelt for months together in one place. The most satisfactory account of the matter is that, while under the sentence of the divine displeasure for forty years, the nation was temporarily rejected by its divine Head, and prohibited from impressing upon their sons the sign of the covenant. See note introductory to verse 2.

6. **Forty years in the wilderness** —This verse assigns the reason why circumcision had not been performed, namely, their disobedience and punishment. As the sentence of exclusion from the favour of Jehovah had now expired, the nation is again admitted to the privilege of using the sign of his covenant. While in exile they were the objects of his care, and even of his supernatural providence, but not of his *approval ;* just as sinners under the Gospel dispensation enjoy the bounty of God, but not the covenant of his pardoning grace. **Till all the people…were consumed**—The word for **people** is that which is always used to designate a heathen nation, a Gentile race, in distinction from the peculiar people, Israel. This confirms the explanation that Israel was excluded from covenant relations during the forty years' wandering. **The Lord sware that he would not show them the land**—That is, cause them to see, *and hence to enter and enjoy, the land.* **A land that floweth with milk and honey**—This phrase represents the great fertility and loveliness of the Land of Promise ; it was a land rich in grass for herds, hence there was an abundance of milk ; it was profuse in flowers, hence bees and wild honey were very plentiful, (Judg. xiv, 8 ; Matt. iii, 4,) and they still are found, in

way. **8** And it came to pass, [3] when they had done circumcising all the people, that they abode in their places in the camp, [l] till they were whole. **9** And the LORD said unto Joshua, This day have I rolled away [m] the reproach of

Egypt from off you. Wherefore the name of the place is called [4] [n] Gilgal unto this day.

10 And the children of Israel encamped in Gilgal, and kept the passover [o] on the fourteenth day of the month at

---

3 Heb. *when the people had made an end to be circumcised.*——*l* See Genesis 34. 25.—— *m* Genesis 34. 14; 1 Samuel 14. 6; see Leviticus 18. 3; chapter 24. 14; Ezekiel 20. 7; 23. 3, 8.—— 4 That is, *Rolling.*——*n* Chapter 4. 19.——*o* Exodus 12. 6; Numbers 9. 5.

---

spite of the lack of cultivation and the desolation of Palestine. Milk and its various products constituted the chief sustenance of the ancient Hebrews. In Palestine the bees do actually deposit honey in the holes of the rocks in so great quantities that it flows out and is gathered in vessels placed beneath.

8. **Circumcising all the people**— Objection is made that it was impossible to circumcise so many, probably six or seven hundred thousand, in one day. But according to the most accurate estimates there were between two and three hundred thousand circumcised men to administer the rite, so that each would have but three or four subjects requiring the ordinance. **They abode in their places in the camp**—Hebrew, *they sat under themselves;* that is, they remained on that spot which was under them when they first sat down. Exod. xvi, 29. **Till they were whole**—According to the Talmud the wound was immediately treated with oil, which diminished the pain and induced a speedy healing. It is not probable that their cure was entirely effected so early as the third day, the passover; nor would it be necessary for them to be free from physical disability in order to celebrate that ordinance, since there were enough who were able to perform the labour of preparing the paschal lamb. For at least one fourth of the men had been previously circumcised, and two small families could unite. Exod. xii, 14.

9. **I rolled away the reproach of Egypt**—The reproach which Egypt has cast upon you; for Egypt is here subjective and not objective. Compare Isa. li, 7; Ezek. xvi, 57, and xxxvi, 15. Many are the explanations of this reproach. Some say it was Egyptian bondage; others, the state of

being uncircumcised, which implies, what cannot be proved, that the Egyptians were circumcised; still others, that the Hebrews were unfit for war. But we find the reproach in Exod. xxxii, 12: " Wherefore should the Egyptians speak, and say, For mischief did he bring them out, to slay them in the mountains, and to consume them from the face of the earth ? " They had been exposed to this reproach for forty years, for God had been destroying them during that time. But with the restoration of covenant relations, whereof circumcision was the sign, the reproach of Egypt is rolled away from them. The malicious taunt is now no longer true. [**Called Gilgal**—The place may have been called Gilgal before this event, and there were other places in the land of the same name; but as the word **Gilgal** means *a wheel* or *circle*, and is so easily associated with the idea of *rolling*, the Israelites naturally gave it the symbolical meaning here stated, because their renewal of the covenant by circumcision had rolled away the reproach of Egypt.]

THE THIRD PASSOVER AND CEASING OF THE MANNA, 10–12.

10. **And kept the passover**— This institution was in memory of their deliverance from the plague which had destroyed the firstborn in Egypt, (Exod. xii,) and was the second feast which had been observed since leaving that land of bondage. The first was at Sinai, in the second year of their journey in the desert. Num. ix. There was no observance of it in the desert subsequent to this, on account of the rejection of Israel from the covenant. See on verse 6 and note introductory to verse 2. **On the fourteenth day of the month**—This was the month Abib, the first month of the

even in the plains of Jericho. **11** And they did eat of the old corn of the land on the morrow after the passover, unleavened cakes, and parched *corn* in the self-same day. **12** And ᵖ the manna ceased on the morrow after they had eaten of the old corn of the land; neither had the children of Israel manna

---

p Exod. 16, 35; Neh. 9. 20, 21; Rev. 7. 16, 17.
q Prov. 13. 22; Isa. 65. 13, 14; John 4. 38.

Hebrew year. After the captivity it was called *Nisan*. The fourteenth of this month corresponded with about the middle of our April.

11. **The old corn of the land—** There is no authority in the Hebrew for the word **old.** They ate of the *produce* of the land. The word **old** was inserted by our translators because it was unlawful to eat of the new grain before the sheaf was waved before Jehovah on the morrow of the Sabbath. Lev. xxiii, 14–16. [But here is a difficulty. *The morrow after the passover* is used in Num. xxxiii, 3, for the fifteenth of Nisan, the day after the evening on which the paschal lamb was eaten. But according to Lev. xxiii. 7, this day was to be celebrated by a holy convocation, and on it no servile work performed. How, then, shall we account for Israel's eating the new fruit of the land on the morrow after the passover? The simplest explanation is that of Keil, who understands the word *passover* here, as in several other places, to mean not simply the paschal supper but the entire feast connected with it, which lasted seven days. **Parched corn—**Ears of grain baked at the fire, an article of food still much relished by the Arabs. See note on Ruth ii, 14.]

12 **Manna—**This was always regarded as a miraculous gift directly from God, and not a product of nature. It is described in Exod. xvi, 14–36, where see notes. It fell upon the encampment six times each week during forty years. As each man had an omer—three quarts—a day, there must have been 15,000,000 pounds a week. The natural product of the Arabian deserts, the tamarisk-manna, called by the same name, differs in the following partic-

any more; but ᵠ they did eat of the fruit of the land of Canaan that year.

13 And it came to pass, when Joshua was by Jericho, that he lifted up his eyes and looked, and, behold, there stood ʳ a man over against him ˢ with his sword drawn in his hand: and Joshua went unto him, and said

---

r Gen. 18. 2; 32. 24; Exod. 23. 23; Zech. 1. 8; Acts 1. 10.——*s* Num. 22. 23.

---

ulars: it is purgative, and not nutritious; it is produced only three or four months, and not all the year; it is found in small quantities; it can be kept good for a long time, and is not corrupted by being kept over the Sabbath; nor would a natural product cease at once and forever. It now ceased because it was no more needed. See chap. i, 11, note.

The Captain of the Lord's Host
Revealed, v, 13–vi, 5.

[The chosen people have now by circumcision renewed their covenant with Jehovah; they have eaten the passover within the limits of the Land of Promise; they have tasted the new corn of the land. The time now approaches for them to proceed to the work of conquest, and the angel of Jehovah appears to Joshua, and reveals the divine plan for the destruction of Jericho.]

13. **When Joshua was by Jericho—**He was apparently making a personal and private *reconnaissance* of the city, which was the key to the whole land of Canaan. See note on chap. ii, 1. **A man over against him—**The subsequent account shows that he was a man only in form. **With his sword drawn—**The sword is a symbol of high executive power. The drawn sword intimates that that power is to be immediately exercised. Hence Joshua's anxiety to know in whose behalf the mysterious stranger has drawn his sword. **Joshua went unto him—**Here is a remarkable display of courage on the part of Joshua. Good men, because of their faith in God, confront danger without fear. **Art thou for us, or for our adversaries?—**The idea of neutrality in the contest does not occur to Joshua

unto him, *Art* thou for us, or for our adversaries? **14** And he said, Nay; but *as* ⁵captain of the host of the LORD am I now come. And Joshua ᵗ fell on his face to the earth, and did worship, and said unto him, What saith my lord unto his servant? **15** And the captain of the LORD's host said unto Joshua,

ᵘLoose thy shoe from off thy foot; for the place whereon thou standest *is* holy. And Joshua did so.

CHAPTER VI.

NOW Jericho ¹ was straitly shut up because of the children of Israel: none went out, and none came in.

---

5 Or, *prince;* see Exod. 23. 20; Dan. 10. 13. 21; 12. 1; Rev. 12. 7; 19. 11, 14.——*t* Gen. 17. 3.

u Exod. 3. 5; Acts 7. 33.——1 Heb. *did shut up, and was shut up.*

---

as a possibility. In God's battles there can be no neutrals. "He that is not with me is against me."

14. **And he said, Nay**—This answer has reference to the last clause, or second part, of the question, "I am not for your adversaries." In the sense that he was not an Israelite, some think that it may be referred to both members of the question. The reading which makes **nay** a pronoun, *to him,* though adopted by the Septuagint and the Syriac, cannot be sustained. **Captain of the host of the Lord**—*Prince of the army of Jehovah.* The army of heaven is here meant, not the Israelitish host. [This prince of the angelic host was not Michael, nor any other created being, but the Word of God, the Divine Logos or Revealer, who in the fulness of time became flesh, (John i,) and even then declared that he came not to send peace on earth, but a sword. Matt. x, 34. Hence in chap. vi, 2, he is called the LORD, (that is, Jehovah,) and hence, too, Joshua was required to put off his shoes, (verse 15,) for, like Moses at the bush, (Exod. iii, 5,) he was standing on ground made holy by the presence of the Holy One. This same angel was "entertained unawares" by Abraham in the plains of Mamre, (Gen. xviii,) just after that patriarch had circumcised his son Ishmael; but before he left him he proved to be his covenant God, Jehovah. It was very meet that this great Prince should now confer with his lieutenant, and give directions for the conquest of the first great city of Canaan which offered resistance to the Hebrew army.] **And did worship**—This act of low obeisance, or of bodily prostration, is commonly practiced in the East to superiors, and does not necessarily involve the rendering

of divine honours. Joshua thought that some distinguished military chieftain had appeared on the theater of war. The fact that the stranger received worship from Joshua without reproof (Rev. xxii, 9) indicates that he was a superior being. How incompatible is this whole account with the rationalistic exegesis which makes the appearance of the Angel only an inward vision or trance! Joshua *sees* the warrior at a distance, *approaches* and *addresses* him, and *receives* a reply. Such a description could not have been rationally given of an internal vision

CHAPTER VI.

There is no more unfortunate division of chapters in the Bible than occurs here. The conversation between the Captain and his lieutenant is cut in twain, and the revelation of the warrior in chap. v is without any perceptible result. But the new chapter should commence at chap. v, 13, and the first verse of chap. vi should be in a parenthesis. Then it will clearly appear that the revelation of the Captain of the Lord's host is an introduction to the history of the conquest of Jericho.

1. **Now Jericho was straitly shut up**—Heb. *shutting* (the gates) *and firmly shut up.* The active participle may describe the act of the people within, and the passive that of the besiegers without. Or the sense may be: Jericho closed her gates, and fastened them up with bolts and bars. Both expressions also indicate the continuance of this condition, which is further explained by the words **None went out, and none came in**—The city was effectually blockaded. On Jericho see note at chap. ii, 1.

2 And the Lord said unto Joshua, See, [a] I have given into thine hand Jericho, and the [b] king thereof, *and* the mighty men of valour. **3** And ye shall compass the city, all *ye* men of war, *and* go round about the city once. Thus shalt thou do six days. **4** And seven priests shall bear before the ark seven [c] trumpets [2] of rams' horns : and the seventh day ye shall compass the city seven times, and

---

a Chap. 2. 9, 24 ; 8. 1.——*b* Deut. 7. 24.

c See Judg. 7. 16, 22.——2 Heb. *of jubilee.*

---

2. The Lord said—The Hebrew word for *Lord* is *Jehovah.* The identity of Jehovah with the Captain of the host of the Lord is too plain to be disputed by any sound biblical scholar. See chap. v, 14, note. **I have given**—The past tense here strongly expresses the certainty of the future event. In the divine mind the act is already accomplished. **Mighty men of valour**—*Heroes of might.* An appositive of Jericho and its king. Their warlike character is here attested by Jehovah.

3. Ye shall compass the city —Here is a peculiar and unprecedented mode of reducing a walled town—to carry a small chest containing, not the enginery of death, but a few religious relics, attended by a band of priests blowing on their trumpets, and followed by the whole army marching in procession. We may not assign with certainty the reason of this strange command, but we plainly see at least four objects attained: (1) The whole army is honoured as a subordinate agent in the conquest of the city. (2) God, the efficient cause, is magnified before all men. (3) His ark and his ministers, by their prominence at the head of the procession, are especially honoured in the eyes of Israelite and Canaanite. (4) A course of proceeding so unmilitary and apparently absurd was a severe test of the faith of the Israelites in Jehovah.

4. Seven trumpets of rams' horns —[Or, *seven trumpets of alarms;* that is, signal trumpets. The Hebrew word here rendered *rams' horns* is יֹבֵל,

yobel, and Fürst still adheres to this explanation, which is also that of the Targum and the Rabbins. But according to Gesenius *yobel* is an onomatopoetic word, signifying *a joyful sound,* (*jubilum,*) and hence some scholars hold that the trumpet of *yobel* was so called because it was used to proclaim through the land the return of the *year of jubilee.* Lev. xxv, 9–13. But long before the sabbatical year was instituted the trumpet that sounded from Sinai was called the *yobel,* (Exod. xix, 13,) and hence it is but natural to infer that the year of jubilee took its name from the trumpet, not the trumpet from the year. The best supported etymology of *yobel* is that which gives it the sense of a *loud and startling sound,* and hence we adopt the rendering *signal trumpet.* In verse 5 occurs the expression *horn of yobel,* so that the words *trumpet* (*shophar*) and *horn* (*keren*) are here used interchangeably. The common opinion is that the *shophar* was a long straight

Ancient Cornets: *a,* from Herculaneum; *b,* from Calmet.

instrument, and the *keren* a crooked one.] Eustathius says that an instrument in the form of a bent trumpet was in use among the Egyptians for the purpose of calling the people together to the sacrifices. It is not quite certain whether the trumpet of jubilee was made of the horn of an ox or of metal; but the latter seems the more probable, since a much larger instrument could be made of metal. The priests on this occasion carried "sonorous metal, blowing martial sounds." "The *seven days'* procession, the *sevenfold* repetition of it on the *seventh* day by *seven* priests, and the use of *seven* trumpets, are unmistakable proofs of the importance of the number *seven.*"—*Keil.* This may be

d the priests shall blow with the trumpets. 5 And it shall come to pass, that when they make a long *blast* with ³ the ram's horn. *and* when ye hear the sound of the trumpet, all the people shall shout with a great shout; and the wall of the city shall fall down ⁴ flat, and the people shall ascend up every man straight before him.

6 And Joshua the son of Nun called the priests, and said unto them, *e* Take up the ark of the covenant, and let seven priests bear seven trumpets of rams' horns before the ark of the LORD. 7 And he said unto the people, Pass on, and compass the city, and let him that is armed pass on before the ark of the LORD. 8 And it came to pass, when Joshua had spoken unto the people, that the seven priests bearing the seven trumpets of rams' horns passed on before the LORD, and blew with the trumpets: and the ark of the covenant of the LORD followed them. 9 And the armed

---

d Num. 10. 8.——3 Heb. *the horn of jubilee.*   4 Heb. *under it.*——*e* Exod. 25. 14; Deut. 20. 2, 4.

---

best explained by observing that the word for **seven** is radically the same as the word for *oath.* Seven, then, was a sacred number. the seal of the covenant. "By this march of seven days, and the sevenfold repetition on the seventh day. with the seven priests blowing the seven trumpets, the host of Israel were to show that they were the people of the covenant." [**The seventh day**—These seven days of marching must have included one Sabbath. and perhaps. as the Rabbins have assumed, the last day of the seven, on which the city fell. was itself the Sabbath. But this solemn marching and carrying of the ark about the doomed city was no ordinary work, such as that contemplated in the prohibition in the fourth commandment. It was rather a service of obedience to a special Divine mandate, and the grand triumph given on the seventh day was, even in that age. a sublime indication that "the Sabbath was made for man, and not man for the Sabbath."] **Seven times**—We have no means of knowing the circumference of Jericho, but allowing that it was five miles. a not unreasonable estimate, the seven marches around it would be thirty-five miles, a distance not exceedingly difficult for a host all aglow with intense enthusiasm, and disciplined to the route by having travelled it for six preceding days. Then, too, they began their travel early in the morning. Verse 15.

5. **All the people shall shout**—This was to take place during the seventh circuit, at a concerted signal. Previous to that signal they were prohibited from uttering a word; the twelve circumambulations were to be in perfect silence. save the sound of the trumpets. **The wall of the city shall fall down flat**—Heb.. *shall fall under itself,* that is, to its very foundations. The portion of the wall which constituted the rear wall of Rahab's house must have been spared. See verse 22. **Ascend up every man straight before him**—The moving column of men was so long that it completely encircled the city. When the wall fell there was a wall of soldiers surrounding it on every side. The command is that this living wall contract by each man's marching over the ruins towards the centre of the city. Escape would be impossible.

THE CONQUEST OF JERICHO, 6–21.

6. **And Joshua . . . called the priests**—The promptness of his unquestioning obedience to a command so unexpected, and so little in accordance with human reason. attests Joshua's unfaltering faith in his great Captain. with whom he had just been in counsel. It is the province of reason to ask who speaks; but when reason acknowledges it is the voice of God. it is her highest function not to sit in judgment upon the message, but to obey.

7. **And he said**—Such in the Hebrew is the marginal reading, while the text is plural, *and they said;* that is. the subordinate officers, to whom Joshua made known the divine plan of the conquest. See chap. i, 10, note. **Him that is armed**—Literally, *the armed one.* The reference is collectively to the armed host of forty thousand from the tribes of Reuben, Gad, and Eastern Manasseh. These, according to chap. iv, 13, marched before the ark of the Lord.

men went before the priests that blew with the trumpets, *f* and the *5* rearward came after the ark, *the priests* going on, and blowing with the trumpets. **10** And Joshua had commanded the people, saying, Ye shall not shout, nor *6* make any noise with your voice, neither shall *any* word proceed out of your mouth, until the day I bid you shout: then shall ye shout. **11** So the ark of the LORD compassed the city, going about *it* once: and they came into the camp, and lodged in the camp. **12** And Joshua rose early in the morning, *g* and the priests took up the ark of the LORD. **13** And seven priests bearing seven trumpets of rams' horns before the ark of the LORD went on continually, and blew with the trum-

pets: and the armed men went before them; but the rearward came after the ark of the LORD, *the priests* going on, and blowing with the trumpets. **14** And the second day they compassed the city once, and returned into the camp. So they did six days. **15** And it came to pass on the seventh day, that they rose early about the dawning of the day, and compassed the city after the same manner seven times: only on that day they compassed the city seven times. **16** And it came to pass at the seventh time, when the priests blew with the trumpets, Joshua said unto the people, *h* Shout; for the LORD hath given you the city. **17** And the city shall be *7* accursed, *even* it, and all that *are* therein,

---

f Num. 10. 25.——5 Heb. *gathering* host.——6 Heb. *make your voice to be heard.*——*g* Deut.

31. 25.——*h* Jer. 7. 20. 22; 2 Chron. 13. 15; 20. 22, 23.——7 Or, *devoted*, Lev. 27. 28; Micah 4. 13.

---

9. **The rearward**—Margin, *the gathering host;* that part of the army which occupies the last place on the march, protecting the front columns, and gathering up the faint and sick. The tribe of Dan had this position in the wilderness. Num. x, 25. Had the ark been at the head of the column, its usual place, it would have been more exposed to capture by a sudden sally of the enemy.

10. **Neither shall any word proceed out of your mouth**—The injunction of silence was necessary that they might distinctly hear the signal for the shout in concert. Moreover, the very silence of a vast army marching in stillness around the city would either lull the inhabitants into a feeling of security, or fill their minds with fearful forebodings of approaching doom.

{ 14. **Six days**—Is there any parallelism between the seven trumpets and downfall of Jericho, and the apocalyptic seven trumpets and overthrow, by Messianic power, of the Mystical Babylon? This, in our view, was the apocalypse of the overthrow of, not the Antichrist, but the anti-Jehovism of Canaan. It is performed at Jericho, the first great Canaanite city taken. And that is utterly destroyed, as token of what was by divine justice due to all the rest. }

15. **About the dawning of the day**—Here not only Joshua rises early, as in verse 12, but also the whole army, because a great day's work was

before them. It is not to be supposed that the entire camp, several millions in number, marched together in this service, but it is probable that the entire military force was engaged.

16. **Shout; for the Lord hath given you the city**—They were to praise the Lord for what he was about to do. Up to this moment it is probable that the soldiers knew nothing of the mode by which the city was to be taken, yet they obeyed with alacrity orders which must have been totally dark with mystery. Verily this is worthy of enrolment among the signal victories of faith. "By faith the walls of Jericho fell down, after they were compassed about seven days." Heb. xi, 30.

17. **The city shall be accursed**—The city, with all its immense wealth, was now put under the ban, and devoted to destruction. To many of the besieging host this was the severest test of their faith and obedience. In oriental usage when a city is stormed the maxim is "To the victors belong the spoils." As symbol of the utter destruction which the Canaanite race had deserved, this first great representative city is made an example of just doom. For the doom of first things, see note on Acts v, 1–11. The anathema was the devotion of any person or thing to God as irredeemable property; the person or animal was to be killed, and the inanimate thing was either completely destroyed, or set apart

to the LORD: only Rahab the harlot shall live, she and all that *are* with her in the house, because [i] she hid the messengers that we sent. **18** And ye, [k] in any wise keep *yourselves* from the accursed thing, lest ye make *yourselves* accursed, when ye take of the accursed thing, and make the camp of Israel a curse, [l] and trouble it. **19** But all the silver, and gold, and vessels of brass and iron, *are* [s] consecrated unto the

LORD: they shall come into the treasury of the LORD. **20** So the people shouted when *the priests* blew with the trumpets: and it came to pass, when the people heard the sound of the trumpet, and the people shouted with a great shout, that [m] the wall fell down [9] flat, so that the people went up into the city, every man straight before him, and they took the city. **21** And they [n] utterly destroyed all that *was* in the city, both man and

---

i Chap. 2. 4.——*k* Deut. 7. 26; 13. 17; chap. 7. 1, 11, 12.——*l* Chap. 7. 25; 1 Kings 18. 17, 18; Jonah 1. 12.——8 Heb. *holiness.*

m Verse 5; Heb. 11. 30.——9 Heb. *under it.* ——*n* Deut. 7. 2; 20. 16, 17; 1 Sam. 15. 3, 8; Psa. 137. 8, 9; Jer. 48. 18; Rev. 18. 21.

---

forever for the purposes of the sanctuary. The exact idea of the anathema, in the words of Hengstenberg, "is the forced dedication to God of those who have obstinately refused to dedicate themselves to him of their own accord, and the manifestation of his glory in the destruction of those who would not, while they lived, serve as a mirror to reflect it, and thus answer the purpose for which the world was created, and for which especially man was formed." Compare Lev. xxvii, 28, note. In the last day all the wicked of the earth shall fall beneath the anathema of the Judge. **Only Rahab** and her kindred were exempt from the curse, for the oath of the spies had now become the oath of their entire nation.

18. **Lest ye make yourselves accursed**—Hebrew, *lest ye both devote and appropriate the accursed thing.* The two acts could not be harmonized. It would be sacrilege to dedicate the whole to Jehovah and then to take possession of a part for their own use. **And make the camp of Israel a curse**—God will not be defrauded. If any one of the camp takes for personal use any thing dedicated to Himself, He will devote the camp to Himself, that is, to destruction. **And trouble it** —By bringing distress, and humiliating defeat in battle.

19. **But all the silver, and gold**— Because the precious metals and vessels of brass and iron were regarded as indestructible by fire, and were needed in the service of the tabernacle, they were put into the treasury of the tabernacle. **Consecrated unto the Lord**—Literally this and the following sentence

read: *Holiness is it to Jehovah, a treasure of Jehovah shall it go.* In Num. xxxi, 21–23, the method is prescribed of purifying metals by fire in order to consecrate them to the service of God.

20. **So the people shouted**—The trumpets gave the signal and then the people shouted. The trumpets had been silent during the speech of Joshua, (verses 17–19,) then came the signal, and the war-cry, and the downfall. How vain the attempt of some to strip this event of the miraculous by ascribing it to an earthquake! How came Joshua to know that an earthquake would occur at that particular juncture? Such knowledge would be a greater miracle. Equally untenable is the theory that the walls had been extensively mined by a people brought up in the desert, in utter ignorance of that method of conducting war. How absurd to imagine that even the most skilful engineer could so undermine a wall that it would stand till a shout should topple it down! Verily, sceptics are the most credulous people in the world. This miracle put into the hand of Joshua the key to Canaan, the strongest city in the land. With no experience in the art of besieging and storming cities, they could not immediately, without the divine aid, have reduced this stronghold. It also gave both Israel and Canaan overwhelming proof of the omnipotence of Jehovah and of his alliance with Joshua.

21. **They utterly destroyed all that was in the city**—The Israelites in this indiscriminate massacre were simply obeying a plain command of God, (Deut. xx, 16, 17,) and hence

woman, young and old, and ox, and sheep, and ass, with the edge of the sword.

22 But Joshua had said unto the two men that had spied out the country, Go into the harlot's house, and bring out thence the woman, and all that she hath, °as ye sware unto her. 23 And the young men that were spies went in, and brought out Rahab, ᵖand her father, and her mother, and her brethren, and all that she had; and they brought

---

o Chap. 2. 14; Heb. 11. 31.

p Chap. 2. 13.

---

the charge of cruelty, if any, must be brought not against Israel, but God. And there have not been wanting men to urge the question, On what principles can the righteousness of God in this case be vindicated? A sufficient answer is furnished in the following considerations, condensed from Dr. Paley's sermon in justification of God's dealings with the Canaanites: (1.) They were destroyed for their excessive, wilful, habitual, and incurable wickedness. Lev. xviii, 24–30. Their "abominable *customs*" show that the grossest vices had become inherent in their national character, and constituted even a *part of their religion*, for they were "done unto their gods." Because of these heinous sins, and not to make way for the Israelites, they were cut off. (2.) God's treatment of these crimes was impartial. The Jews, the chosen and favoured people, are told that for like sins the land shall "vomit you out also." "As the nations which the Lord destroyed before your face, so shall ye perish." (3.) God suffered long with the Canaanites. In the days of Abraham, four generations before, it was said, "The iniquity of the Amorites is not yet full:" (Gen. xv, 16;) for this reason that patriarch was not put in possession of their country. They had not profited by the pure example of Abraham, Isaac, and Jacob, nor had they taken warning from the fate of Sodom and Gomorrah. (4.) If the destruction be just, the manner is of little importance, whether by earthquake, pestilence, or famine, which spare neither age nor sex, or by the hand of their enemies. In all national punishments the innocent are of necessity confounded with the guilty. The Israelites were God's sheriffs, charged with the duty of inflicting capital punishment upon an incorrigible nation. Without the command from God they would have sinned in this act, the same as a man would sin who should kill a fellow man from motives of private resentment, and not by a warrant from the chief magistrate. (5.) There was a peculiar fitness in the destruction of the Canaanites by the agency of Joshua. The people of those ages were affected by no proof of the power of their gods so deeply as by their giving them victory in war. All the neighbouring nations, for whose admonition this dreadful example was intended, were hereby convinced not only of the supreme power of the God of Israel, but also of his utter abhorrence of the abominations for which the Canaanites were destroyed. (6.) Vices of all kinds, especially licentiousness, are astonishingly infectious. If any of these idolatrous tribes were spared they would taint the Hebrews. A little leaven leaveneth the whole lump. Hence, "Thou shall utterly destroy them, that they teach you not to do after all their abominations, which they have done unto their gods." Deut. xx, 17, 18. Moreover, this growing corruption might have polluted the whole ancient world if it had not received this signal and public demonstration of God's indignation.

The Salvation of Rahab, 22–25.

22. **Joshua had said** — The indefinite past tense of the original is here very properly rendered by our pluperfect, *had said*. See verse 17, where these instructions are given.

23. **And her brethren** — This term must be understood to include the sisters spoken of in chap. ii, 13. **All that she had** — This expression seems most naturally to include goods, and not kindred only. The neuter gender in the Septuagint and Vulgate supports this interpretation, and why should we deny that they were per

out all her [10]kindred, and left them without the camp of Israel. **24** And they [q]burnt the city with fire, and all that *was* therein: [r]only the silver, and the gold, and the vessels of brass and of iron, they put into the treasury of the house of the LORD. **25** And Joshua saved Rahab the harlot alive, and her

father's household, and all that she had; and [s]she dwelleth in Israel *even* unto this day; ~~because~~ she [t]hid the messengers, which Joshua sent to spy out Jericho.

26 And Joshua adjured *them* at that time, saying, [u]Cursed *be* the man before the LORD, that riseth up and buildeth

---

10 Heb. *families.*——*q* Deut. 13. 16; **2 Kings** 25 9; Rev. 18. 8.——*r* Verse 19.

s See Matt. 1. 5.——*t* James 2. 25. *u* 1 Kings 16. 34; Mal. 1. 4.

---

mitted to save all their portable possessions? We suppose that the spies had with them a large company of assistants, to carry her household furniture to the camp. It was honourable on the part of Joshua that she should suffer no loss, and that her faith should be profitable for the life that now is. **All her kindred**—Heb., *all her families;* that is, all who were related to Rahab, and also their families. God honours the family institution which he has ordained. He saves by families not only in the Old Dispensation, as in this case, and Noah, and many others, but also in the New, as in the case of whole households admitted to baptism. **Left them without the camp** — They were not prepared ceremonially to dwell among the Hebrews. It was not lawful for uncircumcised men, nor for females who had not publicly espoused the Jewish faith, to enter the camp, which was regarded as sacred because of the ark. This separation for a season would induce them to lay aside all their pagan habits, which an immediate reception might have confirmed.

25. She dwelleth in Israel even unto this day—This account must have been written during the lifetime of Rahab, when many were living who could have disputed the miracles if they had not occurred. Those who assert that this book was written several centuries later are driven to such an arbitrary interpretation as that her descendants continued to dwell in Israel unto this day.

[Rahab was the first Canaanite convert to the Hebrew faith, and is, accordingly, highly honoured in Hebrew history and Jewish tradition. She was married to Salmon, whom a ro-

mantic imagination has very plausibly identified with one of the two spies whose lives she saved at Jericho. She became an honoured mother in Israel, from whom sprang David and his Messianic son. Matt i, 5. The prominence given by Matthew to the adoption of Gentile women, like Rahab and Ruth, into the Messiah's genealogy, is a prophetic indication of the Gospel catholicity, in which Jew and Gentile, bond and free, are seen to be one in Christ.]

JOSHUA'S ADJURATION AND FAME, 26–27.

26. And Joshua adjured them— Bound them with an oath; caused them to swear. This solemn charge, attended with all the solemnity of an adjuration, was designed to prevent Israel and his posterity from erecting again the walls which had been thrown down by the power of Jehovah. Joshua would have these prostrate defences of the wicked city a perpetual and impressive memorial of punished sin, and of the power and justice of Jehovah. We do not understand that the oath bound the Hebrews not to erect houses, but simply the walls and gates: for we find, in Judges iii, 13, the city of palms —the usual appellation of Jericho— spoken of as inhabited. Also, that in 2 Sam. x, 5, David orders his outraged embassy to "tarry in Jericho until their beards be grown." **Cursed be the man before the Lord**—That is, *Jehovah beholding* and *being judge.* The curse is pronounced by divine sanction, and will fall at his command upon the daring man who shall attempt to restore these fallen walls, and thereby destroy their monumental significance. **In his firstborn**—That is, *at the expense of his life.* The meaning, evi-

this city Jericho: he shall lay the foundation thereof in his firstborn, and in his youngest *son* shall he set up the gates of it. **27** ᵛSo the Lord was with Joshua; and ʷhis fame was *noised* throughout all the country.

---

v Chap. 1. 5.——*w* Chap. 9. 1, 3.——*a* Chap. 22. 20.

dently, of this strong poetic expression is, that the builder of the walls would suffer the loss of all his offspring, from the oldest to the youngest. [The words of the curse are in the form of poetic parallelisms, and may be rendered thus:

Cursed be the man before Jehovah,
Who rises up and builds this city of Jericho.
In his firstborn shall he lay its foundation,
And in his younger son shall he set up its gates.

Possibly this rhythmical passage, like that cited in chap. x, 13, was taken from the book of Jasher.] For a striking fulfilment of this prophetic curse, see 1 Kings xvi, 34, where we find that Hiel accomplished this work, and suffered the penalty predicted five hundred and fifty years before.

27. So the Lord was with Joshua —The promise made to Joshua in chap. i is fulfilled. **His fame was noised**—True fame has been styled the shadow of greatness. He who demonstrates that God is with him cannot dwell in obscurity.

CHAPTER VII.

The Trespass and Punishment of Achan, 1–26.

[After the fall of Jericho the prestige of Israel was exceedingly great. The name of Jehovah was a terror to the idolatrous nations of the land, and the chosen people, glorying in his matchless power and their own wondrous triumphs, were in danger of forgetting that his wrath burns against every appearance of evil, and would fall as fiercely on an offender in the camp of Israel as on the armies of the aliens. Hence the severe and solemn lesson taught by the sin and punishment of Achan.]

1. But the children of Israel committed a trespass—Many have found great difficulty here. There was but one

CHAPTER VII.

BUT the children of Israel committed a trespass in the accursed thing: for ᵃ¹Achan, the son of Carmi, the son of ²Zabdi, the son of Zerah, of the tribe of Judah, took of the accursed

---

1 *Achar,* 1 Chron. 2. 7.——2 Or, *Zimri,* 1 Chron. 2. 6.

personal sinner. How can the whole nation, then, be charged with sin? Calvin, dissatisfied with the many different explanations, advises that "we suspend our decisions till when the books are opened, and the judgments, now holden in darkness, are clearly explained." It is certain that the crime of one had robbed the nation of that innocence which is pleasing to God. Such are the relations of human society that a community is punished for the sins of a part of its constituents. National punishments are inflicted in this life because nations do not exist after death. It follows, therefore, that while a nation may suffer from the sin of an individual, that suffering is temporal, and not eternal, to those who are not personally involved in the guilt. ["The Scriptures teach that a nation is one organic whole, in which the individuals are merely members of the same body, and are not atoms isolated from one another and the whole. The State is there treated as a divine institution, founded upon family relationships, and intended to promote the love of all to one another, and to the invisible Head of all. As all, then, are combined in a fellowship established by God, the good or evil deeds of an individual affect beneficially or injuriously the whole society."—*Keil.* All this is simply an admonitory form in which Jehovah places the divine administration of justice. Each man who suffers is worthy of death for his own sin, and no wrong is done to any. See note on Matt. xxiii, 35.] **In the accursed thing**— In appropriating to private use that which had been solemnly consecrated to God, or devoted to destruction. See note, chap. vi, 17, 18. **Achan**— Called in 1 Chron. ii, 7, *Achar, the troubler of Israel.* **Son of Carmi**—His genealogy is thus traced out in view of the method of his detection. Com-

thing: and the anger of the LORD was kindled against the children of Israel.

2 And Joshua sent men from Jericho to [b] Ai, which *is* beside Bethaven, on

b Gen. 12. 8, *Hai;*   Neh. 11. 31, *Aija.*

pare verses 16–18. He seems to have been a descendant of Judah in the fifth generation. **And the anger of the Lord was kindled against the children of Israel**—The entire community has become infected with the guilt of one of its members.

2. [**From Jericho to Ai**—A distance of about fifteen miles, and an ascent of more than 3,000 feet above the plain of the Jordan valley. See map below. **Ai, which is beside Bethaven, on the east side of Bethel**—This precise statement, together with that of chap. viii, 11, 12, that there was a valley on the north, and another on the west, capable of concealing five thousand men, would seem to have been sufficient to enable travelers easily to identify the precise location of **Ai**. But after all their search such men as Robinson, Stanley, and Tristram failed to reach any satisfactory conclusion. Robinson and Tristram assigned as the probable site a place with ruins just south of Deir Duwan, and about an hour distant (south-east) from Bethel; but in the spring of 1866 Captain Wilson and Lieutenant Anderson spent several days in examining every hill-top and almost every acre of ground for several miles east, north, and south of Bethel, and the result

was the identification, beyond any reasonable doubt, of Ai with Et-Tel, an eminence a little south-east of Bethel, covered with heaps of stones and ruins. In chap. viii, 28, where it is said, "Joshua made it a heap forever," the Hebrew word for *heap* is *Tel,* (תל,) which strikingly confirms this identification. See further notes on chap. viii, 11, 12, 28. Whether Ai was rebuilt or not, the name occurs again in the history of Israel. "Men of Ai" returned from Babylon with Zerubbabel, (Ezra ii, 28,) and the name is probably to be recognized in the *Aiath* of Isa. x, 38, and *Aija* of Neh. xi, 31.] **Bethel**—*house of God*—was a well-known city and holy place in Central Palestine, and was originally called Luz. It was named by Jacob on awakening from that sleep in which he had a vision of the opened heavens. Gen. xxviii, 19, note. Here also God blessed him when he had returned from Padan-aram. After the conquest Bethel was the gathering place of the people to ask counsel of God. Here was an altar for sacrifices. Jeroboam chose Bethel as one of the seats of the false worship which he instituted. It is about twelve miles north of Jerusalem, and its ruins are still pointed out under the scarcely altered

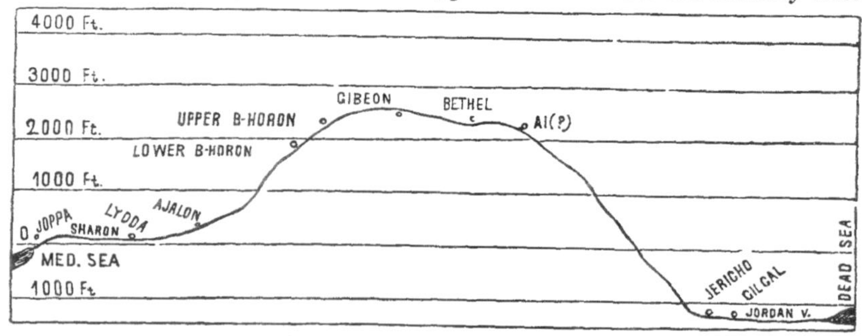

PROFILE SECTION OF CENTRAL PALESTINE.

name of *Beitin.* [**Bethaven** was in the mountains of Benjamin, east of Bethel, and westward from Michmash. 1 Sam. xiii, 5. The name means *house of nothingness,* or *vanity,* and was,

perhaps, so called from the idolatry practised there. Its site has not been discovered, but Capt. Wilson suggests its identity with the ruins called Khurbet An, westward from Michmash, and

the east side of Bethel, and spake unto them, saying, Go up and view the country. And the men went up and viewed Ai. 3 And they returned to Joshua, and said unto him, Let not all the people go up; but let [3] about two or three thousand men go up and smite Ai; *and* make not all the people to labour thither; for they *are but* few. 4 So there went up thither of the people about three thousand men; *c* and they fled before the men of Ai. 5 And the men of Ai smote of them about thirty and six men:

for they chased them *from* before the gate *even* unto Shebarim, and smote them [4] in the going down: wherefore *d* the hearts of the people melted, and became as water. 6 And Joshua *e* rent his clothes, and fell to the earth upon his face before the ark of the Lord until the eventide, he and the elders of Israel, and *f* put dust upon their heads. 7 And Joshua said, Alas, O Lord God, *g* wherefore hast thou at all brought this people over Jordan, to deliver us into the hand of the Amorites, to destroy us? would

---

3 Heb. *about two thousand men, or about three thousand men.*——c Lev. 26. 17; Deut. 28. 25.——4 Or, *in Morad.*——d Chap. 2. 9, 11; Lev. 26. 36; Psa. 22. 14.——e Gen. 37. 29, 34.——f 1 Sam. 4. 12; 2 Sam. 1. 2; 13. 19; Neh. 9. 1; Job 2. 12. ——g Exod. 5. 22; 2 Kings 3. 10.

---

not far from Et-Tel.] **Go up and view the country**—As in the case of Jericho, spies were probably sent to reconnoitre Ai, and not an armed company.

3. **Let not all the people go up**—The spies set a very low estimate upon the military strength of the city. Disasters often happen to armies from this cause. **For they are but few**—That is, comparatively. But the character of the **few,** and their excellent position for defence, were left out of the account. Their numbers were probably under-rated also, for after the conquest of the city the slain numbered twelve thousand. Chap. viii, 25.

4. **They fled before the men of Ai**—Having made their assault in perfect confidence of success, and having met an unexpected repulse, they became panic-stricken, and fled in disorder.

5. **About thirty and six men**—The disaster, though shameful, was much lighter than might have been expected to attend such a rout. **Even unto Shebarim**—That is, *the stone quarries* or *ruins*, the situation of which cannot be determined. Captain Wilson suggests that it may be identical with some extensive ruins north-east of Bethel, called Deir Sheba. **In the going down**—Or, *the declivity.* Heb., *Morad.* Perhaps the descent into the wady, (note, verse 2,) which is hemmed in on both sides with precipitous cliffs, is meant. Both the ruins (*shebarim*) and the declivity (*morad*) were evidently well known places in the time of the writer of this book, but not of sufficient importance to survive in the memory of many genera-

tions. **The hearts of the people melted**—This dismay was not on account of the magnitude of the disaster to the arms of Israel, but because it betokened the withdrawal of their Great Ally, Jehovah. Well may a nation tremble when it sees itself forsaken of God!

6. **Joshua rent his clothes**—This was an expressive oriental symbol of intense sorrow, fear, anger, or despair. The loose, flowing, outer robe was well adapted to this action, and this alone was rent. Joshua felt that the defeat had a deep significance, and must have a moral cause; hence he goes to God to inquire. **Fell to the earth...before the ark**—Over the cover of the ark was the Divine Presence. Ask Judaism the direct way to God, and she points to the mercy-seat between the cherubim. **Put dust upon their heads**—The eastern nations are noted for using actions, rather than words, in expression of strong emotion. Dust or ashes sprinkled upon the head indicates deep mourning and true penitence.

7. **Alas,...wherefore hast thou at all brought this people over Jordan**—This is not the language of distrust, but of distress. It is the tearful wail of a great soul in deepest humiliation and gloom. Joshua unburdens his troubled mind, and reasons with God only as one having the utmost confidence in him can reason. The urgency of his expostulation and the importunity of his plea evince faith in God. He cannot think that such miracles as the passage of the Jordan and the conquest

to God we had been content, and dwelt on the other side Jordan! **8** O Lord, what shall I say, when Israel turneth their [5] backs before their enemies! **9** For the Canaanites and all the inhabitants of the land shall hear *of it*, and shall environ us round, and [h] cut off our name from the earth: and [i] what wilt thou do unto thy great name? **10** And the LORD said unto Joshua, Get thee up;

wherefore [6] liest thou thus upon thy face? **11** [k] Israel hath sinned, and they have also transgressed my covenant which I commanded them: [l] for they have even taken of the accursed thing, and have also stolen, and [m] dissembled also, and they have put *it* even among their own stuff. **12** [n] Therefore the children of Israel could not stand before their enemies, *but* turned *their* backs before their ene-

---

5 Heb. *necks.*——h Psa. 83. 4.——i See Exod. 32. 12; Num. 14. 13.——6 Heb. *fallest.*

k Verse 1.——l Chap. 6. 17, 18.——m See Acts 5.1,2. n See Num. 14. 45; Judg. 2. 14.

---

of Jericho are to lead the chosen nation to destruction. **Amorites**—See note on ii, 10. **Would to God we had been content**—"To all human view it would have been better for us to have remained on the other side of Jordan, and we shall be strongly prompted to wish that that had been the case, for it will be inferred from the event that thy sole purpose in bringing us hither was to deliver us into the hands of the Amorites."—*Bush.*

8. **What shall I say**—Joshua, as the Lord's agent and captain, is perplexed to show a reason for the unexpected defeat. **When Israel turneth**—Or, *inasmuch as Israel has turned.* How is such defeat possible to a people in covenant with Jehovah?

9. **And cut off our name**—Our enemies will be encouraged to make a combined assault, and destroy our communications with eastern Palestine. **And what wilt thou do unto thy great name?**—That is, *with regard to thy great name.* Exalted and true views of God are necessary to elevate man and restore in him the image of God. Reverence for him is the basis of all true holiness. The preservation of the glory of God's name in order that monotheism should finally be the religion of the earth was, according to God's plan, the very mission of Israel. Joshua therefore appropriately argues, Will God defeat that plan, and upset the whole of Israel's future history? It does not detract from this prayer to say that the successive arguments used to move God are eminently human—such as a man would address to his fellow. Moses, in his entreaty, for his nation, uses the same argument. Num. xiv, 13–19; Deut. ix, 28.

10. **Get thee up**—The tone of this answer indicates the divine indignation at Israel's sin, and implies that entreaty for Jehovah's favour, before putting away that sin, is impertinence, and an offence to him, as sacrifices and supplications of *impenitent* sinners always are. Prov. xv, 8. Israel is here viewed as an unrepentant sinner; Joshua is the head of Israel, hence the tone of anger in which he is addressed. The spirit of God's reply is, "This is no time for prayer, but for purifying the camp. Look for the cause of your defeat not in my sovereignty but in your sin."

11. **Israel hath sinned**—For the sense in which the sin of an individual is that of a nation, see note on verse 1. Jehovah then rehearses the aggravated character of that sin. It was a treacherous violation of covenant obligations into which they had entered, (Exod. xix, 8; xxiv, 7;) it was a sacrilege, inasmuch as a consecrated thing had been put to a private use; it was theft, because the appropriation had been made clandestinely: it was a lie, acted if not spoken. "The first three clauses describe the sin in its relation to God; the following three refer to the actual nature of the sin itself, as theft, concealment, and misappropriation to their own use of the stolen goods."—*Keil.*

12. **Therefore the children of Israel could not stand before their enemies**—In the moral government of God there is a causal connexion between moral and natural evil, between sin and suffering. But how few the national leaders who have eyes to see the relation which a nation's righteous character sustains to its victory in war and its prosperity and greatness in

nies, because °they were accursed: neither will I be with you any more, except ye destroy the accursed from among you. **13** Up, ᴾsanctify the people, and say, ᑫSanctify yourselves against to-morrow: for thus saith the LORD God of Israel, *There is* an accursed thing in the midst of thee, O Israel: thou canst not stand before thine enemies, until ye take away the accursed thing from among you. **14** In the morning therefore ye shall be

brought according to your tribes: and it shall be, *that* the tribe which ʳthe LORD taketh shall come according to the families *thereof;* and the family which the LORD shall take shall come by households; and the household which the LORD shall take shall come man by man. **15** ˢAnd it shall be, *that* he that is taken with the accursed thing shall be burnt with fire, he and all that he hath: because he hath ᵗtransgressed

---

o Deut. 7. 26; chap. 6. 18.——*p* Exod. 19. 10.
         q Chap. 3. 5.

r Prov. 16. 33.——*s* See 1 Sam. 14. 38, 39.
         t Verse 11.

---

peace! The atheistic apothegm of Napoleon, that Providence always favours the strongest battalions, is still believed by the statesmen of even Christian nations. God. as the disposer of human events, finds too little recognition in camps, courts. and cabinets. **Neither will I be with you any more—** This declaration proves that the strong promise of chap. i, 5, was conditioned on the fidelity of Israel.

13. **Up…sanctify yourselves**—This mode of address indicates the critical nature of the exigency, which demanded immediate action to prevent further disaster. There cannot be too great haste in putting ourselves right in the sight of God. In order to prepare for the scrutiny which the Lord was to exercise upon all the camp, the entire people were to perform the ablutions and observances required by the law. Jehovah required these washings whenever he came near to them in order to impress them with his own holiness. Exod. xix. 10. 11; see chap. iii, 5, note.

14. **Ye shall be brought according to your tribes**—God could have disclosed to Joshua the sinner as well as the sin. by direct revelation, without this review of the whole camp. But he chose the latter method as far more impressive, since it awakened the interest of all the people, exhibited the magnitude of the crime, and clearly set forth the omniscience of Jehovah, and their personal amenability to him. Representatives of each tribe were to come to the tabernacle, or to pass in review before the ark. **The tribe which the Lord taketh**—The word **taketh**, as we may see from 1 Sam. xiv, 42, is the technical term used for de-

cision by lot. "The lot is cast into the lap, but the whole disposing thereof is of the Lord." Prov. xvi. 33. White pebbles and one black one may have been cast into a sack or urn, and some man from each tribe appointed to draw them out—the black pebble indicating the tribe, clan, family, or individual whom the Lord designated. Decision by lot is mentioned frequently in the Old Testament, and once in the New. Acts i, 24–26. It recommends itself as a sort of appeal to the Almighty, free from all influence of passion or bias. **Families . . . households—** The tribes, says Keil. were founded by the twelve sons of Jacob and the two sons of Joseph, who were placed on an equality with them by adoption. Whenever Levi was reckoned, Joseph was counted as one tribe; whenever Levi was omitted, Joseph was counted as two. The tribes were divided into clans, of which the sons, grandsons, or great grandsons of the twelve were the heads. The clans were again divided into groups of **families**—Heb. *fathers' houses*—taking their name from the sons, grandsons, etc., of the heads of the clans. This last division was subdivided into **households,** composed of individuals. The distinction between the clans and fathers' houses was not very definitely preserved.

15. **He…shall be burnt with fire, he and all that he hath**—As the anathema was to be executed by fire, and as the guilty man has made himself and all his possessions anathema, he is to be destroyed with fire. See note on verse 24. The body, rendered lifeless by stoning, (verse 25,) and not the living

the covenant of the LORD, and because he "hath wrought [7] folly in Israel. **16** So Joshua rose up early in the morning, and brought Israel by their tribes; and the tribe of Judah was taken: **17** And he brought the family of Judah; and he took the family of the *Zarhites: and he brought the family of the Zarhites man by man; and Zabdi was taken: **18** And he brought his household man by man; and Achan, the son of Carmi, the son of Zabdi, the

son of Zerah, of the tribe of Judah, *was taken. **19** And Joshua said unto Achan, My son, *give, I pray thee, glory to the LORD God of Israel, *and make confession unto him; and *tell me now what thou hast done; hide *it* not from me. **20** And Achan answered Joshua, and said, Indeed I have sinned against the LORD God of Israel, and thus and thus have I done: **21** When I saw among the spoils a goodly Babylonish garment, and two

---

u Gen. 34. 7; Judg. 20. 6.——7 Or, *wickedness.* ——*v* Gen. 38. 30; Num. 26. 20; 1 Chron. 2. 7.—— *w* 1 Sam. 14. 42.

x See 1 Sam. 6. 5; Jer. 13. 16; John 9. 24.—— *y* Num. 5. 6, 7; 2 Chron. 30. 22; Psa. 51. 3; Dan. 9. 4.——*z* 1 Sam. 14. 43.

---

man, was to be burned. Burning alive is not found in the Mosaic law. **Wrought folly in Israel—Folly** is a very appropriate name for sin, since every sin proceeds from real intellectual stupidity, short-sightedness, and fatuity, which the Greeks expressed by a word signifying *missing the mark.* In the eye of true reason the devil himself is a simpleton, and all his followers doltishly reject divine instruction, and stupidly go down to hell, imagining that God does not see their sins, and will not punish the guilty.

16. **Early in the morning**—In all hot countries during the heated months early morning is the time for business. Note, Luke xxi, 38. **By their tribes** —Representatively; see verse 14, note. **And the tribe of Judah was taken—** It was indicated by lot that the sinner belonged to that tribe.

17. **The family of Judah**—Some codices read *families of Judah*, but the singular is to be preferred. The meaning is the tribe, or collective family. **He took the family of the Zarhites** —The lot, under Divine guidance, designated this division of Judah as containing the criminal.

18. **Achan...was taken** — God might have instantaneously revealed the sinner, but he chose to sift the nation thus gradually in order that the moral sense of every man might be awakened, and that the conscience of Achan, when he saw the network of conviction and punishment closing in upon him, might prompt him to confession. But he remained impenitent till he found himself within the grasp of the Divine arrest.

19. **My son**—The expression denotes the pity and tenderness of Joshua's heart towards the unhappy Achan. He is by the finger of God convicted of an awful crime, but the crime itself is yet unknown to Joshua. The Scriptures abundantly show how both God and his ministers may, in certain relations, be tender towards a criminal, while, in other relations, they must punish with awful severity his crime. **Give...glory to the Lord**— This is not a formal judicial oath, but rather a solemn appeal to the conscience of the sinner, in the presence of the all-seeing God, to acknowledge his sin. Confession of sin vindicates the Divine administration, and justifies the infliction of the penalty. Compare Ezra x, 11, which, in the original, reads "*give glory*," instead of "*make confession.*" In the day of judgment "every tongue shall confess," but, as in the case of Achan, no sweet joy of forgiveness will ensue.

20. **Indeed I have sinned**—The Hebrew original, as well as the Greek and Latin versions, make the *I* emphatic: I, and I only, have sinned.

21. **A goodly Babylonish garment** —[Literally, *a mantle of Shinar, one of excellence.* The mention of this garment indicates that Jericho had enriched itself by commerce with Babylon, in the land of Shinar. Gen. xi, 2. This was rendered easy by the caravans of merchantmen, such as that to which Joseph was sold, (Gen. xxxvii, 25–28,) which frequently must have passed near Jericho on their journeys between Egypt and the East.] The

hundred shekels of silver, and a [8] wedge of gold of fifty shekels weight, then I [a] coveted them, and took them; and, behold, they *are* hid in the earth in the midst of my tent, and the silver under it. **22** So Joshua sent messengers, and they ran unto the tent: and, behold, *it was* hid in his tent, and the silver under it. **23** And they took them out of the midst of the tent, and brought them

---

8 Heb. *tongue.*——*a* Exod. 20. 17; 1 Kings 1. 2; Hab. 2. 9; Luke 12. 15.

---

original intimates that it was a splendid mantle. Some think it was a military cloak, embroidered with brilliant colors; others, that it was a kingly robe, woven with gold. It is probable that its appearance dazzled the eye of Achan, and through the eye awakened covetousness in his heart. [Herodotus

BABYLONIAN APPAREL.

(i, 195) says: "The dress of the Babylonians is a linen tunic reaching to the feet, and above it another tunic made in wool, besides which they have a short white cloak thrown around them." The Babylonian cylinders furnish us with representations of a flounced robe, reaching from the neck to the feet.] **And two hundred shekels of silver**—The word shekel signifies *weight*, generally a definite weight of unstamped gold, silver, brass, or iron.

ANCIENT SHEKEL.

Here it may mean definite pieces of silver passing current, with the weight marked. In different periods the shekel varied in value. The shekel of the sanctuary differed from the shekel of the king. Its usual value was about sixty-two and one half cents. The whole value of the silver was about $125, when a dollar had nearly ten times the purchasing power that it now has. **A wedge of gold of fifty shekels weight**—The shekel of gold was about five and a half dollars, so that this oblong or tongue-shaped bar was worth $275. **And the silver under it**—That is, under the Babylonish garment. All the stolen goods· were probably placed in some box or bag, and buried where no human eye could see them. The frankness and apparent penitence of this confession affects our hearts with sorrow for the sad fate of Achan. It lacked but two elements — spontaneity and seasonableness — which will be lacking in the confession of every impenitent sinner before the judgment seat of Christ. The whole philosophy of temptation and sin is here strikingly illustrated. In the sacking of Jericho Achan, unobserved by any witness, finds, possibly in the king's palace, a beautiful robe and a quantity of gold and silver. The splendour of the garment and the glitter of the precious metals struck his eye and awakened desire. Instead of turning away his eyes, he continued to look and to desire, till desire ripened into volition, and this into action. "When lust hath conceived it bringeth forth sin, and sin, when it is finished, bringeth forth death."

22. **They ran unto the tent**—The interests of the entire nation, involved in this affair, require prompt and energetic measures. The theft itself, its disastrous consequences at Ai, and the supernatural detection of the criminal, had awakened an intense excitement, which caused the haste of the messengers.

unto Joshua, and unto all the children of Israel. and ⁹laid them out before the Lord. **24** And Joshua, and all Israel with him, took Achan the son of Zerah, and the silver. and the garment, and the wedge of gold, and his sons, and his daughters, and his oxen, and his asses, and his sheep, and his tent, and all that he had: and they brought them unto ᵇthe valley of Achor. **25** And Joshua said, ᶜWhy hast thou troubled us? the Lord shall trouble thee this day. ᵈAnd all Israel stoned him with stones, and burned them with fire, after they had

---

⁹ Heb. *poured.*——*b* Verse 26; chap. 15. 7. ᶜ Chap. 6. 18; 1 Chr. 2. 7; Gal. 5. 12.——*d* Deut. 17.5.

---

23. **Unto all the children of Is-rael**—Representatively ; that is, unto the elders. **Laid them out before the Lord**—"As a sign," says Keil, "that they belonged to Jehovah on account of the ban." They were before the Lord's eyes when covered up in the earth. But now they are publicly displayed before the ark of the covenant, the symbol of Jehovah's presence.

24. **Joshua, and all Israel with him**—The objection of Colenso, that **all Israel** was a body too numerous to perform many acts recorded of them, is sufficiently met by the remark that the heads of the tribes and clans are constructively "all Israel." **And his sons, and his daughters**—These were taken. some say, not to be executed with their father. but to be witnesses of his execution. [But this is inadmissible. Were **his oxen, and his asses, and his sheep, and his tent,** taken to witness his execution? The narrative clearly conveys the impression that all Achan's family and possessions perished with him. Compare also chap. xxii, 20. Why Achan's family and property should all be destroyed for his sin is a question to be answered by reference to that archaic jurisprudence which dealt with families rather than with individuals. In the Patriarchal system of government the father was absolute lord and representative of the entire household. His children and possessions were identified with him in praise or in punishment. And this judicial idea of Patriarchism was also carried over into Mosaism. The family was sometimes punished rather than the individual. the latter being utterly absorbed in the former, and such family punishment sometimes continued through many generations. Exod. xx, 5; xxxiv, 7 ; Num. xiv, 18. Hence the punishment of Achan's children for their father's sin must not be judged by the standards of an age which has not "occasion any more to use the ancient proverb, The fathers have eaten sour grapes, and the children's teeth are set on edge." Ezek. xviii, 2, 3.] **Valley of Achor**—So called by *prolepsis.* or anticipation, (see ver. 26, note,) for the punishment of Achan gave it its name. That this valley was among the hills is evident from the Hebrew verb, *they caused them to ascend into the valley* of Achor. But its location is now a matter of conjecture. Jerome locates it to the north of Jericho.

25. **Why hast thou troubled us?**—The verb here used has, in the Hebrew, (*achar,*) a sound much like Achan's name. See note on verse 26. **And all Israel stoned him**—Here note the propriety of requiring the whole nation by their various representatives to participate in the execution of the law. The great principle embodied is this : The execution of civil law rests largely upon public opinion. When this becomes so corrupt that it will not uphold the law, it becomes a dead letter on the statute book. [**Stoned him ....burned them....had stoned them**—This interchange of singular and plural pronouns does not show that only Achan was stoned, and not his children, but may indicate that he was the person most prominent in the punishment. To urge from this change of number that only Achan was stoned would oblige us to urge that the rest were burned alive without having first been stoned. Two different Hebrew words are here rendered **stoned,** רגם and סקל. The former seems to mean in this place *to pelt with stones,* the latter *to cover with stones.* So we may more accurately render, *All Israel pelted him with stones, and burned them with fire, and covered them with stones.* Per-

stoned them with stones. **26** And they
*raised over him a great heap of stones
unto this day. So ʳthe LORD turned
from the fierceness of his anger. Wherefore the name of that place was called,
ᵍThe valley of ¹⁰Achor, unto this day.

CHAPTER VIII.

AND the LORD said unto Joshua,
ᵃFear not, neither be thou dis-

ᵉChap. 8. 29; 2 Sam. 18. 17; Lam. 3. 53.——
ᶠDeut. 13. 17; 2 Sam. 21. 14.——ᵍVerse 24; Isa.
65. 10; Hos. 2. 15.

---

haps here is an intimation, too, that
they stoned Achan with a fiercer violence than they did his family and possessions.]

26. **And they raised over him a
great heap of stones**—A monument
of everlasting reproach. Michaelis
says it is still a prevalent custom in the
East to throw stones, as a mark of reproach and disgrace, upon the graves
of criminals. **That place was called,
The valley of Achor**—This name signifies *trouble, disturbance*, and is derived
from the verb which Joshua uses twice
in verse 25. Hence the propriety of
the name.

CHAPTER VIII.

CAPTURE OF AI, 1–29.

1. **Fear not**—Joshua had need of
reassurance and encouragement after
the disasters and humiliation which
Israel had suffered for the sin of Achan.
As shines the sun emerging from behind a thunder cloud, so the returning
mercy of Jehovah upon the camp of
Israel. **Take all the people of war
with thee**—How different from the
counsel of the spies, (chap. vii, 3,) " Let
not all the people go up, but let about
two or three thousand men go up."
The Lord could, indeed, have given Ai
into the hands of two or three thousand as easily as to all, but he would
not encourage Israel in a rash, impru-
dent dependence on Omnipotence. It
appears from verse 3 that the expression **all the people of war,** like the oft-
recurring phrase, " all Israel," is not to
be taken in its widest import. It is
probable that the whole camp was put
in preparation, and the whole force was

mayed: take all the people of war with
thee, and arise, go up to Ai: see, ᵇI
have given into thy hand the king of
Ai, and his people, and his city, and his
land: **2** And thou shalt do to Ai and
her king as thou didst unto ᶜJericho
and her king: only ᵈthe spoil thereof,
and the cattle thereof, shall ye take for
a prey unto yourselves: lay thee an ambush for the city behind it. **3** So Joshua

---

10 That is, *Trouble.*——ᵃDeut. 1. 21; 7. 18;
31. 8; chap. 1. 9.——ᵇChap. 6. 2.——ᶜChap. 6. 21.
——ᵈDeut. 20. 14.

---

reviewed, and thirty thousand of the
most suitable were detached for this
expedition, while the rest of the army
was held in reserve. **Go up to Ai**—
The march from Jericho to Ai was actually an ascent, but the term **go up** is
often used in a military sense of an
advance against a city or nation where
the advance is not an actual ascent.
Have given—The conquest of Ai was
a foregone conclusion in the Divine
mind. Compare chap. vi, 2, note.

2. **Only the spoil thereof. . .shall
ye take**—The spoils of Jericho had
been devoted wholly to the Lord, as
the first fruits of the conquest of
Canaan. But the spoils of Ai and of
the other conquered cities (Deut. vi,
10–11) are now to be appropriated unto the conquerors. The people and
their king are to be slain and their city
subverted. There was, henceforth, to
be no temptation to the sin of Achan.
Had he waited obediently and refrained
from the accursed thing he might now
have innocently enriched himself. So
sin generally misses the mark. **Lay
thee an ambush**—If war itself is ever
justifiable, it is right to use the mind
as well as the hand, strategy as well
as brute force. It is certain that a
contest of wit is as proper as a contest
of muscle. Says Calvin: " Those are
pronounced the best generals whose
success is due less to force than to
skilful manœuvres. It is, of course,
understood that neither must treaties
be violated, nor faith broken in any
other way." **Behind it**—As Joshua
was east of Ai, the ambuscade, by a
flank movement up one of the numerous ravines, was to be made on the
west side of the city. See note on ver. 9.

arose, and all the people of war, to go up against Ai: and Joshua chose out thirty thousand mighty men of valour, and sent them away by night. 4 And he commanded them, saying, Behold, *e* ye shall lie in wait against the city, *even* behind the city: go not very far from the city, but be ye all ready: 5 And I, and all the people that *are* with me, will approach unto the city: and it shall come to pass, when they come out against us, as at the first, that *f* we will flee before them, 6 (For they will come out after us,) till we have

e Judges 20. 29.

f Judges 20. 32.

3. Joshua arose . . . to go up—That is, set himself about the preliminary arrangements necessary for the march. **Chose out thirty thousand**—There is some apparent confusion in the details of this movement of Joshua. Some eminent commentators think that the entire army of more than six hundred thousand fighting men (Num. xxvi, 51) was engaged in this enterprise. The difficulties of this interpretation are: (1) the impossibility of handling advantageously so vast a body of soldiers in a country cut up by deep and narrow mountain gorges; (2) The exposure of the camp left behind them; (3) The presence of so vast an array before Ai would so appal the inhabitants that they would not venture to sally out and attack it; (4) The extreme difficulty of hiding so large an ambuscade as that of thirty thousand men **not very far from the city.** Some expositors have even supposed that there were two ambuscades, one of thirty thousand and the other of five thousand. But if so, verses 9 and 12 would argue that both were in the same place, namely, "between Bethel and Ai," on the west side of Ai, and this is hardly supposable. Further, in verses 19 and 21 mention is made of only one ambush. The other theory is, that this number of men were all who were engaged. These were divided into two corps—one of five thousand for the ambush and the other of twenty-five thousand for the feigned assault. The latter theory being more reasonable, and involving less difficulties, is assumed by us. [On this hypothesis the order of events must be understood as follows: Joshua, having made all necessary arrangements, arose early one morning, and, accompanied by the elders, went up with the thirty thousand men who were, in this siege, **all the people of** war, and encamped on the north side of Ai. Verses 10–11. This march occupied the day, so that it was evening when they approached Ai. That same night Joshua sent the five thousand men to lie in ambush on the west side of the city, (verses 4, 9, 12,) but he and the twenty-five thousand remained encamped in the valley north of Ai. Ver. 13. The next day the king of Ai, not knowing Joshua's stratagem, hasted out early with his people to attack the Israelites, but was caught in the snare prepared to deceive him, and he and his people and city were utterly ruined. On the apparent confusion of the narrative, see remarks in the Introduction on the style of the Hebrew historians.] **And sent them away by night**—A portion of them, five thousand in number. A part is here loosely put for the whole. See verse 12, rendering the verb *took, had taken,* as does the Vulgate.

4. **He commanded them**—That is, the five thousand who were to form the ambuscade. To these the words from this verse on through verse 8 are addressed. But of course all these plans for the battle were also made known to the rest of the army.

5. **All the people**—The soldiers are often spoken of by Homer as "the people." **We will flee**—This was no uncommon stratagem for decoying the garrison of a walled town into the open fields. See Livy's description of the capture of Fidenæ by the Romans, book i, chap. 14. There is always danger of military disorganization on the part of the soldiers making this movement, unless they are let into the secret of the commander, as they were in the present instance.

6. **For they will come out after us**—So infatuated are they over their recent victory that our greater num-

1 drawn them from the city; for they will say, *They flee before us, as at the first: therefore we will flee before them. **7** Then ye shall rise up from the ambush, and seize upon the city: for the LORD your God will deliver it into your hand. **8** And it shall be, when ye have taken the city, *that* ye shall set the city on fire: according to the commandment of the LORD shall ye do. h See, I have commanded you. **9** Joshua therefore sent them forth; and they went to lie in ambush, and abode between Bethel and Ai, on the west side of Ai: but Joshua lodged that night among the people. **10** And Joshua rose up early in the morning, and numbered the people, and went up, he and the elders of Israel, before the people to Ai. **11** i And all the people, *even the people* of war that *were* with him, went up, and drew nigh, and came before the city, and pitched on the north side of Ai: now *there was* a valley between them and Ai. **12** And

1 Heb. *pulled.*——*g* Exod. 14. 3; 15. 9; John 20. 32; Eccles. 9. 12.——*h* 2 Sam. 13. 28.——*i* Verse 5.

bers will not be likely to awe them from coming out against us. **They flee before us, as at the first—**It is a wise general who makes a former defeat aid him in securing a future victory.

8. **Ye shall set the city on fire—**We are not to understand that the entire city is to be immediately *destroyed* by fire, for in that case there would be a loss of the promised spoil. A part of the city was set on fire as a signal, and the smoke was to signify to Joshua that it was time to stop the feigned retreat and return to the city. Afterwards the entire city was pillaged and destroyed. **According to the commandment of the Lord—**This is found in the second verse, "as unto Jericho." **See, I have commanded you—**Be impressed with the fact that this is a momentous military order, and on your perfect obedience victory hinges.

9. **Between Bethel and Ai—**This region is greatly cut up with gorges and ravines, "and," says Dr. Thomson, "as I passed from Bethel towards Michmash, (southeasterly,) I could easily understand how Joshua's ambush of five thousand men could be hid between Ai and Bethel." [**On the west side of Ai—**A short distance west of Et-Tel, says Captain Wilson, "and entirely concealed from it by rising ground, is a small ravine well suited for an ambush, one of the branches of the main valley, which runs close to Et-Tel, and protects its northern face— the same into which the army of the Israelites descended the night before the capture of the city. On the hills to the north, beyond the valley, Joshua encamped before making his final ar-

rangements for the attack, (verse 11,) and it seems probable that he took his stand at some point on the hillside while the battle was raging, for there is a most commanding view over the whole scene, not only up the lateral valley, in which the ambush was placed, but also down by the way of the wilderness. Verse 15. He would thus be able at the same time to control the feigned flight of the Israelites, and signal the ambush (verses 18, 19) to rise up quickly and seize the city."] **Joshua lodged that night among the people—**That is, among the twenty-five thousand who encamped for the night on the north side of Ai in the valley. Verses 11, 13. The night here mentioned is to be understood as identical with that mentioned in verses 3 and 13.

10. **And Joshua rose up early—**This must be regarded as a repetition of verse 3, after the custom of oriental historians. **Numbered the people—**Reviewed the troops (thirty thousand) with whom he intended to capture Ai. **Went up—**From the Ghor, or Jordanic Valley, to the interior of Palestine, there is a steep ascent. Compare note on Luke x, 30. Ai was distant from Jericho about fifteen English miles. **And the elders—**As a council of war. Joshua's impetuous and rapid movements were attended by a wise senate.

11. **A valley between them and Ai—**The Hebrew reads *the valley*, the article intimating that it was well known. It was the main valley, of which the ravine in which the ambush was laid was a branch. See note on verse 9.

he took about five thousand men, and set them to lie in ambush between Bethel and Ai, on the west side [2] of the city. **13** And when they had set the people, *even* all the host that *was* on the north of the city, and [3] their liers in wait on the west of the city, Joshua went that night into the midst of the valley. **14** And it came to pass, when the king of Ai saw *it*, that they hasted and rose up early, and the men of the city went out against Israel to battle, he and all his people, at a time appointed, before the plain; but he [k] wist not that *there*

were liers in ambush against him behind the city. **15** And Joshua and all Israel [l] made as if they were beaten before them, and fled by the way of the wilderness. **16** And all the people that *were* in Ai were called together to pursue after them: and they pursued after Joshua, and were drawn away from the city. **17** And there was not a man left in Ai or Bethel, that went not out after Israel: and they left the city open, and pursued after Israel. **18** And the Lord said unto Joshua, [m] Stretch out the spear that *is* in thy hand toward Ai; for I

---

2 Or, *of Ai.*——3 Heb. *their lying in wait,* Verse 4.

k Judg. 20. 34; Eccles. 9. 12.——*l* Judg. 20. 36, &c. *m* Exod. 8. 5; 17. 11.

---

12. And he took about five thousand—The Hebrew has no separate form for the pluperfect tense, hence we are justified in rendering an indefinite past tense by the pluperfect when the context requires it, as the Vulgate has rendered this—*had taken* and *had set.*

13. Joshua went that night into the midst of the valley—That is, the valley on the north of Ai. Verse 11, note. This movement was executed very late in the night, probably just before the dawn of day, when he was descried by the watchmen approaching the city in front.

14. At a time appointed—In Judg. xx, 38, the same word is translated *an appointed sign.* This makes good sense here; but Gesenius and Fürst both say that it is here to be rendered, *an appointed place* in Joshua's line, upon which the attack was to be made. This place is mentioned immediately afterwards as **the plain,** that is, the Arabah, *the desert,* which is spoken of in verse 15 under the name of *the wilderness.*

[15. **Made as if they were beaten** —The original simply reads *were beaten.* Keil renders it *suffered themselves to be beaten.* **The wilderness**—The eastern slope of the mountains of Judah towards Jericho and the Dead Sea. Captain Wilson says that on the east of Et-Tel " the ground, which at first breaks down rapidly from the great ridge that forms the backbone of Palestine, swells out into a small plain three quarters of a mile broad, before

commencing its abrupt descent to the Jordan valley."]

16. **And all the people**—That is, all capable of military service. We read in verse 24 that some were killed in the city.

17. **Or Bethel**—This small city, three miles distant on the west, had probably concentrated its military strength at Ai, as the next probable point of attack by Joshua after the conquest of Jericho; for we cannot conceive of their separate and concerted action, with a large undiscovered ambuscade between them. Our interpretation is confirmed by the next statement, **and they left the city**—not cities—**open.** We have no further mention in this book of the conquest of Bethel, except that its king is in the list of those subdued by Joshua, in chap. xii, 16. "It was not taken at that time, and seems long to have resisted the invaders. At last it fell before the arms, not of the little tribe of Benjamin, within whose territory it was included, but of the powerful house of Joseph, who attacked it from the north, and who thus acquired possession of it. Judg. i, 23-25."—*Stanley.*

18. **The Lord said**—As there were probably no facilities for consulting the Lord by means of the urim and thummim, we infer that there was an immediate communication to Joshua of this divine command. **Stretch out the spear**—This was the concerted signal for the ambush to arise and seize the city. The Hebrew word for **spear** has been variously explained. See note on

will give it into thine hand. And Joshua stretched out the spear that *he had* in his hand toward the city. **19** And the ambush arose quickly out of their place, and they ran as soon as he had stretched out his hand: and they entered into the city, and took it, and hasted and set the city on fire. **20** And when the men of Ai looked behind them, they saw, and, behold, ⁿthe smoke of the city ascended up to heaven, ^oand they had no ⁴power to flee this way or that way: and the people that fled to the wilderness turned back upon the pursuers. **21** And when Joshua and all Israel saw that the ambush had taken the city, and that the smoke of the city ascended, then they turned again, and slew the men of Ai.

22 And the other issued out of the city against them; so they were in the midst of Israel, some on this side, and some on that side: and they smote them, so that they ^plet none of them remain or escape. **23** And ^qthe king of Ai they took alive, and brought him to Joshua. **24** And it came to pass, when Israel had made an end of slaying all the inhabitants of Ai in the field, in the wilderness wherein they chased them, and when they were all fallen on the edge of the sword, until they were consumed, that all the Israelites ^rreturned unto Ai, and smote it with the edge of the sword. **25** And *so* it was, *that* all that fell that day, both of men and women, *were* twelve thousand, *even* all the men of Ai.

---

n Gen. 19. 28; Rev. 18. 9.——o Job 11. 20; Psa. 48. 5, 6.

4 Heb. *hand.*——p Deut. 7. 2.——q 1 Sam. 15. 8. r Num. 21. 24.

---

1 Sam. xvii, 6. The translator of the Vulgate, and several others, have rendered it *shield.* Others suppose that a shield was elevated on the spear. Gesenius suggests that the spear supported a small flag, like that of the modern lance. This could be seen by the distant liers in wait, who were, doubtless, instructed to watch for the signal. **Toward the city**— An act symbolical of the terrible blow which was now to ruin it forever.

19. **And set the city on fire** —Not only for its destruction, but also for a signal to the army which was feigning a retreat to turn upon their pursuers, whose place of safety was now cut off. In verse 28 the burning of the city occurs after the pillage, but that is to be understood of the completion and consequence of what the ambush had begun.

20. **And they had no power to flee**—[Literally, *there was not in them two hands to fly.* Keil makes the word rendered *two hands* mean *on both sides,* that is, it was not in them to flee on either side, or in either direction. But this explanation hardly holds good in connection with the expression בָּהֶם, *in them.* We prefer, therefore, the common version, which takes *hands* metaphorically for *capability, power* for ac-

tion or flight.] They were appalled by the revelation of the plot, and stupified by sudden terror. Their wives, children, houses, and possessions were in the hands of a merciless foe, and they themselves were in a ravine completely shut in before and behind by Joshua's army.

22. **They let none of them ... escape**—Considering the Israelites' superior numbers, their advantage in the strife, and the panic of the men of Ai, their total destruction was an easy matter. Rarely in those times were prisoners taken in battle. The sword devoured utterly.

23. **And the king of Ai they took alive**—Kings were anciently spared in battle, either to grace the triumph of the victor, or for the accomplishment of some political end, or, as in this case, for a more formal and impressive execution. The king of Bethel (chap. xii, 16) was, perhaps, killed in this battle, and left among the common dead, so that no special notice of his death is here recorded.

24. **Smote it with the edge of the sword**—The non-combatant population, without regard to age or sex, were indiscriminately slain. For several considerations in justification of the total excision of the Canaanites, see note on chap. vi, 21.

[25. **Twelve thousand**—Some expositors have argued that these twelve thousand were only the military force

26 For Joshua *drew not his hand back, wherewith he stretched out the spear, until he had utterly destroyed all the inhabitants of Ai.   **27** 'Only the cattle and the spoil of that city Israel took for a prey unto themselves, according unto the word of the LORD which he "commanded Joshua.   **28** And Joshua burnt Ai, and made it 'a heap for ever, *even a* desolation unto this day.   **29** *And the king of. Ai he hanged on a tree until eventide : * and as soon as the sun was down, Joshua commanded that they should take his carcass down from the tree, and cast it at the entering of the gate of the city, and ' raise thereon a great heap of stones, *that remaineth* unto this day.

---

s Exod. 17. 11, 12.——*t* Num. 31. 22, 26.——*u* Verse 2.——*v* Deut. 13. 16.——*w* Chap. 10. 26;

Psa. 107. 40; 110. 5.——*x* Deut. 21. 23; chap. 10. 27.——*y* Chap. 7. 26; 10. 27.

---

of Ai; but this would imply a population of fifty or sixty thousand; a number far too large for a comparatively small city among the hills. Compare chap. vii, 3.   This verse clearly affirms that the twelve thousand included **all that fell that day, both of men and women.**]

26. **Joshua drew not his hand back**—The uplifted spear was not only a signal for the assault of the city, but also for its continuance till the conquest was completed.   We see no good reason for regarding this act as symbolic of prayer, as was the lifting up of Moses' hands when Israel fought with Amalek. Exod. xvii, 11.

27. **A prey unto themselves**—Joshua's army was now, like Sherman's on his grand march to the sea, a moving column cut off from its base of supplies.   Hence it must live upon spoils.

28. **A heap for ever**—[The word translated **heap** is בֵל, *Tel*, and strikingly confirms Capt. Wilson's identification of the site of Ai with the mound still bearing, after the lapse of ages, the name *Et-Tel, the ruined heap.* Compare note on vii, 2.]   Because the meaning of Ai is a *heap of ruins* the Rationalists build up a theory that the history of its conquest is a myth, growing out of ruins of unknown origin. But the city destroyed by Joshua may have taken the name of Ai or Hai, *the ruins,* from the ruins of a more ancient city out of which it may have been built.   **Unto this day**—This clause seems awkward, coming immediately after **for ever,** but it shows that the word *for ever* sometimes has a limited reference.   Perhaps, however, the historian, or some later editor, meant by the former clause, closing

with **for ever,** to express Joshua's purpose to make Ai a perpetual desolation, and by the latter clause to indicate its fulfilment.   The name of Ai appears again, after a thousand years, as inhabited. Neh. xi, 31.   But it was probably on another site, just as there were an Old and a New Troy, an Old and a New Tyre.

29. **The king of Ai he hanged**—For the reason, see note on verse 23.   **On a tree**—The Septuagint says, on a double tree, which the Vulgate renders, a fork-shaped gibbet.   **Until eventide**—This was in accordance with the law, (Deut. xxi, 23,) "that the land be not defiled."   Among the ancient Israelites hanging alive seems not to have been practiced, but, as Deut. xxi, 22, implies, the victim was first slain and then hanged.   Comp. chap. x, 26; 2 Sam. iv, 12.   **At the entering of the gate**—Probably the dead body was cast into a pit.   Thus the Septuagint translates this passage.   **A great heap of stones**—See note on chap. vii, 26.

THE MEMORIAL ALTAR AND SERVICE ON MOUNT EBAL, 30–35.

[This passage is one of those peculiarly interesting narratives of sacred history which serve to bind the Bible to the hearts of devout believers.   But the whole account has been hastily pronounced by some critics an interpolation by a later hand, the main argument being that Joshua had not yet carried his conquests as far north as Mount Ebal.   It is possible, indeed, that the narrative may have been inserted here out of its proper place, (for chronological order seems not to have been sought after by our author,) and to a critic's eye it might appear more appropriate, as some suggest, at the

30 Then Joshua built an altar unto the LORD God of Israel *in mount Ebal, **31** As Moses the servant of the LORD commanded the children of Israel, as it is written in the *book of the law of Moses, an altar of whole stones, over which no man hath lifted up *any* iron: and *they offered thereon burnt offerings unto the LORD, and sacrificed peace offerings. **32** And *he wrote there up-

*Deut. 27. 4, 5.——*a* Exod. 20. 25; Deut. 27. 5, 6.

b Exod. 20. 24.——*c* Deut. 27. 2, 8.

close of chap. xi. But the criticisms which make the passage an interpolation, or hold it to be out of place here, are based on uncertain and unwarrantable assumptions, and there are several considerations which make it more probable that the narrative is in its proper chronological order. Joshua improved the first possible opportunity to obey the commandment of Moses, which required Israel, "on the day when they passed over Jordan," (Deut. xxvii, 2,) to do what is here recorded. Of course the commandment, literally understood, imposed an impossibility, for Mount Ebal could not be reached by the Israelitish camp on the very day they crossed the Jordan. The spirit and import of the commandment were that the first possible opportunity be taken for it. Jericho and Ai were the centers of two powerful kingdoms that lay directly in the way from the Jordan to Mount Ebal, and these must first be conquered. Then, as the miraculous passage of the Jordan had so awed the Canaanites that Joshua could circumcise the people and celebrate the passover unmolested in the plains of Jericho, so the destruction of Ai enabled him to proceed at once to Mount Ebal, and without opposition erect the memorial altar there. Keil supposes that after this the camp of Israel was pitched at the Gilgal which lies about half way between Bethel and Mount Ebal. But see note on chap. ix, 6. Keil's hypothesis is unnecessary, especially as no account at all is given of the march of Israel either to or from Mount Ebal, and it is therefore as easy to *suppose* they marched back to the Jordan Gilgal as to the mountains of Ephraim.]

30. **Mount Ebal**—The mountain, nearly eight hundred feet high, which rises in steep, rocky precipices on the north side of the narrow valley in which lay the city, Shechem, and which was confronted on the south by Mount Gerizim. See on verse 33, and on John v, 4.

31. **An altar of whole stones**— That is, stones on which no tool of iron had been used to chisel down or polish. According to the law of Exod. xx, 25, a stone altar must not be built of hewn stones, for the touch of an iron tool upon it was regarded as a pollution. And an unhewn stone would the better symbolize that Living Stone, (1 Pet. ii, 4.) cut out of the mountain without hands, (Dan. ii, 45,) which has become the head of the corner, (Eph. ii, 20,) and certainly owes none of its excellence to human culture or polish.

32. **He wrote there upon the stones**—Whether these stones were the same as those of which the altar was built, or others, erected solely for the purpose of inscription, is not positively determined either by this passage or that of Deut. xxvii, 2–8. But the more probable opinion, and the one adopted by most expositors, is that it was a separate monument of stones on which the law was written. According to the original command, (Deut. xxvii, 4,) the stones were to be smeared with cement, and the words to be written upon it. At first thought this would seem to lack the chief quality of a memorial, durability. But travelers in the east assert that such inscriptions are as lasting as those cut in the rock. Says Dr. Thomson: "A careful examination of Deut. xxvii, 4, 8, and Josh. viii, 30–32, will lead to the opinion that the law was *written upon,* or *in,* the plaster with which these pillars were coated. This could be done, and such writing was common in ancient times. I have seen numerous specimens of it certainly *two thousand years old,* and still as distinct as when they were first inscribed on the plaster. In this hot climate, where there is no frost to dissolve the cement, it will continue hard and unbroken for thousands of years, which

on the stones a copy of the law of Moses, which he wrote in the presence of the children of Israel. **33** And all Israel, and their elders, and officers, and their judges, stood on this side the ark and on that side, before the priests the Le-vites, [d] which bare the ark of the cove-nant of the Lord, as well [e] the stranger, as he that was born among them; half of them over against mount Gerizim, and half of them over against mount Ebal; [f] as Moses the servant of the Lord

d Deut. 31. 9, 25.——e Deut. 31. 12.

f Deut. 11. 29; 27. 12.

is certainly long enough. The cement on Solomon's pools remains in admi-rable preservation, though exposed to all the vicissitudes of climate, and with no protection. The cement in the tombs about Sidon is still perfect, and the writing entire, though acted upon for perhaps two thousand years by the moist damp air always found in caverns." Respecting the mode of writing on the cement, he says: "What Joshua did, therefore, when he erected these great stones at Mount Ebal, was merely to write *in* the still soft cement with a stile, or, more likely, *on* the polished surface, when dry, with red paint, as in ancient tombs." **A copy of the law of Moses**—The chief difficulty which critics have here is in the size of the work, if the whole of the *Torah*, or Mosaic law, is to be deemed as thus inscribed. The Hebrew word for **copy** is *mishneh*, (מִשְׁנֶה,) and signifies a *rep-etition*, a *duplicate*, "an apograph next to the original." The Septuagint and the Vulgate translate it by the word *Deuter-onomy*, which, though literally meaning *a repetition of the law*, had already ac-quired a narrower signification. Several Rabbins make the incredible statement that the whole law, word for word, was written on the monuments, in seventy different languages, that all the people of the earth might be able to read it! Clarke and Bush suppose "that only a copy of the blessings and curses, re-corded in Deut. xxvii and xxviii, was written." But Keil well says, "To limit 'the law' to the blessings and curses is out of the question, for these are not 'the law,' but motives added to impel, or rather adjure, the people to keep the law inviolate." [The opinion of Grotius seems at first very plausible, that the Decalogue is meant, for it con-tains the essence of the whole law, all else being accessory to it. But against it is the insuperable objection, that to

call "the words of the covenant"—"the ten words," (Exod. xxxiv, 28; Deut iv, 13,) which are ever associated with "the two tables of the testimony"—to call these **a copy of the law of Moses** would be inexplicably strange. In the absence of any specific statement it is impossible to decide the question posi-tively, but we incline to the view of Hengstenberg, Keil, and others, that the so-called "second law" is meant, which is embodied in Deuteronomy, between chap. iv, 44, and chap. xxvi, 19, omitting, of course, the exhortations and historical incidents with which it is now associated in the Book of Deuter-onomy. This would be the essence of all the law of Moses.]

33. **As well the stranger**—The entire body of Israelites, by descent and by adoption, were present. The latter were more commonly called *pros-elytes*, but sometimes *strangers*. **Over against Mount Gerizim**—The multi-tude did not stand on the summits of the mountains, but on their slopes. That they could all hear when thus stand-ing is sufficiently attested by modern travellers. Says Stanley: "The vale of Shechem is far from broad, not ex-ceeding in some places a few hundred feet." [Says Tristram: "The acoustic properties of this valley are interesting. A single voice might be heard by many thousands, shut in and conveyed up and down by the enclosing hills. In the early morning we could not only see from Gerizim a man driving his ass down a path on Mount Ebal, but could hear every word he uttered as he urged it on; and, in order to test the matter more certainly, on a subsequent occasion two of our party stationed themselves on opposite sides of the valley, and with perfect ease recited the commandments antiphonally."] Dr. W. M. Thomson writes, respecting this impressive scene: "This was, beyond

VALLEY OF SHECHEM.

had commanded before, that they should bless the people of Israel. **34** And afterward ^ghe read all the words of the law, ^hthe blessings and cursings, according to all that is written in the book of the law. **35** There was not a word of all that Moses commanded, which Joshua read not before all the congregation of Israel, ⁱwith the women, and the little ones, and ^kthe strangers that ⁵were conversant among them.

g Deut. 31. 11; Neh. 8. 3.——h Deut. 28. 2, 15, 45; 29. 20, 21; 30. 19.——i Deut. 31. 12.——k Verse 33. ——5 Heb. *walked*.

question or comparison, the most august assembly the sun ever shone upon. I never stand on the narrow plain, with Ebal and Gerizim rising on either hand to the sky, without involuntarily recalling and reproducing the scene. I have shouted to hear the echo, and then fancied how it must have been when the loud-voiced Levites proclaimed from the naked cliffs of Ebal, ' Cursed be the man that maketh any graven or molten image, an abomination unto Jehovah;' and then the tremendous AMEN, tenfold louder, from the mighty congregation, rising and swelling, and reaching from Ebal to Gerizim and from Gerizim to Ebal."

CHAPTER IX.

THE CANAANITES CONFEDERATED, 1, 2.

1. **All the kings**—Palestine was divided into many petty sovereignties, the heads of which were dignified by this title. **This side Jordan**—Literally, *beyond Jordan*, but meaning here, as the context shows, the west side of Jordan. See note on chap. i, 14. **In the hills**—Or, *in the mountain*. The reference is to the entire mountain range which forms the backbone of Palestine. **In the valleys**—Or, *in the Shephelah*. This word designates the maritime plain of Philistia, and might well be translated *the low countries*. **Great sea**—The Mediterranean. **Coasts... over against Lebanon**—The Phenician plain. Canaanites from even these remoter parts joined this confederacy. On the Canaanitish tribes here mentioned, see note on chap. iii, 10. **Heard thereof**—Not of the demonstration at

CHAPTER IX.

AND it came to pass, when all the kings which *were* on this side Jordan, in the hills, and in the valleys, and in all the coasts of ^athe great sea over against Lebanon, ^bthe Hittite, and the Amorite, the Canaanite, the Perizzite, the Hivite, and the Jebusite, heard *thereof;* **2** That they ^cgathered themselves together, to fight with Joshua and with Israel, with one ¹accord.

3 And when the inhabitants of ^dGib-

a Num. 34. 6.——b Exod. 3. 17; 23. 23.——c Psa. 83. 3, 5.——1 Heb. *mouth*.——d Chap. 10. 2; 2 Sam. 21. 1, 2.

Ebal and Gerizim, but of the rapid conquests of Joshua. The word **thereof,** supplied by our translators, is better omitted.

2. **Gathered themselves together** —It is not singular that rival and jealous States did not combine till the dread of a victorious foe, already in the heart of their territory, compelled them to unite for their common safety. Had wise statesmanship dwelt in their councils, their confederated hosts would have confronted Joshua on the banks of the Jordan. [**To fight with Joshua**—How Joshua suddenly surprised and conquered the southern nations of this confederacy is told in chap. x, and how he subdued the northern tribes, and others who escaped from the south, will be found in chap. xi. Meantime the writer turns aside to narrate the league of the Gibeonites, which served as the immediate occasion of Joshua's war with the five Amoritish kings.]

THE FRAUD AND PUNISHMENT OF THE GIBEONITES, 3–27.

3. **Gibeon**—This was called " a great city." Chap. x, 2. It was the capital of the Hivites, and was situated five miles north by west from Jerusalem, at the head of the pass of Bethhoron. It was the key of central Palestine. Three adjacent cities were leagued with it, (verse 17,) and seem to have formed with it a kind of republic; at least it was not under a king, but was equal in rank to " one of the royal cities." Chap. x, 2. " It stands on one of those rounded hills which characterize especially the western for-

eon *heard what Joshua had done unto Jericho and to Ai, **4** They did † work wilily, and went and made as if they had been ambassadors, and took old sacks upon their asses, and winebottles, old, and rent, and bound up; **5** And

old shoes and clouted upon their feet, and old garments upon them; and all the bread of their provision was dry *and* mouldy. **6** And they went to Joshua ‡ unto the camp at Gilgal, and said unto him, and to the men of Israel,

e Chap. 6. 27.——*f* Gen. 34. 13; 1 Kings 20. 31, 33; Luke 16. 8.——*g* Chap. 5. 10.

---

mation of Judea."—*Stanley.* It is by all travellers identified with the modern village El-Jib—a corruption of Gibeon. "It is a very fair and delicious place," says Mandeville, "and it is called Mount Joy, because it gives joy to pilgrims' hearts; for from that place men first see Jerusalem." Here, where it overlooked the wide domain of Israel, the sacred tabernacle was set up for many years under David and Solomon. 1 Kings iii, 3, 4. El-Jib is a moderately sized village of irregularly placed houses, chiefly composed of old mossy ruins.

4. [**They did work wilily**—Literally, *Then did also they by stratagem.* The *also* seems to refer here most naturally to what Joshua had done to Ai. As he used cunning and strategy in the capture of that city, so did also they practice strategy in making a league with Israel. Others, we think less correctly, take *also* (נָם) as an adversative here, expressing the contrast between the action of the Gibeonites and the other Canaanites.] **As if...ambassadors**—Suing for peace. The more distant cities think only of war; the nearest, on whom the next blow must fall, seek for peace; perhaps their popular form of government also influenced them toward a pacific policy. [The Hebrew word translated, **made as if they had been ambassadors,** (Hithpael of צִיר,) occurs nowhere else; but Keil and others defend this meaning, given in the English version. Others, however, with Gesenius, argue that " since no other trace of this form or signification exists in Hebrew or Aramæan, it is better to read, with six MSS., יִצְטַיָּדוּ, *they provided themselves with food* for the journey, as in verse 12; which is also expressed by the ancient versions."] **Old sacks**—The traveller's equipage in Syria, anciently and at the present day, comprises food and drink,

kitchen utensils, tents, bedding, etc., all stowed away in sacks and transported on the backs of asses. **Old sacks** would give the impression of a long journey. **Winebottles**—These were goat-skins, nearly whole, cured in a peculiar manner. When worn through, a temporary expedient for mending them was to gather up the skin about the hole and tie it like the mouth of a bag. By this means the mending becomes very manifest.

5. Old shoes and clouted—Or, as the Hebrew, *shoes fallen into pieces,* and *botched* or *cobbled.* In long journeys the traveller walks up the hills that he may spare the heavily laden beast. These shoes in tatters and patches indicate many a walk, and hence a long journey. [The somewhat antiquated English word **clouted,** from the Anglo-Saxon *clut, a little cloth* or *patch,* accurately expresses the sense of the Hebrew טָלָא, to *patch,* to *mend.* It may be used of patching with cloth, leather, or other material.] **Old garments upon them**—That is, *upon themselves,* and not upon their feet. **Dry and mouldy**—The Vulgate says, instead of **mouldy,** *broken up into crumbs,* and this seems to be the true rendering. The Septuagint adds *offensive to the smell.* Ancient inns or caravanserais provided the sojourner with lodging only; hence he must carry his food. See note on chap. ii, 1.

[**6. The camp at Gilgal**—In the absence of any hint that this was altogether a different place from the Gilgal near Jericho, where Joshua first pitched his camp, it seems rather arbitrary and unnecessary, with Keil and Van de Velde, to maintain that this Gilgal must be identified with the modern Jiljilia, in the mountains of Ephraim. If, after the capture of Ai, or after the memorial service at Mount Ebal, Joshua had pitched his camp in a new spot, and especially at another place

h We be come from a far country: now therefore make ye a league with us. 7 And the men of Israel said unto the i Hivites, Peradventure ye dwell among us; and k how shall we make a league with you? 8 And they said unto Joshua, l We *are* thy servants. And Joshua

said unto them, Who *are* ye? and from whence come ye? 9 And they said unto him, m From a very far country thy servants are come, because of the name of the LORD thy God: for we have n heard the fame of him, and all that he did in Egypt, 10 And o all that he did

---

h 2 Kings 20. 14.——*i* Chap. 11. 19.——*k* Exod. 23. 32; Deut. 7. 2; 20. 16; Judg. 2. 2.

l Deut. 20. 11; 2 Kings 10. 5.——*m* Deut. 20. 15. *n* Exod. 15. 14; Josh. 2. 10.——*o* Num. 21. 24, 33.

---

bearing the name *Gilgal*, it is inexplicably strange that no mention is anywhere made of a fact so noticeable and important. Further, the expressions in chap. x, 7, 9—Joshua *ascended* and *went up from Gilgal*—most naturally indicate the ascent from the Jordan valley to the interior of Palestine, (see note on chap. viii, 10,) and show that the writer still had in mind the Gilgal near Jericho; for to understand the expressions in a military sense is hardly admissible. Keil's only weighty argument is, that it would have been folly in Joshua, after having penetrated into the heart of the country, to go back again to the eastern border, and leave the Canaanites at liberty to move at pleasure through the conquered territory. But this whole argument rests on the assumption that Joshua would, of course, endeavour to *keep* the conquered Canaanites in subjection by the presence of his camp and army in the centre of the land, or else by establishing garrisons in the conquered districts—a thing which we have no evidence was ever done during the wars of the conquest. Keil's argument is therefore altogether insufficient, and rests solely on a critic's assumption of what *Joshua ought to have done*.] **From a far country—** They had heard that all the Canaanites had been doomed to extermination. See verse 24. To avoid such a fate they represented that they dwelt beyond the limits of Canaan. By this means they hoped to negotiate a treaty of peace, and even an alliance with the invincible invader. That such a treaty with nations beyond the limits of Canaan was lawful, see Deut. xx, 10, 11.

7. **Said unto the Hivites—**The inhabitants of Gibeon were Hivites. See chap. xi, 19. **Peradventure ye dwell among us** — The suspicions

of the Hebrews are awakened, as they well might have been. Their Canaanitish speech must have betrayed them. **How shall we make a league with you ?—**This question strongly implies the impossibility of such an act, because it had been expressly forbidden, (Exod. xxiii, 32; xxxiv, 12; Deut. vii, 2,) on the ground of the ensnaring and corrupting influence of pagan allies.

8. **We are thy servants** — This expression hardly implies that these Gibeonites anticipated their destiny of serfdom, as some suppose; it is rather a common oriental mode of speech by which inferiors becomingly address a superior. Compare Gen. xliii, 28; xliv, 7. **Who are ye ?—**Joshua seeks to draw from them their nationality and their country, but he is baffled by their vague reply.

9. **Because of the name of the Lord thy God—**⟨ The word LORD, in capitals, here as elsewhere in the Old Testament, is the Hebrew Jehovah, the proper name of the God of Israel, as Baal was the god of the Canaanites. These Canaanite-Gibeonites, assuming that Baal and Jehovah are two rival national deities, are proposing to make submission, and even, if needs be, to transfer their allegiance to the latter, who has shown himself by his victories to be the mightier god of the two. ⟩ **And all that he did in Egypt—**They are too cunning to say that they have heard of the miraculous crossing of the Jordan, of Jericho's downfall, and the capture of Ai. This would intimate that they were so near as to become cognizant of these recent events. So they speak of events forty years ago in Egypt, and many months ago beyond the Jordan. ⟨ Thereby fulfilling God's words to Pharaoh, that he had raised him up to make his name declared throughout all the earth.

to the two kings of the Amorites, that *were* beyond Jordan, to Sihon king of Heshbon, and to Og king of Bashan, which *was* at Ashtaroth. **11** Wherefore our elders and all the inhabitants of our country spake to us, saying, Take victuals [2] with you for the journey, and go to meet them, and say unto them, We *are* your servants: therefore now make ye a league with us. **12** This our bread we took hot *for* our provision out of our houses on the day we came forth to go unto you; but now, behold, it is dry, and it is mouldy: **13** And these bottles of wine, which we filled, *were* new; and, behold, they be rent: and these our garments and our shoes are become old by reason of the very long journey. **14** And [s] the men took of their victuals, [p] and asked not *counsel* at the mouth of the Lord. **15** And Joshua [q] made peace with them, and made a league with them, to let them live: and the princes of the congregation sware unto them.

---

2 Heb. *in your hand.*——3 Or, *they received the men by reason of their victuals.*——p Num. 27. 21; Isa. 30. 1. 2; Judg. 1.1; 1 Sa. 22. 10; 23. 10, 11; 50. 8; 2 Sa. 2. 1; 5. 19.——q Chap. 11. 19; 2 Sa. 21. 2.

Exod. ix, 16. And wonderfully have these words been fulfilled. }

10. **Amorites ... Sihon ... Heshbon ... Og ... Bashan**—See note on chap. ii, 10. **Which was at Ashtaroth**—The word **which** (according to old English) refers to Og, and should be rendered *who*. This royal city of Og was in Bashan, and named from Ashtoreth, the Greek Astarte, the Oriental Venus, who was worshipped there. **Ashtaroth** is the plural form of *Ashtoreth*, and the place perhaps took this form of the name from the many Astarte-images used in her worship there. It lies six miles north-west of Edrei, and, according to Robinson, is the modern Tell-Astereh. After its capture it was assigned to the Levites.

11. **Our elders**—The popular character of their government, with a senate of elders at its head, appears quite distinctly in this verse.

12. **This our bread**—To confirm their statements they exhibit their dry, crumbled bread, wine skins and apparel sadly the worse for wear, knowing well the influence which such ocular proofs have over the human mind.

14. **The men**—The chiefs in Joshua's camp with whom the Gibeonites conferred. **Took of their victuals** —But it is not said that the men of Israel ate of these victuals. Yet, as it is a custom among the Arabs to eat the victuals of a guest, as a sign of peace and friendship, this may have been the purpose of their taking the provision of these Gibeonites. This passage has puzzled all the interpreters. The marginal reading in our English Bible is ingenious, but it is not sus-

tained by the Hebrew, "*they received the men by reason of their victuals.*" Nor did they make a treaty with them by eating their food, for this was not customary. More plausible is the theory that they took their bread into their hands to examine it. But we would suggest that the real meaning may be, *they presumed* the truth of the story *from their victuals.* The original word for *took* is sometimes used for mental acts. **And asked not counsel at the mouth of the Lord**—A momentous question was settled with no reference to the Divine will, and that, too, on a point in regard to which Jehovah's commands were very explicit—alliance with aliens. Compare note and references on verse 7. Jehovah, who had made special arrangements for communicating with his people through the urim and thummim, was slighted and ignored. These Israelitish princes have had many imitators in the senates and cabinets of Christian lands. How rarely is God consulted by statesmen, even in affairs in which the destiny of a nation is involved!

15. **Peace**—He solemnly pledged the faith of his people to abstain from war against their commonwealth. **A league**—This is a step beyond peace; an alliance, binding the two parties to mutual assistance in defensive, if not offensive, war. **Princes of the congregation**—Called, in verses 6 and 7, *men of Israel*, that is, representative men, consisting of heads of families and elders of the people. **Sware**— The Hebrew princes appealed to God in their oaths in such phrase as, "The God of Abraham judge;" "As Jeho-

16 And it came to pass at the end of three days after they had made a league with them, that they heard that they *were* their neighbours, and *that* they dwelt among them. **17** And the children of Israel journeyed, and came unto their cities on the third day. Now their cities *were* [r] Gibeon, and Chephirah, and Beeroth, and Kirjath-jearim. **18** And the children of Israel smote them not, [s] because the princes of the congregation had sworn unto them by the LORD God

of Israel. And all the congregation murmured against the princes. **19** But all the princes said unto all the congregation, We have sworn unto them by the LORD God of Israel: now therefore we may not touch them. **20** This we will do to them; we will even let them live, lest [t] wrath be upon us, because of the oath which we sware unto them. **21** And the princes said unto them, Let them live; but let them be [u] hewers of wood and drawers of water unto all

---

[r] Chap. 18. 25, 26, 28; Ezra 2. 25.——[s] Psa. 15. 4; Eccles. 5. 2.

[t] See 2 Sam. 21. 1; 2, 6; Ezek. 17. 13, 15, 18, 19; Zech. 5. 3, 4; Mal. 3. 5.——[u] Deut. 29. 11.

---

vah liveth:" "God do so to me and more also;" "God knoweth," and similar formulas.

16. **At the end of three days**— The Gibeonites themselves probably notified Joshua, after three days, that they were dwelling in their vicinity. This precaution was necessary as a safeguard against a sudden attack by Joshua. They held the pass of Beth-horon, the key of Central and Western Palestine, which a sagacious foe would seek to wrest from their hands.

17. **Gibeon**—See verse 3, note. There were three other cities on federal relations with Gibeon. **Chephira,** literally, *the village,* is in the mountains on the western confines of Benjamin, east of Nicopolis, and about two miles east of Yalo, the ancient Aijalon. Dr. Robinson discovered it under the scarcely altered name of *Kefir.* **Beeroth,** a Hebrew word for *wells,* was known to Eusebius, and his description of its position agrees perfectly with that of the modern el-Bireh, ten miles north of Jerusalem, on the great road to Shechem. It is a favourite resting-place for caravans at the end of the first day's journey from Jerusalem, and contains a population of about seven hundred. **Kirjath-jearim** — *City of forests,* called also, in chap. xviii, 14, *City of Baal,* the great Canaanite deity. It was celebrated as the abode of the ark for twenty years, (1 Sam. vii, 2,) and is still a resort of pilgrims from all Judea. Dr. Robinson identifies it with the modern Kuriet-el-Enab, *city of grapes,* on the road from Jaffa to Jerusalem, and about ten miles northwest of the latter city. In chap. xviii, 28, it is called merely Kirjath.

18. **The congregation murmured** —This entire land had been promised to them for an inheritance. A part of that long-promised inheritance, to which they had for many years looked forward with hope, was now suddenly snatched from them as they were just entering on its possession. The manner in which this had been done aggravated their disappointment, and increased their indignation against the princes who had permitted themselves to be so duped, and the Hebrew people to be cheated out of its divine legacy. Another reason for their murmuring was the imprudence of the chiefs of Israel in entering into a treaty like this without consulting Jehovah.

19. **Now therefore we may not touch them**—So strong was their respect for their oath that they would hold as valid a contract made on fraudulent representations. According to natural justice and the laws of our modern civilization, they would have been justified in treating their oath as null and void. Most expositors are of this opinion; and Calvin goes so far as to charge the princes with a new violation of the will of God, because they now " obstinately maintain, upon the pretext of their oath, the promise which they had foolishly made."

20. **Lest wrath be upon us**—By neglecting to consult God they had brought themselves into a state of moral perplexity. They were in a strait between their oath and the plain command of God, strengthened by the murmurs of the people.

21. **Hewers of wood and drawers of water**—We will keep our oath to

the congregation; as the princes had *promised them. **22** And Joshua called for them, and he spake unto them, saying, Wherefore have ye beguiled us, saying, *We are very far from you; when* ye dwell among us? **23** Now therefore ye *are* cursed, and there shall none of you be freed from being bondmen, and hewers of wood and drawers of water for the house of my God. **24** And they answered Joshua, and said, Because it was certainly told thy servants, how that the LORD thy God commanded his servant Moses to give you all the land, and to destroy all the inhabitants of the land from before you, therefore we were sore afraid of our lives because of you, and have done this thing. **25** And now, behold, we *are* in thine hand: as it seemeth good and right unto thee to do unto us, do. **26** And so did he unto them, and delivered them out of the hand of the children of Israel, that they slew them not. **27** And Joshua made them that day hewers of wood and drawers of

---

v Verse 15.——*w* Verses 6, 9.——*x* Verse 16.——
y Gen. 9. 25.——4 Heb. *not be cut off from you.*
——*z* Verses 21, 27.——*a* Exod. 23. 32; Deut. 7. 1, 2.

b Exod. 15. 14.——*c* Gen. 16. 6.——5 Heb. *gave,*
or *delivered to be;* 1 Chron. 9. 2; Ezra 8. 20.——
d Verses 21, 23; 1 Chron. 9. 2; Ezra 8. 20.

---

the letter: they shall live, but live as slaves. Upon the "great high place" of Gibeon the tabernacle was set up at a later period, (1 Chron. xvi, 39,) and there it remained till it was removed to Jerusalem by Solomon. From beneath this eminence water and wood for the service of the tabernacle were constantly carried up, requiring the labour of a large number of people. Stanley says: "They hewed the wood of the adjacent valley and drew the water from the springs and tanks which in its immediate neighbourhood abound, and carried them up to the Sacred Tent, and there attended the altar of the Lord." Respecting the drudgery of this menial service, Dr. Thomson, while passing through this very region of the Gibeonites, says: "I was forcibly reminded of one item in the sentence of condemnation pronounced upon them for their cunning deception—that they should be hewers of wood—by long files of women and children carrying on their heads heavy bundles of wood. It is the severest drudgery, and my compassion has often been enlisted in behalf of the poor women and children who daily bring loads of wood to Jerusalem from these very mountains of the Gibeonites. To carry water, also, is very laborious. The fountains are far off, in deep wadies with steep banks; and a thousand times have I seen the feeble and the young staggering up long and weary ways, with large jars of water on their heads. It is the work of slaves." **As the princes had promised them**—They had promised life,

not servitude. This promise was kept by successive generations, till Saul rashly killed some and planned the general massacre of the rest. Seven of Saul's descendants atoned for this breach of the covenant with their lives. 2 Sam. xxi, 1–9. At the time of Saul's massacre they were so identified with Israel that the historian was obliged to insert a note explaining their origin.

23. **Ye are cursed**—Bondage, even to the best of masters and to the most honourable kind of labour, is a curse. If slavery were ever a blessing to a pagan nation, by bringing it into a knowledge of the true religion, this would have been such a case; but Joshua pronounces even such bondage, though far above chattel slavery, a curse.

24. **It was certainly told thy servants**—This information could have been brought by spies sent from Canaan to ascertain the intentions of so formidable a mass of people marching through the wilderness toward Palestine. The language of both nations was nearly the same. **We were sore afraid**—They had grounds for their great fear, in view of the fate of their brethren, the Amorites east of the Jordan.

26. **And delivered them**—The people were clamorous for their blood. Joshua shows his great courage and fidelity to his convictions by resisting the pressure of the outraged and excited populace, who in mobocratic madness would have swept away a weaker ruler.

27. [**Joshua made them**—Rather, as the margin, *gave them*; that is, ap-

water for the congregation, and for the altar of the LORD, even unto this day, [e]in the place which he should choose.

CHAPTER X.

NOW it came to pass, when Adonizedek king of Jerusalem had heard how Joshua had taken Ai, and had ut-

e Deut. 12. 5.——a Chap. 6. 21.——b Chap. 8. 22, 26, 28.——c Chap. 9. 15.

pointed them to the service named. Jewish tradition and most commentators agree that these Gibeonites, thus given to perform the menial service of the sanctuary, were the original caste or order who in later times were known as *the Nethinim*, that is, *the given ones.* See 1 Chron. ix, 2; Ezra ii, 43; viii, 20, notes.] **For the congregation, and for the altar**—They were never to be required to render personal service, nor to be employed for private purposes. **In the place which he should choose**—Here is strong incidental evidence that the sanctuary had not, at the time this history was written, been permanently established at Jerusalem.

CHAPTER X.

FIVE KINGS WAR AGAINST GIBEON, 1-5.

1. **Adoni-zedek**—The name means *lord of justice.* Compare the kindred word *Melchizedek, king of justice.* Gen. xiv, 18. All that is known of this Amorite king and his four confederates is recorded in this chapter. Alarmed at the victories of Joshua and the defection of Gibeon, his nearest neighbour on the north, he aroused the kings in the south, and combined them against the seceding state. This drew Joshua to the aid of his ally, and to the discomfiture of his confederated foes, and the execution of Adoni-zedek and his four royal associates. **Jerusalem**—This is the first time that undisputed mention is made in the Bible of this celebrated city. Probably the Salem in Gen. xiv, 18, is Jerusalem, although Jerome contends that Salem was in the southern part of Galilee, near Scythopolis. Jerusalem is called " Jebus " and the " city of the Jebusites " in Judges and some later books. It became the metropolis

terly destroyed it; [a]as he had done to Jericho and her king, so he had done to [b]Ai and her king: and [c]how the inhabitants of Gibeon had made peace with Israel, and were among them; **2** That they [d]feared greatly, because Gibeon *was* a great city, as one of the [1]royal cities, and because it *was* greater than

d Exod. 15. 14, 15, 16; Deut. 11. 25.——1 Heb. *cities of the kingdom.*

of the Hebrews under David at a comparatively late date, after the nation had gone through the period of the Judges and entered on the Monarchy. Bethel, Hebron, and Shechem were ancient holy places when the Jebusite was still possessing Jerusalem. It is a little south of the centre of Palestine, thirty-two miles from the coast and eighteen from the Jordan, and is two thousand six hundred feet above the level of the sea. It is surrounded on three sides by hills still higher, from which it is separated by precipitous ravines, which rendered it, before the invention of gunpowder, almost impregnable. " It is on the ridge, the broadest and most strongly marked ridge, of the backbone of the complicated hills which extend through the whole country, from the plain of Esdraelon to the desert. Every wanderer, every conqueror, every traveller, who has trod the central route of Palestine from north to south, must have passed through the table-land of Jerusalem. It was the water-shed between the streams, or, rather, the torrent beds, which find their way eastward to the Jordan and westward to the Mediterranean."—*Stanley.* See note, Matt. ii, 1. **And were among them**—That is, were having amicable intercourse with the Israelites.

2. **They feared greatly**—The loss to the Amorites of so powerful a commonwealth as Gibeon, and its alliance with Joshua, was a sufficient cause of fear, aside from the fact that Joshua, now securely established in this central position, had completely cut off northern from southern Palestine, so that he could conquer each in detail. **As one of the royal cities**—It was not a royal capital, but as important. The fact that so large a city, in their

Ai, and all the men thereof *were* mighty. 3 Wherefore Adoni-zedek king of Jerusalem sent unto Hoham king of Hebron, and unto Piram king of Jarmuth, and unto Japhia king of Lachish, and unto Debir king of Eglon, saying, 4 Come up unto me, and help me, that we may smite Gibeon: *e* for it hath made peace with Joshua and with the children of Israel. 5 Therefore the five kings of the Amorites, the king of Jerusalem, the king of Hebron, the king of Jarmuth, the king of Lachish, the king of

Eglon, *f* gathered themselves together, and went up, they and all their hosts, and encamped before Gibeon, and made war against it.

6 And the men of Gibeon sent unto Joshua *g* to the camp to Gilgal, saying, Slack not thy hand from thy servants; come up to us quickly, and save us, and help us: for all the kings of the Amorites that dwell in the mountains are gathered together against us.

7 So Joshua ascended from Gilgal, he, and *h* all the people of war with

---

e Verse 1; chap. 9. 15.——*f* Chap. 9. 2.   *g* Chap. 5, 10; 9. 6.——*h* Chap. 8. 1.

---

immediate vicinity, renowned for bravery, had submitted to the invader without striking a blow, was indeed appalling.

3. **Hebron**—This city, one of the most ancient in the world, is situated among the mountains of Judah, twenty miles south of Jerusalem. It is two thousand eight hundred feet above the Mediterranean, and is the highest town in Palestine, being six hundred feet above Jerusalem. Hence the appropriateness of the expression in chap. xx, 7: "Hebron in the mountain of Judah." It was well known when Abraham sojourned there, nearly four thousand years ago. Its original name was *Kirjath-Arba*, the city of Arba, and it was sometimes called *Mamre*. Ritter argues that the original name was Hebron, and that this name was restored after the expulsion of the Anakim. Chap. xv, 14. It is now called by the Mohammedans *El-Khulil*, "the Friend," that is, of God—the designation of Abraham, whose tomb, the cave of Machpelah, is still here, one of the historic· remains in the Holy Land of which travellers have no doubts. It is enclosed within a mosque. The present population is about ten thousand. **Jarmuth** was a town in the low country of Judah, but not so far west as the plain. It was southwest from Jerusalem about eighteen miles. Robinson found here a hamlet called *Yarmûk*, which doubtless represents the ancient capital of **Piram**, and contains among the hewn stones of its ruins some traces of its ancient greatness. **Lachish**, probably the modern Um-Lakis, is about fifteen miles

west of Hebron, on the lower range of hills, so far below the summit of Hebron that it is called "the plain." It was rebuilt after Joshua destroyed it, and in the reign of Hezekiah was taken by Sennacherib. The siege is mentioned in 2 Chron. xxxii, 9, and a plan of the city and its capture is portrayed on slabs found by Layard at Nineveh. See notes and cuts at 2 Kings xviii, 14; xix, 8. **Eglon** was about eight miles west by north from Lachish on the plain. Its name is supposed to survive in Ajlan, a shapeless mass of ruins covering a round hillock. In translating this verse the Septuagint has erroneously called this place *Adullam*.

THE GIBEONITES APPEAL FOR AID, 6.

6. **Save us**—As soon as the hostile army of the confederated Amorites pitched their camp before their walls the Gibeonites sent to Joshua for aid. It was of the first importance that Joshua should rescue them and retain their allegiance. Had the Gibeonites been neglected by Joshua they would have been either forced into a league with the Amorites, or defeated by their superior numbers.

JOSHUA'S NIGHT-MARCH TO GIBEON, 7–9.

7. **Ascended**—This expression (repeated in verse 9) most obviously has reference to the ascent from the Jordan valley to the interior of Palestine. See notes on chap. viii, 10; ix, 6. **All the people of war** is an expression limited by its appositive in the next clause, **all the mighty men of valour**, which is the Hebrew way of saying, *all the bravest men of the army.*

him, and all the mighty men of valour.
8 And the LORD said unto Joshua,
'Fear them not: for I have delivered
them into thine hand; *k* there shall
not a man of them stand before thee.

i Chap. 11. 6; Judg. 4. 14.——*k* Chap. 1. 5.

8. Fear them not—He was constrained to aid Gibeon not only by
military necessity, but also by the encouraging assurance of the Lord that
he should be victorious. As Joshua
up to this time had fought only single
cities, he needed additional assurance
when he was about to meet for the
first time the allied armies of Canaan.

9. Suddenly—Because Joshua believed the words of Jehovah he made

9 Joshua therefore came unto them suddenly, *and* went up from Gilgal all
night.

10 And the LORD ¹discomfited them
before Israel, and slew them with a

l Judg. 4. 15; 1 Sam. 7. 10, 12; Psa. 18. 14; Isa. 28. 21.

a bold and sudden movement. Great
faith is essential to a great captain.
Went up from Gilgal all night—
He had marched over this route several times before, and was familiar
with it. The distance from Gilgal to
Gibeon was about the same as that
from Gilgal to Ai, fifteen miles. See
chap. viii. 9, note. This night march
was a memorable prelude to the most
astounding miracle of history.

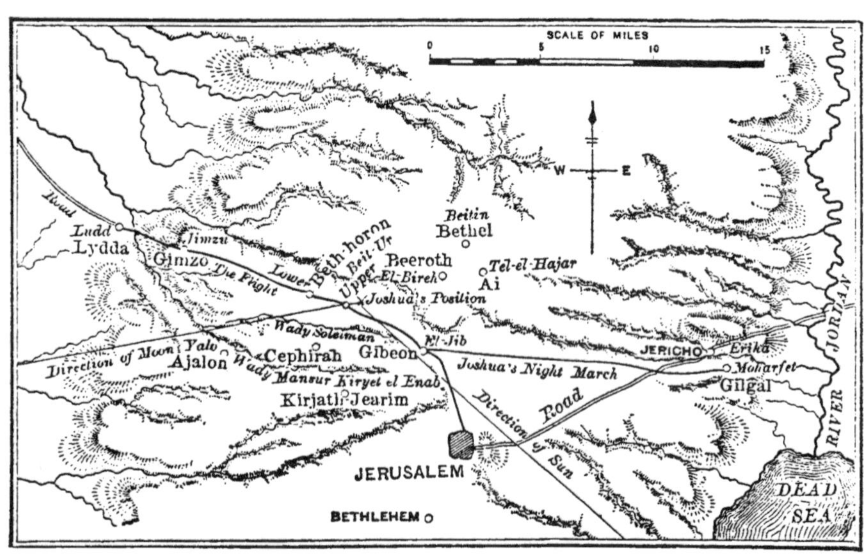

JOSHUA'S BATTLE-FIELD AT GIBEON.

THE GREAT BATTLE OF GIBEON AND
BETH-HORON, 10, 11.

["The battle of Beth-horon, or Gibeon," says Stanley, "was one of the most
important in the history of the world;
and yet so profound has been the indifference, first of the religious world,
and then (through their example or
influence) of the common world, to
the historical study of the Hebrew
annals, that the very name of this
great battle is far less known to most
of us than that of Marathon or Can-
næ. It is one of the few military

engagements which belong equally
to ecclesiastical and to civil history,
which have decided equally the fortunes of the world and of the Church."]

**10. And the Lord discomfited
them**—The victory is ascribed not to
Joshua but to the Lord. He had inspired the great Hebrew chieftain with
confidence to strike a sudden blow,
probably in the early morning dawn,
and the panic-stricken enemy fled in
confusion. There is no need of supposing, with some expositors, that God
made use of thunder and lightning, or

great slaughter at Gibeon, and chased them along the way that goeth up [m] to Beth-horon, and smote them to [n] Azekah, and unto Makkedah. **11** And it came to pass, as they fled from before Israel, *and* were in the going down to Beth-horon, [o] that the LORD cast down great stones from heaven upon them unto Azekah, and they died: *they were* more which died with hailstones than *they* whom the children of Israel slew with the sword.

---

m Chap. 16. 3, 5. —— n Chap. 15. 35.   o Psa. 18. 13, 14; 77. 17; Isa. 30. 30; Rev. 16. 21.

---

any other terrific natural phenomena, to discomfit the Amorite host early in the morning. The sudden assault of Joshua with his battalion of picked men was sufficient to produce such a result. God is often said to do that which is done through the agency of men. The issue of battles, like every other human event, is in the hands of Almighty God. In the sphere of mind there is a field for divine interposition, breathing courage into one army and dismay into the other. Hence many of the most wonderful triumphs in the world's history have been achieved by the weaker army. **Beth-horon**—The house of caves. Upper Beth-horon is on an elevation northwest of Gibeon, higher up, and is at the head of a ravine through which there is a steep pass to Lower Beth-horon and to the plain of Sharon. The flight of the Amorites was toward this pass up the long ascent, **the way that goeth up.** Then came the second stage of the flight down the steep ravine, **in the going down to Beth-horon** the lower. **Azekah** was a town in the rich agricultural plain into which the valley of Aijalon opens westward. Its position has not yet been recognized. **Makkedah** is supposed to be in the same plain, but its situation has hitherto eluded discovery.

11. **The Lord cast down great stones.** — Some have supposed that this was a shower of meteoric stones, but before the statement is concluded **hailstones** are mentioned. Neither of these, considered by itself, is a miraculous event; but either of them occurring at that particular crisis in the flight, and falling only on the foes of Israel, must be regarded as supernatural. Both meteoric stones and hail may have fallen. I have before me the account of a shower of stones in Normandy, in France, in 1803. The stones fell with a hissing noise from a small rectangular cloud, which did not seem to move, and they were scattered over a tract of country eight miles long by three broad. Above two thousand were collected, the largest weighing seventeen and a half pounds. In the Yale College cabinet may be seen a similar stone, weighing sixteen hundred and thirty-five pounds, which fell in Arkansas. Others are found in South America, one whose estimated weight is fifteen tons. The most reasonable hypothesis is, that these stones are fragments of small invisible planets moving through space, drawn within the sphere of the earth's attraction. That a shower of such projectiles may have been directed by the Ruler of the universe to fall on the descent to Lower Beth-horon while his foes were fleeing from Joshua is not an incredible supposition to one who believes in a personal God. There are many instances of hail storms so violent as to be destructive of life, aside from that recorded in Exodus, (ix, 23–26,) a plague so destructive to all who were unsheltered. In our own country, in Jackson, La., 1834, within ten minutes, a little after midnight, a great number of cattle were killed by the hailstones, and much damage was done to the houses and woods. Sir Robert Wilson describes a terrible thunder and hail-storm at Marmorice Bay, Asia Minor, while the British fleet were at anchor there in February, 1801. It continued, at intervals, two days and nights to pour hailstones as large as walnuts, deluging the camps with a torrent of them till the earth was covered two feet deep. In August, 1831, there was a hail-storm so violent that two boatmen in a village on the Bosphorus were killed, and many others were severely wounded, by balls of ice of a pound weight. Sudden showers

12 Then spake Joshua to the LORD in the day when the LORD delivered up the Amorites before the children of Israel, and he said in the sight of Israel, ⁹Sun, ²stand thou still upon Gibeon; and thou, Moon, in the valley of

---

9 Isa. 28. 21; Hab. 3. 11.

2 Heb. be silent.

---

of hail are not unusual in Palestine. The destructiveness of this shower of hail to the Amorites only, and its occurrence at this time, mark it as a miraculous event. **The Lord cast down great stones from heaven,** by intensifying and controlling natural agencies.

THE SUN AND MOON STAND STILL, 12–15.

We are not to regard these remarkable verses as giving an unauthentic and merely poetical description of the victory, as rationalistic expositors teach, but rather a parenthesis thrown into the narrative, by the author himself, or by a later hand, and taken from the book referred to in verse 13. This may be clearly seen from the statement in verse 15, that Joshua returned to Gilgal, which he did not do until the close of the campaign, as stated in verse 43. On the supposition that verse 15 is the conclusion of the quotation all the confusion is cleared up. We may admit that this quotation from the Book of Jasher was inserted here some time after the Book of Joshua was otherwise completed. The Book of Jasher was not completed, possibly not composed, until the time of David. See note on verse 13. But from this admission it does not follow that the passage is unhistorical, or to be explained merely as poetry.

12. Then spake Joshua to the Lord—What Joshua said to the Lord we do not know, unless we are to construe the command to the sun and moon as Joshua's prayer, "O Lord, let the sun stand still." But it is more probable that the great captain, standing on the mountain summit, and seeing his fugitive enemies hastening for their lives far down in the valley below, ejaculated a prayer to Jehovah for supernatural aid, and that he was, in answer to prayer, suddenly endowed with the gift of faith to believe that the laws of the universe would be suspended at his command. The difference between the *grace* of faith and the *gift* of faith is this: The trust which Joshua reposed in God's promise at Gilgal, verse 8, was an exercise of the *grace* of faith, which has a moral character, inasmuch as its opposite, a disbelief of God's word, would have been sin; while the *gift* of faith is an extraordinary endowment, enabling the possessor to ask for things for which he has no specific promise, the non-exercise of which faith would not be sinful, inasmuch as it does not discredit God's word. The Lord had never promised to arrest the sun in answer to Joshua's command. Hence it would have been the highest presumption for Joshua to command a thing so extraordinary on the ground of God's general promises. But being endowed with this miraculous *gift* of faith, the act of Joshua in giving orders to the sun and moon to halt in their march through the heavens—given, doubtless, in the name of Jehovah—becomes perfectly proper. **He said in the sight of Israel**—That is, in their presence, or in sight of the army. This was done in their presence, in order that they might know to what cause to attribute so remarkable an occurrence, and might glorify God, who had given such power to a man. They could afterward attest to their children the truth of an event of which they had been eye-witnesses. **Sun, stand thou still upon Gibeon**—[Verse 12 and the first part of verse 13 may be thus poetically rendered:

Then spake Joshua to Jehovah,
In the day of Jehovah's giving the Amorite
In the presence of the sons of Israel;
And he said in the eyes of Israel:
Sun, in Gibeon be still,
And moon, in the valley of Aijalon.
Then still was the sun,
And the moon stood,
Until a nation should take vengeance on its enemies.]

Various have been the theories devised to explain the manner of this stupendous miracle. Some assert that the passage is merely a poetical interpolation to adorn the narrative and heighten its effect. They allege that it is never quoted in the catalogues of Old Testament miracles. To this we reply, that, as we never find any exhaustive catalogues of those miracles, the omission of this proves nothing. The writer of the Epistle to the Hebrews omits the striking and unquestioned miracle of the passage of the Jordan. See Heb. xi, 29–30. Others explain this miracle as merely a poetical statement of the fact that the Israelites, in answer to Joshua's prayer, were endowed with power to do two days' work in one; a theory too absurd to call for sober refutation. There are others who insist that the earth's motion on its axis was actually arrested, causing a cessation of the apparent diurnal revolution of the sun and moon. Our objection to this theory is, that it involves several secret miracles. A sudden check in the velocity of rotation of the earth on its axis would violently throw down objects on its surface, especially near the equator. If a resisting force were gradually applied, like a brake to a car-wheel, Prof. Mitchell has ascertained that "in forty seconds the motion might cease entirely, and the change would not be sensible to the inhabitants of the earth, except from the appearance of the heavens." But this would require a direct interposition of a secret miracle to keep the ocean, which is sustained at a higher level in the equatorial regions by the centrifugal force, from flowing toward the poles, and from submerging much of the continents, and to keep the Mediterranean Sea from dashing over Palestine. Again: By the recent discovery of the correlation of forces it has been demonstrated that a force requisite to arrest the revolution of the earth must convert momentum into heat equal to that generated by the burning of a mass of anthracite coal fourteen times as large as the globe itself. Another secret miracle would be required to prevent this universal confla-

gration. But secret miracles, so far as we know, have no place in the divine system, since they cannot authenticate a revelation, or demonstrate to man the interposition of God's hand in the course of nature. We, therefore, with a large number of commentators and Christian philosophers, adopt the theory that the standing still of the sun and moon was *optical*, and not literal —that we have a description of phenomena as presented to the eyes of the spectators. The language of the Scriptures is evidently popular, and not scientific; as when they speak of the earth as standing still and the sun as rising and setting. By the supernatural refraction, or bending of the rays of light, the sun and moon might maintain a stationary appearance for several hours. Even by natural refraction we daily see the sun before he has risen above, and after he has gone below, the horizon. The miraculous receding of the shadow on the dial of Ahaz (2 Kings xx, 11; Isa. xxxviii, 8) was probably caused by a similar supernatural refraction of the sun's rays. This explanation of these astronomical miracles involves the principle which is found in nearly all miracles, namely, the intensifying of some natural agency rather than the violation of any natural laws. As in the case of the widow's cruse and the feeding of the multitudes, new oil and new loaves were not created, but that which was in existence was multiplied, so do we believe that instead of a new and strange force brought to bear on nature the natural law of refraction was intensified in both of these miracles.

There is no astronomical difficulty in the statement of the positions of the sun and the moon at that time. To Joshua, standing at Upper Beth-horon, the direction of Gibeon was southeast, which would also be the direction of the sun in the early part of the day, at which time the moon might have been in the southwest, above the valley of Aijalon, approaching its setting. See map of the scene of the battle, page 74. To the question why Joshua should ask for

ᵠAijalon. **13** And the sun stood still, and the moon stayed, until the people had avenged themselves upon their enemies. ʳ*Is* not this written in the book of ˢJasher? So the sun stood still in the midst of heaven, and hasted not to go down about a whole day. **14** And there

was ᵗno day like that before it or after it, that the LORD hearkened unto the voice of a man: for ᵗthe LORD fought for Israel. **15** ᵘAnd Joshua returned, and all Israel with him, unto the camp to Gilgal.

16 But these five kings fled, ᵛand

ᵠ Judg. 12. 12.——ʳ 2 Sam. 1. 18.——3 Or, *The upright?*——ˢ See Isa. 38. 8.

ᵗ Deut. 1. 30; verse 42; chap. 23. 3.——ᵘ Verse 43. ᵛ Psa. 48. 4, 6; 139. 7, 10: Amos 9. 2; Rev. 6. 15.

---

the day to be lengthened while more than half the day was still unspent, we reply that the account does not say that he asked for such a miracle. He " spake to the Lord." We are left to supply the subject-matter of his prayer, which would most naturally be for aid to annihilate God's foes. He receives no answer, but is suddenly endowed with the gift of faith that at his command to the sun and moon God will work an unheard-of miracle, for the demonstration of his sovereignty over physical law, and of his interest in his people.

It is quite probable that the sun and the moon, the gods of so many pagan nations, were the divinities of the Canaanites, to whom they were then appealing for aid against the victorious Hebrews. If this be true, there is a peculiar appropriateness in this miracle, strikingly demonstrating to both armies the superiority of the God of Joshua.

The absence of any account of this miracle in the annals of other nations should have little weight with us, since the records of nearly all the contemporaneous nations have perished, and none of them have histories containing complete accounts of that early period.

13. **The book of Jasher**—This was a poetical book in praise of the heroes of the theocracy—a collection of national songs. Both its name and extant fragments seem to show that it was composed to celebrate upright men in Israel, like Joshua and Jonathan. **Jasher** signifies the *upright*. It was probably written in the reign of David, or soon after. It may have been compiled gradually through a long course of years, one national song after another being added to the collection, but it certainly was not completed till David's time, for it contained

his elegy on Saul and Jonathan. See 2 Sam. i, 18. Fürst is of the opinion that **Jasher** is a collective term for Israelites, and that it should be translated *the book of the Israelites*, that is, the national book. We are ignorant of its author or compiler. If it had been divinely inspired, Providence would doubtless have preserved it for the benefit of mankind. The modern works bearing its title are later and spurious. **About a whole day**—The exposition of Bush, who translates this passage *as at the perfect day*, signifying only that the sun did not go down at its usual time at the close of the day, but pretty soon after, is rather far-fetched. The Vulgate version, " *Nor was there before nor afterward so long a day*," contains the true explanation of this expression, namely, that the day was greatly extended, perhaps nearly doubled in length. A study of the whole chapter, and a consideration of the many acts performed by Joshua and his army, would seem to require about two days for their accomplishment.

14. **No day like that**—No day was ever before or since supernaturally extended at the command of man. God had often before this hearkened unto the voice of man, but never before to the voice of a man inspired with miracle-working faith to control the movements of the heavenly bodies.

15. **And Joshua returned**—This must be regarded as the close of the quotation from the book of Jasher. The writer of that book drops all the further acts of the campaign, and speaks of its conclusion. See note introductory to verse 12.

THE PURSUIT AND SLAUGHTER OF THE AMORITES, 16-21.

16. The thread of the narrative, broken at the end of verse 11 by the

hid themselves in a cave at Makkedah.
17 And it was told Joshua, saying,
The five kings are found hid in a cave
at Makkedah. **18** And Joshua said,
Roll great stones upon the mouth of the
cave, and set men by it for to keep
them: **19** And stay ye not, *but* pursue
after your enemies, and 4 smite the hind-
most of them; suffer them not to enter
into their cities: for the LORD your God
hath delivered them into your hand.
20 And it came to pass, when Joshua
and the children of Israel had made an
end of slaying them with a very great
slaughter, till they were consumed, that
the rest *which* remained of them entered
into " fenced cities. **21** And all the
people returned to the camp to Joshua

at Makkedah in peace: ˣ none moved
his tongue against any of the children
of Israel.
22 Then said Joshua, ʸ Open the
mouth of the cave, and bring out those
five kings unto me out of the cave.
23 And they did so, and brought forth
those five kings unto him out of the
cave, the king of Jerusalem, the king
of Hebron, the king of Jarmuth, the
king of Lachish, *and* the king of Eglon.
24 And it came to pass, when they
brought out those kings unto Joshua,
that Joshua called for all the men of
Israel, and said unto the captains of the
men of war which went with him, Come
near, ᶻ put your feet upon the necks of
these kings. And they came near, and

---

4 Heb. *cut off the tail.*——*w* Hos. 8. 14.
x Exod. 11. 7.——*y* 1 Sam. 15. 32.

ᶻ Psa. 107. 40; 110. 5; 149. 8, 9;
Isa. 26. 5, 6; Mal. 4. 3.

---

quotation from the Book of Jasher,
is here resumed. **Five kings**—See
verse 3. **A cave**—Caves still abound
in that region. Beth-horon signifies a
house of caves. Travellers relate that
these hiding places are found in all
parts of Palestine. "The rocks are
perforated in every direction with
'caves' and 'holes' and 'pits,' crevices
and fissures sunk deep in the rocky
soil."—*Stanley.*

18. **Roll great stones**—The cave
when thus barricaded would require
but a small guard. The rest of the
men could be employed in the pursuit.
The golden hour for the victor is the
time when his enemies are fleeing dis-
ordered and panic-stricken. The vig-
orous commander in such an hour
neglects even his own wounded and
dying that he may make his victory
decisive.

19. **Pursue after your enemies**—
The excitement of such a victory would
in a wonderful manner keep up the
strength of the soldiers, and perhaps
supernatural vigour was also imparted
to them. **For the Lord . . . hath delivered**—Compare notes on chap. vi, 2;
viii, 1. But though the enemies' destruction is a foreseen certainty in the
Divine Mind, the conditions, **pursue,
smite,** are insisted on.

20. **Till they were consumed**—
That is, utterly defeated, demoralized,
and dispersed. **That the rest which
remained**—These words and the rest

of this verse should be put in paren-
theses and rendered, *And the survivors
escaped from them and went into fortified cities.* The sense of this passage
is, therefore, well expressed by Keil:
"Only a remnant of them was left, and
they took refuge in the fortified cities." The parenthesis thus qualifies
the clause **till they were consumed.**

21. **All the people**—The army that
had pursued the foe. **None moved his
tongue**—Or, *pointed his tongue.* None
uttered an impious or threatening word
against Israel. The enemy was reduced to the most abject silence. This
is the Hebrew way of expressing the
complete subjection of all that region.
Compare Exod. xi, 7.

THE FIVE KINGS EXECUTED, 22–27.

24. **Called for all the men of
Israel**—This must be limited to the
bravest warriors; those only were at
Makkedah; the rest of the people
were at Gilgal. See verse 7, note, also
verse 43. A grand assembly of the
army was made for the formal humiliation and public execution of the five
kings. It was desirable to make the
execution as impressive as possible.
**Put your feet upon the necks of
these kings**—Symbolical actions are
very common in the East, such as passing under yokes and kissing the conqueror's feet, and in case of extreme
and perfect subjection the victor proclaimed his triumph by treading on the

put their feet upon the necks of them. [f] as he did unto the king of Jericho.
25 And Joshua said unto them, [a] Fear **29** Then Joshua passed from Makkedah, and all Israel with him, unto Libnah, and fought against Libnah: not, nor be dismayed, be strong and of good courage: for [b] thus shall the LORD do to all your enemies against whom ye fight. **26** And afterward Joshua smote them, and slew them, and hanged them on five trees: and they [c] were hanging upon the trees until the evening. **27** And it came to pass at the time of the going down of the sun, *that* Joshua commanded, and they [d] took them down off the trees, and cast them into the cave wherein they had been hid, and laid great stones in the cave's mouth, *which remain* until this very day.

28 And that day Joshua took Makkedah, and smote it with the edge of the sword, and the king thereof he utterly [e] destroyed, them, and all the souls that *were* therein; he let none remain: and he did to the king of Makkedah

29 Then Joshua passed from Makkedah, and all Israel with him, unto Libnah, and fought against Libnah: **30** And the LORD delivered it also, and the king thereof, into the hand of Israel; and he smote it with the edge of the sword, and all the souls that *were* therein; he let none remain in it; but did unto the king thereof as he did unto the king of Jericho. **31** And Joshua passed from Libnah, and all Israel with him, unto [g] Lachish, and encamped against it, and fought against it: **32** And the LORD delivered Lachish into the hand of Israel, which took it on the second day, and smote it with the edge of the sword, and all the souls that *were* therein, according to all that he had done to Libnah. **33** Then Horam king of Gezer came up to help Lachish; and Joshua smote him and his people,

---

a Deut. 31. 6, 8; chap. 1. 9.——*b* Deut. 3. 21; 7. 19.
c Chap. 8. 29.——*d* Deut. 21. 23; chap. 8. 29.

e Deut. 7. 16; 20. 16, 17.——*f* Chap. 6. 21.
g 2 Chron. 11. 9; Micah 1. 13.

---

neck of his conquered foe. This impressive act inspirited the Israelites, and struck terror into their enemies yet unconquered. Some regard this as the fulfilment of the prophecy of Moses in Deut. xxxiii, 29. It also explains the expression, "to make one's enemies his footstool." Psa. cx, 1.

25. **Thus shall the Lord do to all your enemies**—Unless ye forfeit my favour by your sin, as in the first battle with Ai. Thus every Christian, if faithful to Christ, will "find his latest foe under his feet at last."

26. **Joshua smote them**—Here observe, they were slain before they were hung. This summary infliction of capital punishment so abhorrent to the humane spirit of our Christian civilization, was in accordance with the character of that age and people, who would have construed mercy as cowardice. European nations in their wars with the semi-barbarous Orientals of modern times are compelled to adopt the severe war-code of those nations. Compare the note on chap. viii, 29. **Hanged them on five trees**—As a mark of further indignity, and to strike the enemy with increased terror. **Until the evening**—See on viii, 29.

27. **Cast them into the cave**—The place of their concealment was made

their sepulchre. **Until this very day** —See note, viii, 28.

CONQUEST OF SOUTHERN PALESTINE, 28–43.

28. **That day**—Joshua and a part of the host **took Makkedah** while the rest were pursuing the flying foe. **Destroyed...all the souls**—All the human beings. For considerations justifying this indiscriminate extermination of the Canaanites, see note, chap. vi, 21.

29. **Libnah,** according to Stanley and Robinson, is the present Tel-el-Sâfieh, which is only a mile from Eleutheropolis, in the plain of Judah; but Van de Velde, with more probability, identifies it with Arak el-Menshyeh, a hill about five miles west of Eleutheropolis, and showing signs of having been an ancient fortified place. But the identity is far from certain. It was a city of Judah (chap. xv, 42) appropriated to the priests, xxi, 13. In the reign of Jehoram it revolted from Judah, (2 Kings viii, 22,) and still later was besieged by Sennacherib. 2 Kings xix, 8.

31. **Lachish**—See verse 3, note.

32. **On the second day**—The second day of the siege.

33. **Horam,** like the other ill-fated kings mentioned in this chapter, has left no other record. **Gezer** must

until he had left him none remaining. **34** And from Lachish Joshua passed into Eglon, and all Israel with him; and they encamped against it, and fought against it: **35** And they took it on that day, and smote it with the edge of the sword, and all the souls that *were* therein he utterly destroyed that day, according to all that he had done to Lachish. **36** And Joshua went up from Eglon, and all Israel with him, unto [h] Hebron; and they fought against it: **37** And they took it, and smote it with the edge of the sword, and the king thereof, and all the cities thereof, and all the souls that *were* therein; he left none remaining, according to all that he had done to Eglon; but destroyed it utterly, and all the souls that *were* there-

in. **38** And Joshua returned, and all Israel with him, to [i] Debir; and fought against it: **39** And he took it, and the king thereof, and all the cities thereof, and they smote them with the edge of the sword, and utterly destroyed all the souls that *were* therein; he left none remaining: as he had done to Hebron, so he did to Debir, and to the king thereof; as he had done also to Libnah, and to her king. **40** So Joshua smote all the country of the hills, and of the south, and of the vale, and of the springs, and all their kings: he left none remaining, but utterly destroyed all that breathed, as the Lord God of Israel [k] commanded. **41** And Joshua smote them from Kadesh-barnea even unto [l] Gaza, [m] and all the country of Goshen, even unto Gibeon.

---

h See chap. 14. 13; 15. 13; Judges 1. 10.
i Chap. 15. 15; Judges 1. 11.

k Deut. 20. 16, 17.——l Gen. 10. 19.
m Chap. 11. 16.

---

have been between the Lower Beth-horon and the sea. It does not seem to have been destroyed by Joshua. Some identify it with the village Jazur, four or five miles east of Joppa, but this is uncertain. [It was an important city of the Canaanites, and fell within the borders of Ephraim, (xvi, 3,) but that tribe failed to drive out the original inhabitants. Judg. i, 19. Subsequently Pharaoh, king of Egypt, captured it, slew its Canaanitish inhabitants, and presented it to his daughter, Solomon's wife. Pharaoh burned the city, but Solomon rebuilt and fortified it. 1 Kings ix, 16, 17.]

34. **Eglon**—See on verse 3.

36. **Hebron**—See on verse 3. As the king of Hebron had been executed at Makkedah, his successor is probably referred to as killed in this siege.

[38. **And Joshua returned…to Debir**—Debir has not been with certainty identified with any modern name. Van de Velde finds it in a place called Dilbeh, six miles southwest of Hebron. Compare Stanley's note at chap. xv, 18. Others suppose it to have been nearer Hebron, on the west. Dr. Rosen places it, with much probability, at Dewirban. Its earlier name was *Kirjath-sepher*, (chap. xv, 15,) which means *book city*, and intimates that the original Canaanitish inhabitants were acquainted with writing and books, and that their city became noted

for learning. The same place is called *Kirjath-sannah* in chap. xv, 49, a name of similar meaning.]

40. **Country of the hills** — The mountain ridge, which is the backbone of the Holy Land, is cut up into hills by ravines which stretch away to the Dead Sea and the Mediterranean. The heads of these valleys often interlap for a considerable distance, forming numerous steep hills. **The south**—The *Negeb*. This term designates that territory which was subsequently occupied by Judah and Simeon, and also a portion of Edom. It is a geographical term, used constantly to designate the land lying to the south of Palestine, and should always be translated *the south country*, as it is in Gen. xx, 1. In later Hebrew writers it extended from Southern Canaan to Arabia Petræa and Egypt. **The vale**—The *shephelah*. This word, with one exception, (xi, 16,) always designates the maritime plain of Philistia, from Joppa to the borders of Egypt. **The springs** — אֲשֵׁדוֹת, slopes where torrents flow together; ravines.

41. [**Kadesh-barnea** was a most important station in the southern border of the Holy Land, the starting-point of the forty years' wandering, the place where Miriam died, and whence the spies went out to explore the Land of Promise. There has been uncertainty

42 And all these kings and their land did Joshua take at one time, [n] because the Lord God of Israel fought for Israel. **43** And Joshua returned, and all Israel with him, unto the camp to Gilgal.

n Verse 14.——*a* Chap.

as to its exact location. Stanley proposes to identify it with Petra, the modern Wady Mousa; Robinson locates it at Ain el-Weibeh, twenty miles northwest of Mount Hor; but more recently Captain Palmer argues for the opinion first maintained by Dr. Rowlands, that the ancient **Kadesh-barnea** is represented by the modern Ain Gadis, a fountain in the plateau of Jebel Magrah, some forty miles west of Mount Hor. This view will probably gain general acceptance.] **Gaza** is still standing, and is a place larger than Jerusalem, situated on the Mediterranean Sea in Southern Palestine. It has been the scene of many remarkable events. See at Gen. x, 19. **Country of Goshen**—A city and district generally supposed to be in the mountains of Judah, though some think that it was on the plain. Its name suggests that it may have been founded by a colony from Goshen in Egypt.

42. At one time—During one campaign, which commenced with the great battle of Gibeon and Beth-horon. **Because the Lord...fought for Israel**—The unprecedented rapidity and success of Joshua's movements is here ascribed to his great ally, Jehovah. The only miraculous interposition in aid of Joshua was on the memorable first day of the campaign; but the marvellous victories obtained in quick succession over a foe which, forty years before, by reason of their stature and the strength of their walled cities struck terror into the hearts of the Hebrew spies, show that God was the author of that courage which now nerved the people, and also of that despair which paralyzed their foes so perfectly that before they could reorganize a combined resistance they were cut off, city by city.

43. All Israel—All who had served in this campaign. **Gilgal**—The old camp in the Jordan valley. See note on chap. ix, 6; also x, 9. The transfer

CHAPTER XI.

AND it came to pass, when Jabin king of Hazor had heard *those things*, that he [a] sent to Jobab king of Madon, and to the king [b] of Shimron,

10. 2.——*b* Chap. 19. 15.

of this statement to verse 15 shows the passage in verses 12–15 to be an interpolation.

CHAPTER XI.

The Great Battle of Merom, 1–15.

["The battle of Beth-horon is represented as the most important battle of the Conquest, because, being the first, it struck the decisive blow. But in all such struggles there is usually one last effort made for the defeated cause. This, in the subjugation of Canaan, was the battle of Merom. Round Jabin were assembled the heads of all the tribes who had not yet fallen under Joshua's sword. As the British chiefs were driven to the Land's End before the advance of the Saxon, so at this Land's End of Palestine were gathered for the last struggle, not only the kings of the north, in the immediate neighbourhood, but from the desert valley of the Jordan south of the Sea of Galilee, from the maritime plain of Philistia, from the heights above Sharon, and from the still unconquered Jebus, to the Hivite who dwelt in the valley of Baal-gad under Hermon."—*Stanley.*]

1. Jabin (signifying *he shall know*, or *he is wise*) was probably the royal title of the kings of Hazor. **Hazor** was a Phenician fortified city in the north of Palestine. It was the principal city of the whole of the North, "the head of all those kingdoms."—Ver. 10. [After its destruction by Joshua it was rebuilt and occupied by another Jabin, who attained vast power, and for twenty years greatly oppressed Israel, (Judges iv, 2, 3,) but was in turn defeated by Barak. It was subsequently fortified by Solomon, (1 Kings ix, 15,) but was afterward captured by Tiglath-pileser, king of Assyria. 2 Kings xv, 29. Travellers are not agreed as to its site. Dr. Thomson thinks it is at the modern Hazere, about twelve miles west of the Lake

and to the king of Achshaph, **2** And to the kings that *were* on the north of the mountains, and of the plains south of Chinneroth, and in the valley, and in the borders *d* of Dor on the west, **3** *And* to the Canaanite on the east and on the west, and *to* the Amorite, and the Hit-

tite, and the Perizzite, and the Jebusite in the mountains, *e* and *to* the Hivite under *f* Hermon *g* in the land of Mizpeh. **4** And they went out, they and all their hosts with them, much people, *h* even as the sand that *is* upon the sea shore in multitude, with horses and chariots very

---

c Num. 34. 11.——*d* Chap. 17. 11; Judges 1. 27; 1 Kings 4. 11.——*e* Judges 3. 3.

f Chap. 13. 11.——*g* Gen. 31. 49.——*h* Gen. 22. 17; 32. 12; Judges 7. 12; 1 Sam. 13. 5.

Merom. Stanley locates it on an eminence just above Cesarea Philippi; Robinson at Tell Khureibeh, a rocky peak three miles west of Lake Merom; and Porter inclines to locate it a few miles south of this, on a bank of the Wady Hendaj.] **Madon** was a leading city in the same vicinity, but its locality is now unknown. **Shimron,** called also Shimron-Merom, (chap. xii, 20,) was the chief place in a small district afterward belonging to Zebulun, eleven miles northeast of Nazareth. Schwarz thinks that it is the same as the modern Semuniyeh, a few miles west of Nazareth. **Achshaph** was in the territory of Asher. Chap. xix, 25. Robinson identifies it with the ruined town now called Kasaf, ten or twelve miles northwest of Lake Merom.

2. **Kings that were on the north of the mountains**—Heb. *on the north in the mountain.* Mount Hermon and its northern extension, called Anti-Libanus, are perhaps here meant. **Chinneroth** was a small enclosed district north of Tiberias, and by the side of the lake to which it subsequently gave the name *Genesareth.* See at Num. xxxiv, 11; notes on Matt. iv, 13. **The valley**—The plain by the Mediterranean, the *shephelah.* See the note on chap. x, 40. **Borders of Dor**—The word for **borders** is used in the Hebrew only in connexion with Dor, and it designates the plain of Sharon at the foot of Carmel. **Dor,** now Tantura, was probably the southern limit of Phenicia. Of its site there is no doubt. "Its situation, with its little harbour enclosed within the wild rocks rising over the shell-strewn beach, and covered by the fragments of the later city of Tantura, is still a striking feature on the desolate shore."—*Stanley.*

3. **Amorite**—See the note on chap. ii, 10. All the tribes here named were

greatly intermingled. They seem to have had no fixed boundaries. The nations of the South, over whom the five kings ruled, are called Amorites. Chap. x, 5. The Jebusites long held fast this stronghold **in the mountains** of Central Palestine, and from it, perhaps, went forth often to trouble Israel. **Hittite**—Chap. i, 4, note. For the other tribes see notes and references at chap. iii, 10. **Under Hermon**—This mountain, "almost the only one which deserves the name in Palestine," is the southern extremity of the eastern range of Lebanon, called Anti-Libanus, and it is the highest point of the whole range. "From the moment that the traveller reaches the plain of Shechem in the interior, nay, even from the depths of the Jordan valley by the Dead Sea, the snowy heights of Hermon are visible. The ancient names of its double range are all significant of this position. It was 'Sion,' 'the upraised;' or 'Hermon,' 'the lofty peak;' or 'Shenir' and 'Sirion,' the glittering 'breastplate' of ice; or, above all, 'Lebanon,' the 'Mont Blanc' of Palestine, the White Mountain of ancient times; the Mountain of the 'Old White-headed Man,' or the 'Mountain of Ice' in modern times."—*Stanley.* Hermon was probably the scene of our Lord's transfiguration. See notes on Matt. xvii, 1. **Mizpeh**—This appellative is commonly preceded by the article, *the watch-tower.* It was a name given to several localities. **The land of Mizpeh** is probably the same as *the valley of Mizpeh,* verse 8, and may be understood either of the tract of Cœle (Hollow) Syria, over which Hermon rises like a watch-tower, or of the plains that stretch off east of Hermon towards Damascus.

4. **Even as the sand that is upon the sea shore**—This exaggerated com-

many. **5** And when all these kings were [1]met together, they came and pitched together at the waters of Merom, to fight against Israel. **6** And the LORD said unto Joshua, [i]Be not afraid because of them: for to morrow about this time will I deliver them up all slain

before Israel: thou shalt hough their horses, and burn their chariots with fire. **7** So Joshua came, and all the people of war with him, against them by the waters of Merom suddenly: and they fell upon them. **8** And the LORD delivered them into the hand of Israel,

---

1 Heb. *assembled by appointment.*

i Chap. 10. 8.

---

parison is in perfect keeping with the style of the Oriental writers. It is to be interpreted rhetorically, and not literally. It is to be expected that an inspired writer will employ the style of his country and age. Josephus reckons this army at three hundred thousand foot, ten thousand horse, and twenty thousand chariots. Anciently **chariots** supplied the place of artillery in modern times, so that among the Egyptians and Syrians the number of

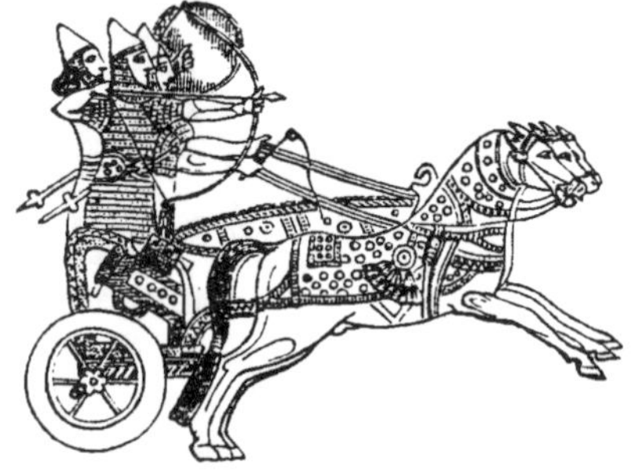

ASSYRIAN CHARIOT.

these indicated their military power. The Hebrews, having been forbidden to multiply horses, did not to any great extent provide themselves with chariots of war till the reign of David. By reason of this lack of chariots in Joshua's army the odds were heavily against him, so that there was occasion for the encouragement which the Lord gives in verse 6.

5. **Waters of Merom**—This first lake through which the Jordan flows was the Samochonitis of Josephus. Its modern name is Huleh. Its name **Merom** occurs nowhere else in the Bible. It is of a triangular shape, and measures about six miles in each direction. It is surrounded by a marshy basin, which is sufficiently elevated on the southwestern margin to afford an encampment and battle-field. It was

the use of "horses and chariots very many" which probably fixed the scene of the encampment on the uplands near by the plain of the lake, along whose level shores they could have full play for their force. See verse 7, note.

6. **Be not afraid**—The vast multitude of enemies provided with war chariots, instruments which Joshua had probably never before encountered in battle, would naturally awaken fear in the Hebrew army and its great leader. To allay this the Lord, whose opportunity is man's extremity, interposes words of cheer and a promise of victory. It is not said that Joshua asked for this, but it was doubtless given in answer to prayer. **To morrow about this time**—Only the God of battles can foretell the very day and hour of his people's triumph. **Thou shalt hough their horses**—They were to disable their horses by cutting the sinews of their legs. For this barbarous treatment of the horse we have in modern English the verb *to hamstring*. As the multiplication of horses was forbidden by God, (Deut. xvii, 16,) they would have been a useless booty. **Burn their chariots**—For they also would have been only a cumbrance to the Hebrews.

7. **Suddenly**—Joshua's victories were achieved by bold and unexpected strokes, appalling and disorganizing the foe by the suddenness of his assault. The Septuagint reads that he fell upon them on the "mountain slopes," or in the hilly region, before they could deploy upon the plain by the lake and use their war chariots to any good purpose. These would only serve to obstruct their movements and impede their flight when attacked among the hills.

8. **The Lord delivered them**—Jehovah is ever recognized as the arbi-

who smote them, and chased them unto [2]great Zidon, and unto [3][k] Misrephoth-maim, and unto the valley of Mizpeh eastward; and they smote them, until

---

2 Or, *Zidon-rabbah.*——3 Or, *Salt pits.*   Heb. *Burnings of water.*——*k* Chap. 13. 6.

---

ter of battles. **Chased them**—W.M. Thomson, who has repeatedly traversed this region, and who has acquired a greater familiarity with it than has any other traveller, thus describes this flight and pursuit: "Those whose homes lay beyond the mountains to the north and east sought them by the great wady of the Upper Jordan, now Wady-et-Teim, or out east of Hermon, in Hauran—the land of Mizpeh. Those from the seacoast of Acre and Carmel fled over these hills and down southwest by Hazor to Misrephoth-maim, (now called Musheirifeh,) on the north border of the plain of Acre. Thence they dispersed along the seaboard to their homes, as far south as Dor. Joshua himself chased a third division along the base of the mountain northward, past Abel-Beth-maachah, through the plain of Ijon, down the tremendous gorge of the Litany, (ancient Leontes,) to the ford at Tamrah, or the bridge at the Khutweh, and thence over the wooded spurs of Jebel Rihan towards great Zidon, behind whose lofty walls the flying host could alone find safety." **Great Zidon**—This city, one of the most ancient of the world, is situated in Phenicia, on the coast of the Mediterranean. It was formerly surrounded by towering walls, and covered a vast area. Its harbour was crowded with ships from every coast, and its magazines enriched by the treasures and luxuries of the distant East, brought to them by caravans. It had a stupendous colonial system. On its coast was built Berytus, (the modern Beyroot,) Gebel, Arvad, Dor, Accho, and many more, besides Tyre, a daughter which subsequently eclipsed the mother in power and wealth.

Zidon planted colonies in Cyprus, the Grecian Isles, Libya, and in Spain. It afterward declined, but never became extinct like Tyre, and now numbers about ten thousand population. **Misrephoth-maim**—The Hebrew literally signifies *the burnings of waters.* Dr. Thomson identifies it with the modern Musheirifeh, on the coast, midway between Tyre and Mount Carmel. It is remarkable for its noble fountains. The ancient and modern names are nearly identical in form and in signification, and both were suggested by the bright and glowing colour of those magnificent cliffs which overhang the sea. The route from Merom to Dor must have been through this place. Here is a difficult pass commanded by a castle, an ancient structure corresponding to which might have afforded safety to the fugitives. **Valley of Mizpeh**—See note on verse 3. **Eastward**—That is, eastward from the scene of battle. The panic-stricken host fled northward to Zidon, westward to Misrephoth-maim, and eastward to the valley of Mizpeh.

ZIDON.

they left them none remaining. **9** And Joshua did unto them [l] as the LORD bade him: he houghed their horses, and burnt their chariots with fire. **10** And Joshua at that time turned back, and took [m] Hazor, and smote the king thereof with the sword: for Hazor beforetime was the head of all those kingdoms. **11** And they smote all the souls that *were* therein with the edge of the sword, utterly destroying *them:* there was not [4] any left to breathe: and he burnt Hazor with fire. **12** And all the cities of those kings, and all the kings of them, did Joshua take, and smote them with the edge of the sword, *and* he utterly destroyed them, [n] as Moses the servant of the LORD commanded. **13** But *as for* the cities that stood still [5] in their

strength, Israel burned none of them, save Hazor only; *that* did Joshua burn. **14** And all [o] the spoil of these cities, and the cattle, the children of Israel took for a prey unto themselves; but every man they smote with the edge of the sword, until they had destroyed them, neither left they any to breathe. **15** [p] As the LORD commanded Moses his servant, so [q] did Moses command Joshua, and [r] so did Joshua; [6] he left nothing undone of all that the LORD commanded Moses.

16 So Joshua took all that land, [s] the hills, and all the south country, [t] and all the land of Goshen, and the valley, and the plain, and the mountain of Israel, and the valley of the same; **17** [u] *Even* from [7] the mount Halak, that goeth up

---

l Verse 6.——*m* Judges 4. 2.——4 Hebrew, *any breath.*——*n* Num. 33. 52; Deut. 7. 2; 20. 16, 17. ——5 Heb. *on their heap.*——*o* Num. 31. 9; Deut. 6. 10, 11; 20. 14.

p Exod. 34. 11, 12.——*q* Deut. 7. 2.——*r* Chap. 1. 7.——6 Heb. *he removed nothing.*——*s* Chap. 12. 8.——*t* Chap. 10. 41.——*u* Chap. 12. 7.——7 Or, *the smooth mountain.*

---

10. At that time—After he had utterly routed and pursued the enemy even to distant cities and villages, and had destroyed their horses and chariots. The pursuit may have lasted several days. **Turned back**—From pursuing the foe. **Smote the king**—Jabin, as soon as defeated, seems to have taken refuge in his capital. Joshua did not stop to take Hazor until after he had utterly dispersed the confederate army.

11. Smote all the souls—For a justification of this severity see on chap. vi, 21.

13. The cities that stood still in their strength, that is, on mounds or eminences, (Heb. עַל־תִּלָּם, *on their hill,*) were retained, since they could be easily defended, while the cities on the plains were razed. But **Hazor,** the head of the confederacy, though in a strong position, must fall, as a penalty for the past and a security for the future.

14. All the spoil of these cities ...Israel took— Save "the graven images of their gods." Deut. vii, 25.

15. He left nothing undone— Joshua here evinces two cardinal virtues: (1) diligent study of the recorded precepts; (2) perfect obedience. Here is the model of all righteous living—the intellect exercised in discovering God's

will, and the heart so imbued with love as to sway the will to execute every dictate of the conscience.

SUMMARY OF JOSHUA'S CONQUESTS, 16–23.

The historian, having finished the account of Joshua's Northern Campaign, here adds, as if concluding his record of the conquest, a general summary of all his work.

16. Took all that land—The whole land of Canaan. **Hills... south country...Goshen...valley** —Comp. chap. x, 40, 41, notes. **The plain**—The *Arabah,* the valley of the Jordan and the Dead Sea. **The mountain of Israel**—The northern part of the great mountain range which runs through Palestine from north to south. Compare note on chapter ix, 1. In verse 21 this phrase is used in contrast with *mountains of Judah,* the southern part of the same range. **Valley of the same** —That is, valley of Israel, not merely the plain of Philistia, but that of Jezreel also.

17. From the Mount Halak—*The bald mount* was south of the land of Canaan, toward Seir or Edom. "It is probably a row of white cliffs, sixty to eighty feet high, which cuts the Arabah obliquely at about eight English miles

to Seir, even unto Baalgad in the valley of Lebanon under mount Hermon: and *all their kings he took, and smote them, and slew them. **18** ^sJoshua made war a long time with all those kings. **19** There was not a city that made peace with the children of Israel, save *the Hivites the inhabitants of Gibeon: all *other* they took in battle. **20** For ^xit was of the LORD to harden their

v Deuteronomy 7. 24; chapter 12. 7.——8 Till 1445; verse 23.——*w* Chapter 9. 3, 7.——*x* Deuteronomy 2. 30; Judges 14. 4; 1 Samuel 2. 25;

to the south of the Dead Sea, and divides the great valley into two parts."—*Keil.* **Baal-gad,** *fortune-bringing Baal,* was evidently a well-known landmark in the time of Joshua, and designates the northern limit of his conquest, but its site has not been certainly identified. Some are disposed to identify it with Baalbek in Cœle-Syria; others with Banias, near Cesarea Philippi.

18. **Joshua made war a long time** —The only note of time in this book is the age of Caleb, forty when a spy to search out the land, (chap. xiv, 7,) and eighty-five at the end of the war. Subtract thirty-nine years in the wilderness after the sending of the spies—Calmet says thirty-eight—and we have six or seven years for the length of the conquest, the first of which was spent in the subjugation of the South. One reason for the length of the war was "lest the beasts of the field increase upon thee." Deut. vii, 22. Another may have been the purpose of God to test their faith in his promises, to bind them together by the endurance of common hardships, and to awaken a strong love for the country purchased at such a cost.

20. **It was of the Lord to harden their hearts**—It is a Hebraism to ascribe to direct divine agency the results of human perverseness, as in the case of Pharaoh. These nations had filled the cup of their iniquity, (Gen. xv, 16,) and their idolatry and crimes demanded punishment. God therefore leaves them to judicial blindness and infatuation, and uses Israel as the rod of his anger to **destroy them utterly.** So their hardened hearts and consequent destruction were but the

hearts, that they should come against Israel in battle, that he might destroy them utterly, *and* that they might have no favour, but that he might destroy them, ^yas the LORD commanded Moses. **21** And at that time came Joshua, and cut off ^zthe Anakim from the mountains, from Hebron, from Debir, from Anab, and from all the mountains of Judah, and from all the mountains of Israel:

1 Kings 12. 15; Romans 9. 18.——*y* Deuteronomy 20. 16, 17.——*z* Numbers 13. 22, 33; Deuteronomy 1. 28; chapter 15. 13, 14.

certain outcome, according to Divine arrangement, of their own, as of every sinner's, free and wilful sinning. But we are not to understand, with Calvin, a miraculous operation of God, urging them on to blind fury. Their own self-induced perversity was a sufficient power for this.

21. **At that time**—During the war, the *long time* mentioned in verse 18. **The Anakim** were a race of giants in Southern Palestine. Some escaped to the Philistines and became the progenitors of Goliath. See references in margin, especially Num. xiii, 22, 33. On **Hebron** and **Debir** see notes on chap. x, 3, 38. **Anab** is probably identical with the place of this name which Dr. Robinson discovered about ten miles south of Hebron. But this could hardly be said to be **in the mountains of Judah,** where chap. xv, 48, 50, also locates it. [**Mountains of Judah and...Israel**—The words **Judah** and **Israel** in this passage do not, as some critics have assumed, betray the hand of a writer who lived after the nation was divided into two rival kingdoms bearing these names. The use of these expressions may easily have grown out of facts existing in Joshua's time. The tribe of Judah first received its allotment, comprising nearly all Palestine south of Jerusalem, and some time elapsed before the rest of Israel —especially seven of the tribes (chap. xviii, 2)—received their allotments. It was therefore perfectly natural at that early time to apply the names here used respectively to the southern and northern parts of the great mountain range of Palestine. The central part of this range, where the sons of Joseph early received their portion, (chaps.

Joshua destroyed them utterly with their cities. **22** There was none of the Anakim left in the land of the children of Israel: only in Gaza, in [a] Gath, [b] and in Ashdod, there remained. **23** So Joshua took the whole land, [c] according to all that the LORD said unto Moses; and Joshua gave it for an inheritance unto Israel [d] according to their divisions by their tribes. [e] And the land rested from war.

a 1 Samuel 17. 4.——*b* Chapters 15. 46.—— *c* Numbers 34. 2, &c.——*d* Numbers 26. 53; chapters 14 to 19.

xvi. xvii.) was sometimes called Mount Ephraim. Chap. xvii. 15.]

22. **Gath**—The city of the giant Goliath had been searched for in vain, till J. L. Porter in 1857 fixed upon the conspicuous hill now called Tell-es-sâfieh, at the side of the plain of Philistia, at the foot of the mountains of Judah, ten miles east of Ashdod and south by east of Ekron. Hither the ark was carried during its captivity, (1 Sam. v, 8,) and hither David twice fled for refuge while persecuted by Saul. 1 Sam. xxi, 10: xxvii, 2. **Ashdod** is the modern Esdud, on a small round hill thickly covered with trees, between Jamnia and Gaza, ten miles south of the former. This, like the two other cities here named, belonged to the Philistines, and was the chief seat of the worship of Dagon. See 1 Sam. v, 1–7, and note on Acts viii, 40.

[23. **Joshua took the whole land** —This verse and chap. xxi, 43–45, seem at first sight not to agree with chap. xiii, 1, and chap. xviii, 3, and there have not been wanting critics to urge that these passages are irreconcilably discrepant. But the discrepancy is only apparent. The key to a proper interpretation is furnished in chap. xxiii, 1–5, where in one and the same passage it is assumed that all the Canaanitish enemies are subdued, and yet some nations are to be expelled and their land possessed by Israel. Plainly the author never meant to say that every Canaanite and every city and hamlet in all Palestine was destroyed by the sword of Joshua. The land was thoroughly subdued, and the Canaanitish power and dominion were utterly broken; but the Lord had

CHAPTER XII.

NOW these *are* the kings of the land, which the children of Israel smote, and possessed their land on the other side Jordan toward the rising of the sun, [a] from the river Arnon [b] unto mount Hermon, and all the plain on the east: **2** [c] Sihon king of the Amorites, who dwelt in Heshbon, *and* ruled from Aroer, which *is* upon the bank of the river Arnon, and from the middle of the river,

e Chap. 14. 15; 21. 44; 22. 4; 23. 1; verse 18.—— *a* Num. 21. 24.——*b* Deut. 3. 8, 9.——*c* Num. 21. 24; Deut. 2. 33, 36: 3. 6, 16.

expressly declared that he would not utterly expel the Canaanites at once, but gradually, lest the beasts of the field multiply against them. The possession by the enemy of a number of isolated cities and districts was not therefore inconsistent with the broad statement of this passage. Compare also notes on chap. xxi, 43–45. **The land rested from war** — A concluding statement of the historical portion of the book, repeated at chap. xiv, 15, and used for the same purpose as here, namely, to form a transition from the history of the wars of the conquest to the more peaceful work of distributing the subjugated land among the several tribes.]

CHAPTER XII.

LIST OF THE TRANS-JORDANIC CONQUESTS, 1–6.

This chapter concludes the general history of the conquests, and is a *resumé* of the triumphs under Moses and Joshua. For the historical facts referred to in the first six verses see Num. xxi, 21–35, and Deut. ii, 26–37; iii, 1–17.

1. **The river Arnon**—This stream is now called Wady el-Mojeb. It runs circuitously for some eighty miles through a romantic rocky valley, and empties into the Dead Sea near the center of its eastern shore. It became the southern boundary of Reuben, but was originally the border between Moab and the Amorites. See on Num. xxi, 13. **Mount Hermon** — See on chap. xi, 3. **The plain on the east** —The Jordan valley east of the river.

2. **Aroer**—See on chap. xiii, 16. **The middle of the river**—The midst

and from half Gilead, even unto the river Jabbok, *which is* the border of the children of Ammon; 3 And [d]from the plain to the sea of Chinneroth on the east, and unto the sea of the plain, *even* the salt sea on the east, [e]the way to

Beth-jeshimoth; and from [1]the south, under [2][f]Ashdoth-pisgah: 4 And [g]the coast of Og king of Bashan, *which was* of [h]the remnant of the giants, [i]that dwelt at Ashtaroth and at Edrei, 5 And reigned in [k]mount Hermon, [l]and in Sal-

d Deut. 3. 17.——*e* Chap. 13. 20.——1 Or, *Teman.*——2 Or, *The springs of Pisgah,* or, *The hill.*——*f* Deut. 3. 17; 4. 49.

g Num. 21. 35; Deut. 3. 4, 10.——*h* Deut. 3. 11; chap. 13. 12.——*i* Deut. 1. 4.——*k* Deut. 3. 8.——*l* Deut. 3. 10; chap. 13. 11.

of the valley of the Arnon. This is "a more exact definition of the previous clause, since the Arnon, which flowed through the middle of the valley, formed the actual boundary; whereas Aroer stood not upon the river itself, but on the northern slope of the valley."—*Keil.* Compare chap. xiii, 16, note. **And from half Gilead**—The word **from** should be omitted both here and in the next verse. Sihon ruled over the southern half of Gilead, Og over the northern half. Verse 5. Gilead is the name of the great mountain region of limestone on the east of the Jordan, stretching from Mount Lebanon nearly to the territory of Moab. **Jabbok** is now the Wady Zurka, which intersects · the mountain range of Gilead, and falls into the Jordan about half way between the Sea of Galilee and the Dead Sea. See on Num. xxi, 24. **Ammon** was a son of Lot, born of incestuous intercourse. Gen. xix, 30–38. The Ammonites at one time possessed the whole country between the rivers Arnon and Jabbok, from the Jordan on the west to the wilderness on the east. They were driven out of it by Sihon, king of the Amorites, and he was in turn expelled by the Israelites. Yet long subsequent to these events the country was popularly called the land of the Ammonites, and was even claimed by them. Judges xi, 12–22. For this reason the Jabbok is still called the **border of the children of Ammon.**

3. [**From the plain**—The **from** here, as in the previous verse, is confusing. The sense and connexion will be better seen in the following literal rendering of the Hebrew: *And (Sihon ruled) the plain, as far as the sea of Chinneroth, eastward, and as far as the sea of the plain, the Salt Sea, eastward, on the way toward Beth-jeshimoth, and from the south under the ravines of Pisgah.* The **plain** is the Jordan valley on the east side from the Dead Sea to the Sea of Galilee.] The **Salt Sea** is so called because of the exceeding saltness of its waters—twenty-six pounds of salt to one hundred of water; and a whole mountain ridge on its southwest shore is composed of rock salt. It is commonly called the Dead Sea because no living thing abides in its waters. It is thirteen hundred feet below the Mediterranean, and has no outlet. The **Sea of Chinneroth** was afterwards called the Sea of Galilee, Sea of Tiberias, and Lake of Gennesaret. See notes and cut at Matt. iv, 13. **Beth-jeshimoth** means *house of desolations.* It was a Moabite city in the desert at the northeastern extremity of the Dead Sea. Schwarz mentions a *Beth-jisimuth* as still existing in that locality, but the spot needs further examination. **Ashdoth-pisgah**—The ravines of Pisgah; the gorges at the foot or on the sides of the mountain through which the torrents flow. Comp. chap. x, 40, note, and Deut. iii, 17. The hill Pisgah was opposite Jericho, on the mountains of Abarim, but no traces of the name have been met with in modern times in that locality. See on Deut. xxxiv, 1.

4. **The coast of Og**—The territory of this king, with its boundaries. **Remnant of the giants**—Or, *of the Rephaim.* A race of giants who once peopled Eastern Palestine. Gen. xiv, 5. On Og's gigantic stature see at Deut. iii, 11. On **Ashtaroth** and **Edrei** see note at chap. xiii, 31.

[5. **Salcah**—A city in the eastern border of Bashan, now called Sulkhad. It stands on a conical hill at the southern extremity of Jebel Hauran. J. L. Porter, writing in 1868, says: "It has long been deserted, and yet, as nearly as I could estimate, five hundred of its

cah, and in all Bashan, ^m unto the border of the Geshurites and the Maachathites, and half Gilead, the border of Sihon king of Heshbon. **6** ⁿ Them did Moses the servant of the LORD and the children of Israel smite: and ^o Moses the servant of the LORD gave it *for* a possession unto the Reubenites, and the Gadites, and the half tribe of Manasseh.

7 And these *are* the kings of the country ^p which Joshua and the children of Israel smote on this side Jordan on the west, from Baal-gad in the valley of Lebanon even unto the mount Halak, that goeth up to ^q Seir; which Joshua ^r gave

unto the tribes of Israel *for* a possession according to their divisions; **8** ^s In the mountains, and in the valleys, and in the plains, and in the springs, and in the wilderness, and in the south country; ^t the Hittites, the Amorites, and the Canaanites, the Perizzites, the Hivites, and the Jebusites: **9** ^u The king of Jericho, one; ^v the king of Ai, which *is* beside Beth-el, one; **10** ^w The king of Jerusalem, one; the king of Hebron, one; **11** The king of Jarmuth, one; the king of Lachish, one; **12** The king of Eglon, one; ^x the king of Gezer, one; **13** ^y The king of Debir, one; the king of Geder, one; **14** The king of Hormah,

---

m Deut. 3. 14.——*n* Num. 21. 24, 33.——*o* Num. 32. 29, 33; Deut. 3. 11, 12; chap. 13. 8.——*p* Chap. 11. 17.——*q* Gen. 14. 6; 32. 3; Deut. 2. 1, 4.—— *r* Chap. 11. 23.

s Chap. 10. 40; 11. 16.——*t* Exod. 3. 8; 23. 23; chap. 9. 1.——*u* Chap. 6. 2.——*v* Chap. 8. 29.—— *w* Chap. 10. 23.——*x* Chap. 10. 33.——*y* Chap. 10. 33.

---

houses are still standing, and from three to four hundred families might settle in it at any moment without laying a stone, or spending an hour's labour on repairs. The circumference of the town and castle together is about three miles." **The Geshurites** were the inhabitants of Geshur, a district on the borders of Bashan and Syria, probably embracing, as Porter concludes, the northern section of the wild and rocky region now known as el-Lejah. **The Maachathites** occupied a region on the north of Palestine, and apparently extending from near the fountains of the Jordan under Hermon eastward to the plain of Damascus and the defiles of the Argob. Both the Geshurites and the Maachathites were warlike peoples, and were not expelled from their coasts by the warriors of Israel. Chap. xiii, 13. On the tribal divisions of this trans-Jordanic territory see notes on chap. xiii, 15–33.]

LIST OF THE KINGS SUBDUED BY JOSHUA, 7–24.

[This list is acknowledged by the most rationalistic critics to be a very ancient document. Ewald speaks of it as " a record of remarkable interest in many ways. Its distinctive antiquity would be sufficiently evident from its enumeration of cities which in those early days were great, and powerful, but which afterwards sank into abso-

lute insignificance, or were never heard of again." It was not improbably composed by Joshua himself. A number of the kings here mentioned are not otherwise known, but so far as the previous history throws light on it this list follows mainly the order of the conquest. On the apparent exceptions see note on verse 16.

From the fulness of this list as compared with the previous history we at once see that it was no object of the compiler of the Book of Joshua to record a complete history of all the wars and conquests of Joshua. He has given a detailed account of only the most important, but enough to show, together with this list, that under the administration of the great captain the whole land was subdued.]

7–13. For **Baal-gad** and **Halak** see chap. xi, 17. For the Canaanitish tribes see chap. iii, 10. **Jericho**—See chap. ii, 1. **Ai and Bethel**—See chap. vii, 2. **Jerusalem**—See chap. x, 1. **Hebron, Jarmuth, Lachish, and Eglon**—See chap. x, 3. **Gezer**—See chap. x, 33. **Debir**—See chap. x, 38. **Geder** is now unknown.

14. **Hormah** — The name of this city was originally *Zephath*, (Judges i, 17,) and a trace of this latter name Dr. Robinson found in the rocky pass es-Sufah in the mountain barrier which completes the plateau of Southern Palestine; but the true identification is with Sebaita, some twenty-five miles south-

one; the king of Arad, one; **15** ₑThe king of Libnah, one; the king of Adullam, one; **16** ₐThe king of Makkedah, one; ᵇthe king of Beth-el, one; **17** The king of Tappuah, one; ᶜthe king of Hepher, one; **18** The king of Aphek, one; the king of ³Lasharon, one; **19** The king of Madon, one; ᵈthe king of Hazor, one; **20** The king of ₑShimron-meron, one; the king of Achshaph, one; **21** The king of Taanach, one; the king of Megiddo, one; **22** ᶠThe king of Kedesh, one; the king of Jokneam of Carmel, one; **23** The king of Dor in the

---

ₑ Chap. 10. 29.——a Chap. 10. 28.——b Chap. 8. 17; Judges 1. 22.——c 1 Kings 4. 10.

3 Or, *Sharon*. Isa. 33. 9.——d Chap. 11. 10. ₑ Chap. 11. 1; 19. 15.——f Chap. 19. 37.

---

west of Beer-sheba. See note on Judg. i, 17. The name **Hormah** commemorates the execution of the ban or curse of utter destruction which Moses pronounced on all the dependencies of Arad, (Num. xxi, 2,) and which Judah and Simeon fulfilled. Judges i, 17. **Arad** still exists in Tell Arad, twenty miles south of Hebron. Dr. Robinson describes it as "a barren-looking eminence rising above the country around." Its king troubled Israel in their desert journey. Num. xxi, 1.

15. **Libnah**—See chap. x, 29. **Adullam** is placed, in chap. xv, 35, among the cities of the valley between Jarmuth and Socho. Eusebius and Jerome place it ten miles east of Eleutheropolis, but its site has not been ascertained.

16. **Makkedah**—See chap. x, 10. **Beth-el**—See chap. vii, 2. [Whether the kings of Beth-el and Makkedah here mentioned were slain at the taking of Ai (compare chap. viii, 17, note) and the battle of Beth-horon (chap. x, 28) is somewhat doubtful. It is expressly said that Joshua took Makkedah and destroyed its king in connexion with the great battle of Beth-horon, and it is also said that the men of Beth-el fought against Israel with the men of Ai. But the order of this list would seem to indicate that these kings fell after Joshua had conquered Southern Palestine and was returning northward. It is possible, however, that Beth-el and Makkedah may have recovered somewhat from their fall while Joshua was in the far south, and when he returned northward gave him battle again. The same may be said of Libnah in the preceding verse compared with chap. x, 30. But on the whole it seems more probable that this list does not mean to chronicle the names

of the cities in the exact order of their conquest.]

17. **Tappuah** and **Hepher** are unknown. The former is enumerated, in chap. xv, 34, among the cities of the valley of Judah, and is distinguished from Beth-Tappuah (xv, 53) in the mountains.

18. **Aphek**—This can hardly be the Aphek of the tribe of Asher (chap. xix, 30) which is mentioned in chap. xiii, 4, but it was probably identical with the Aphek not far from Jezreel, where the Philistines gathered their forces before the fearful battle of Gilboa. 1 Sam. xxix, 1. Its site has not been certainly identified. **Lasharon** is mentioned here only and is now unknown. Some think tne first syllable is not an integral part of the name, but would read *king of Sharon*. But this is unlikely.

19, 20. On the cities mentioned in these verses see chap. xi, 1.

[21. **Taanach** — In the Scripture **Taanach** and **Megiddo** are generally mentioned together. They were the two most distinguished cities in that rich tract of land which forms the western portion of the great Plain of Esdraelon. **Taanach** is still found in the ruins of Taanuk, which are on an elevated mound near the base of the hills of Manasseh, the southeastern part of the Carmel range, and about six miles southwest of the city of Jezreel. **Megiddo** also is identified with the modern el-Lejjun, four or five miles northwest of Taanach. Both these places were chiefly famous for their association with the wars of Israel. Taanach was assigned to the Levites. Chap. xxi, 25.

22. **Kedesh** — This city is commonly called *Kedesh-Naphtali*, because it was in the territory of that tribe. It

ᵍcoast of Dor, one; the king of ʰthe nations of Gilgal, one; **24** The king of Tirzah, one: all the kings thirty and one.

CHAPTER XIII.

NOW Joshua ᵃwas old *and* stricken

g Chap. 11. 2.——*h* Gen. 14. 1, 2; Isa. 9. 1.—— *a* See chap. 14. 10; 23. 1.——1 Heb. *to possess it,*

was both a city of refuge (chap. xx, 7) and a Levitical city. Chap. xxi, 32. Hence. as the name indicates, it was *the holy place of Naphtali,* a sanctuary and asylum for all Northern Palestine. Here the tribes assembled, at the call of Barak, to war with Jabin's hosts. Judges iv, 10. From its exposed position on the northern frontier it was among the first to fall into the hands of the Assyrian invaders. 2 Kings xv, 29. Its ruins, still bearing the name *Kedes,* lie on the top and slopes of a round hill in a little plain among the mountains a few miles northwest of Lake Merom.]

Jokneam was also a Levitical city in the tribe of Zebulun, (chap. xix, 11; xxi, 34,) and was identified by Robinson with Tell Kaimon, an eminence close to the northern base of Mount Carmel, and on the south bank of the Kishon, a mile from the river. On **Carmel,** see note on chap. xix, 26.

23. **Dor**—See chap. xi, 2. [**King of the nations of Gilgal**—This intimates that Gilgal was a capital whose sovereign ruled several surrounding tribes. This **Gilgal** must be distinguished both from that in the Jordan valley and that in the hills of Ephraim. It was probably the *Galgulis* of Eusebius and Jerome, on the Mediterranean plain, about eighteen miles northeast of Joppa, and near to Antipatris. It is supposed by Robinson and others to be the same as the modern village of Jiljulieh, two miles southeast of the site of Antipatris.]

24. **Tirzah** is chiefly famous for having become at a later period the royal residence of the first kings of Israel. See 1 Kings xiv, 17, note. Robinson identifies it with the modern Telluzah, a large village a few miles north of Shechem, in a sightly and commanding position, and surrounded by immense groves of olive trees.

in years; and the LORD said unto himᵉ Thou art old *and* stricken in years, and there remaineth yet very much land ¹to be possessed. **2** ᵇThis *is* the land that yet remaineth: ᶜall the borders of the Philistines, and all ᵈGeshuri,

Deut. 31. 3.——*b* Judges 3. 1.——*c* Joel 3. 4.—— *d* Verse 13; 2 Sam. 3. 3; 13. 37, 38.

PART SECOND.

DIVISION AND SETTLEMENT OF CANAAN.

CHAPTERS XIII–XXIV.

CHAPTER XIII.

LIST OF UNCONQUERED CITIES AND DISTRICTS, 1–6.

1. **Joshua was old**—It was time for Joshua to be placed on the retired lists. Since he could not vigorously carry on the war, and no great captain had been raised up, it was deemed by God better that the delicate question of division should be made by Joshua, whose influence and authority would go far towards an amicable partition of the land. Joshua was now about one hundred years old. [**Much land to be possessed**—The writer proceeds (verses 2–6) to name the unconquered districts. Joshua had effectually subdued Palestine, and gained for Israel a firm and lasting foothold there. It does not militate against this fact that there remained still unsubdued a number of scattered cities and provinces in various parts of the land. See note on chap. xi, 23. It is usual, when a land is invaded and subdued, for the unconquered tribes to forsake the plains and seek refuge in the hills; but the unconquered nations here enumerated abode chiefly in the plains.]

2. **All the borders of the Philistines**—This territory is in the southern part of the Holy Land, lying on the Mediterranean. It was a confederacy of five powerful cities, Gaza, Ashdod, Ashkelon, Gath, and Ekron. These enemies of the sea-coast afterwards gave great trouble to the Hebrews. The **Philistines,** according to Gen. x, 14, sprang from Mizraim. See note, Acts viii, 40. **All Geshuri**—Hebrew, *all the Geshuri.* These are not to be confounded with the Geshurites of

3 [e] From Sihor, which *is* before Egypt, even unto the borders of Ekron northward, *which* is counted to the Canaanite: [f] five lords of the Philistines; the Gazathites, and the Ashdothites, the Eshkalonites, the Gittites, and the Ekronites; also [g] the Avites: **4** From the

south, all the land of the Canaanites, and [2] Mearah that *is* beside the Sidonians, [h] unto Aphek, to the borders of [i] the Amorites; **5** And the land of [k] the Giblites, and all Lebanon toward the sunrising, [l] from Baal-gad under mount Hermon unto the entering into Hamath.

[e] Jer. 2. 18.——[f] Judges 3. 3; 1 Sam. 6. 4, 16; Zeph. 2. 5.——[g] Deut. 2. 23.——[2] Or, *The cave.*

[h] Chap. 19. 30.——[i] See Judges 1. 34.——[k] 1 Kings 5. 18; Psa. 83. 7; Ezek. 27. 9.——[l] Chap. 12. 7.

chap. xii, 5, but were a nomadic and predatory people of the desert south of Philistia. David invaded their country and smote them while he dwelt at Ziklag. 1 Sam. xxvii, 8.

3. **Sihor** is not, in this passage, the Nile, as some have supposed, but rather the Wady el-Arish or Rhinocorura, **which is before Egypt,** that is, east of Egypt, constituting the southern boundary of Canaan. It is also called "the river of Egypt." Chap. xv, 4. **Ekron,** the most northerly city of the Philistines, is represented by the modern village of Akir twenty-four miles west of Jerusalem, containing about fifty mud houses, without a remnant of antiquity except two large, finely built wells. **[Which is counted to the Canaanite**—As all that belonged to the Canaanite was now to be divided among the nine and one half tribes of Israel, it was important to know the whole extent of their ancient territory. The Philistines were not of Canaanitish but Egyptian origin, being descended from Mizraim. Gen. x, 14. They seem to have expelled the original Canaanites, and dwelt in their coasts by the sea.] **Gazathites, and Ashdothites**—See chap. xi, 22, note. **Eshkalon** stood upon the Mediterranean, about fifteen miles north of Gaza. Retaining nearly the same name, it now consists of very thick walls and ruins of temples and theatres. **Gittites**—People of Gath. **Avites**—An early, but probably not an aboriginal, people in Philistia.

4. **[From the south**—This is to be connected with **the Avites** in the preceding verse, and stands in contrast with **northward** in the same verse. The Masoretic pointing is here noticeably wrong. Verses 2 and 3 describe the unconquered territory in the south, from its northern limit, Ekron, to its southern, the land occupied by the

Avites; verses 4–6 describe the northern lands.] **Mearah** belonged to the Sidonians. The word **beside** is a mistranslation. **Mearah** signifies a *cavern.* Its location is a matter of conjecture. **Aphek** is identified by Gesenius with Aphaca of classical times, famous for its temple of Venus. Its modern name is Afka, situated some eighteen miles northeast of Beyroot. It was assigned to the tribe of Asher. Chap. xix, 30. **To the borders of the Amorites**— This is taken by most interpreters to refer to the land of Bashan, which formerly belonged to the Amorites and was ruled by Og.

[5. **Giblites**—Inhabitants of Gebal, the Gyblos of the Greeks, the modern Jebail, situated on the seacoast at the foot of the northern slopes of Lebanon, and about seventeen miles north of Beyroot. A multitude of gray granite columns are built into the modern walls and houses, choke up the harbour, and lie scattered over the surrounding fields, and they attest the antiquity of the town. The **Giblites** were employed in building Solomon's temple, (1 Kings v, 18, note,) and, according to Ezek. xxvii, 9, were skilled in shipbuilding. **Baal-gad**—See on chap. xi, 17. **Hamath** was probably founded by the youngest son of Canaan, (Gen. x, 18,) and so was one of the oldest cities in the world. In Amos vi, 2, it is called "the great." Its king Toi made peace with David, (2 Sam. viii, 9,) but Solomon seems to have subjugated the kingdom and made it a part of his own empire. 2 Chron. viii, 3. It early fell into the hands of the great Assyrian conquerors. 2 Kings xviii, 34. It still exists, in the beautiful valley of the Orontes, about sixty miles southeast of Antioch, and has a population of 30,000. It lies on both sides of the river, and is

6 All the inhabitants of the hill country from Lebanon unto [m] Misrephoth-maim, *and* all the Sidonians, them [n] will I drive out from before the children of Israel: only [o] divide thou it by lot unto the Israelites for an inheritance, as I have commanded thee.

7 Now therefore divide this land for an inheritance unto the nine tribes, and the half tribe of Manasseh, **8** With whom the Reubenites and the Gadites have received their inheritance, [p] which Moses gave them, beyond Jordan eastward, *even* as Moses the servant of the LORD gave them; **9** From Aroer, that *is* upon the bank of the river Arnon, and the city that *is* in the midst of the river, [q] and all the plain of Medeba unto Dibon; **10** And [r] all the cities of Sihon king of the Amorites, which reigned in Heshbon, unto the border of the children of Ammon; **11** [s] And Gilead, and the border of the Geshurites and Maachathites, and all mount Hermon, and all Bashan unto Salcah; **12** All the kingdom of Og in Bashan, which reigned

---

m Chap. 11. 8.——*n* See chap. 23. 13; Judges 2. 21, 23.——*o* Chap. 14. 1, 2.——*p* Num. 32. 33; Deut. 3. 12, 13; chap. 22. 4.——*q* Verse 16; Num. 21. 30.——*r* Num. 21. 24, 25.——*s* Chap. 12. 5.

---

noted for the immense wheels, eighty feet in diameter, which are turned by the rapid current and used for irrigation. **The entering into Hamath** is a geographical term used to designate the northern border of Israel. Num. xxxiv, 8; 1 Kings viii, 65; 2 Kings xiv, 25. It was evidently some great pass connected with the Lebanon mountains, but which one has been a matter of dispute. Robinson and Porter identify it with the depression between the northern end of Lebanon and the Nusairiyeh mountains, which opens westward, towards the coast of the Mediterranean. But as the Israelites never occupied territory so far north as that, most sacred geographers identify this **entering** with the southern opening into the great valley of Coele-Syria. This is by far the most notable *entrance into* the ancient kingdom and land of Hamath.]

6. **Misrephoth-maim**—See chap. xi, 8, note. **Them will I drive out** —God's promises of good to man are all grounded on the implied condition of his obedience and faithful co-operation. This promise never was fulfilled, through the failure of the Hebrew nation to maintain an all-conquering faith in their divine Ally. **Divide thou it** —The pronoun **it** is to be referred to the *land* in the first verse, and the intervening verses are to be read parenthetically. Without a special command, Joshua, who supposed that all the land must be first conquered, would not have dared to allot territory still held by the enemy. **By lot**—A difficulty here arises. The land was to be apportioned by lot, and yet, according to Num. xxvi, 53–56, it was also to be divided according to the size of the tribes. The best solution of this difficulty is the supposition that the **lot** only determined the relative *location* of each portion, (Num. xxxiii, 54,) while the *extent* and *bounds* were to be fixed by a board of commissioners. See chap. xiv, 1, note. The manner of the lot is unknown, but probably there were two urns, one containing the names of the tribes, and the other the location of the portions; then by drawing one card or pebble from each urn, the question would be decided by the divine Providence, which directed the lots. The **lot** thus publicly drawn would allay jealousies and prevent disputes. As the result was in exact harmony with Jacob's prophecy in his dying hour two hundred and fifty years before, and in striking fulfilment of Moses' prediction just before his death, it would confirm the Israelites' faith in Jehovah, who had inspired these predictions, and so guided the lots as to secure their accomplishment.

THE TRANS-JORDANIC ALLOTMENTS REVIEWED, 7–14.

8. **With whom**—That is, with the half tribe of Manasseh—not the same half which received its portion of territory west of the Jordan, opposite their Eastern brethren, but the other half.

9–12. On the places named in these verses see the notes on verses 16–31, where the tribal territories are fully described.

in Ashtaroth and in Edrei, who remained of [t] the remnant of the giants : [u] for these did Moses smite, and cast them out. **13** Nevertheless the children of Israel expelled [v] not the Geshurites, nor the Maachathites: but the Geshurites and the Maachathites dwell among the Israelites until this day.   **14** [w] Only unto the tribe of Levi he gave none inher-

itance; the sacrifices of the LORD God of Israel made by fire *are* their inheritance, [x] as he said unto them.

15 And Moses gave unto the tribe of the children of Reuben *inheritance* according to their families.   **16** And their coast was [y] from Aroer, that *is* on the bank of the river Arnon, [z] and the city that *is* in the midst of the river, [a] and

---

t Deut. 3. 11; chap. 12. 4.——*u* Num. 21. 24, 35. ——*v* Verse 1.——*w* Num. 18. 20, 23, 24; chap. 14. 3, 4.——*x* Verse 33.——*y* Chap. 12. 2.——*z* Num. 21. 28.——*a* Num. 21. 30; verse 9.

---

13. Expelled not the Geshurites —See chap. xii. 5.   Geshur and Maacah so late as David's time were small independent States. 2 Sam. iii, 3; xiii, 37.   The contrast between the radical policy of Moses and the conservative policy of the children of Israel in respect to these States seems to imply a censure upon the Israelites.

14. Only unto the tribe of Levi —Moses did not give any inheritance to the nine and a half tribes, not from lack of purpose, but from lack of opportunity.   But the Levites he excluded from a territorial allotment by an express prohibition to Joshua.   They received scattered cities with a narrow margin of pasture lands, but no separate share of the land.   See chap. xxi. **Sacrifices** is here used, in a broad sense, to include all offerings, even those, like the show bread, which were eaten and not burned.   The Vulgate has it *sacrificia et victimae*.   They were to receive a tenth of the fruits of the field, the trees, and the cattle.   Twelve tribes received allotments because the two sons of Joseph were each reckoned as a tribe.

REUBEN'S LOT, 15–23.

[From this point on through chapter xix follows a minute description of the territorial possessions assigned by Joshua to the tribes of Israel, and, while to a modern reader these chapters may appear as a dry and tiresome list of names, we should remember that they were as necessary and important as are the details of a modern deed of real estate to prevent future litigation.   These lists of cities and borders were evidently compiled from the most ancient registers, and in all probability are substantially identical

with those written by Joshua's own hand, or under his supervision and direction.   Their minuteness not only shows the care of the commissioners who determined them, but also the progress already made in the art of mensuration.   See notes on xviii, 4, 9.

15. **Children of Reuben** — In Num. xxxii the children of Reuben and Gad are represented as petitioning Moses for an allotment on the east of Jordan, and they received their portion chiefly between the Arnon and the Jabbok.   This district is now called the Belka, and Burckhardt describes the country and climate as exceedingly picturesque and delightful. "In the Belkan mountains we were refreshed by cool winds, and everywhere found a grateful shade of pine, oak, and wild pistachio trees, with a scenery more like that of Europe than any I had yet seen in Syria.   The superiority of the pasturage of the Belka over that of all southern Syria is the cause of its possession being much contested.   The Bedouins have this saying: 'Thou canst not find a country like the Belka.'"   Reuben and Gad had much cattle, and no wonder they desired a possession in these rich and delightful pasture lands.

16. **Aroer**—A city on the northern **bank of the river Arnon,** and on the southern border of the territory conquered from Sihon, king of the Amorites.   Compare Num. xxi, 26.   Its ruins, called *Araayr*, were discovered by Burckhardt on the summit of a lofty wall of rock overlooking the ancient Arnon.   It is to be distinguished from the Aroer before Rabbah (verse 25) and the Aroer in the south of Judah. 1 Sam. xxx, 28.   **The city that is in the midst of the river** is a subject

all the plain by Medeba; **17** Heshbon, and all her cities that *are* in the plain; Dibon, and [3] Bamoth-baal, and

Bethbaal-meon, **18** [b]And Jahaza, and Kedemoth, and Mephaath, **19** [c]And Kirjathaim, and [d]Sibmah, and Zareth-

---

3 Or, *The high places of Baal, and house of Baal-meon;* see Num. 32. 38.

b Num. 21. 23.——*c* Num. 32. 37.
d Num. 32. 38.

---

of dispute. Some think it is the city Aroer itself. Others conjecture that Aroer consisted of two parts, or an upper and lower city, one on the high bank of the river, and the other in the valley below, where it may have been surrounded by the waters of the stream. Others think it was a city at the junction of the Arnon and one of its tributaries, where Burckhardt saw a hill with ruins on it. Keil thinks that it was Ar of Moab, and at that junction *Ar Moab* is located on Menke's map. **Plain by Medeba**—"The whole plain of Medeba was occupied by the Reubenites; but the city itself was, perhaps, strongly fortified, and suffered to remain, like many in western Palestine, in the hands of its old inhabitants. Its ruins still exist, and bear their old name under the Arabic form *Madeba.* They lie about four miles southeast of Heshbon, with which they are connected by an ancient paved road. The city occupied a low hill, a mile and a half in circumference. The whole site is covered with ruins; not a solitary building remains standing. The plain around it, though now desolate, is fertile, and thickly dotted with ancient cities."—*J. L. Porter.*

17. **Heshbon**—The ancient capital of Sihon, king of the Amorites. See on Num. xxi, 26–28. Its ruins, some twenty miles east of the Jordan at the spot where it empties into the Dead Sea, still bear the name of *Hesban.* It was on the summit and sides of a low hill that rises from the undulating plain, and commands a wide prospect. After its capture by the Israelites it was rebuilt by the tribe of Reuben, (Num. xxxii, 37,) and afterwards assigned to the Levites. Chap. xxi, 39. **Dibon**—A city three miles north of the Arnon, captured and occupied by the Israelites after they defeated Sihon. Num. xxi, 30. It was rebuilt by the tribe of Gad, and called *Dibon-gad.* Num xxxii, 34; xxxiii, 45. In Isa.

xv, 9, it is called *Dimon.* It is identified with extensive ruins still bearing the name of *Diban.* Both Medeba and D.bon are mentioned on the famous Moabite stone recently discovered near this place. See note on 1 Kings xvi, 23. **Bamoth-baal**—That is, *high places of Baal,* so called, probably, because it had been a noted place of Baal worship. Knobel regards this place as identical with the modern Jebel Attarus, a mountain a few miles northwest of Dibon, but the true site of the place is as yet only a matter of conjecture. **Bethbaal-meon** — Called also *Baal-meon* (Num. xxxii, 38) and *Beon.* Num. xxxii, 3. It was evidently also associated with the worship of Baal. Its ruins are found in the modern *Main,* a few miles southwest of Medeba and a little north of the Wady Zerka.

18. **Jahaza** — Written also *Jahaz.* It was the place of the decisive battle of the Israelites with Sihon, (Num. xxi. 23,) and seems to have been on the confines of the desert, to the southeast of Heshbon, but its site has not been discovered. **Kedemoth** was also a city of this eastern desert, but as this region has not yet been explored its exact situation is not known. **Mephaath** is always mentioned in connexion with the two cities prevously named, but, like them, is unknown. In the time of Eusebius it was the station of a Roman garrison to check the wandering Arabs of the desert.

19. **Kirjathaim**—The word means *the double city,* and in the English version is sometimes written *Kiriathaim.* In its plain Chedorlaomer and his confederate kings smote the Emim in the days of Abraham. Gen. xiv, 5. There is some uncertainty as to its site, but J. L. Porter very plausibly identifies it with Kureijat, a ruined town on the southwestern slope of Jebel Attarus. **Sibmah**—From Isa. xvi, 8, 9, and Jer. xlviii, 32, this place seems to have been famous for the cultivation of the vine.

shahar in the mount of the valley,
20 And Beth-peor, and *e* *4* Ashdoth-pisgah, and Beth-jeshimoth, **21** *f* And all the cities of the plain, and all the kingdom of Sihon king of the Amorites, which reigned in Heshbon, *g* whom Moses smote *h* with the princes of Midian, Evi, and Rekem, and Zur, and Hur, and Reba, *which were* dukes of Sihon, dwelling in the country. **22** *i* Balaam also the son of Beor, the *5* soothsayer,

did the children of Israel slay with the sword among them that were slain by them. **23** And the border of the children of Reuben was Jordan, and the border *thereof*. This *was* the inheritance of the children of Reuben after their families, the cities and the villages thereof.

24 And Moses gave *inheritance* unto the tribe of Gad, *even* unto the children of Gad according to their families.

---

e Deut. 3. 17; chap. 12. 3.——4 Or, *Springs of Pisgah*, or, *The hill*.——*f* Deut. 3. 10.

g Num. 21. 24.——*h* Num. 31. 8.——*i* Num. 22. 5; 31. 8.——5 Or, *diviner*.

According to Jerome it was hardly five hundred paces distant from Heshbon, but no trace of its name has yet been found among the ruined cities of that district. **Zareth-shahar**—This place was in a **mount of the valley,** that is. a mountain overlooking the valley of the Jordan and Dead Sea. Seetzen conjectured that its name still lingered in the ruins of *Sara*, a little northwest of Jebel Attarus, and near the mouth of the Wady Zerka.

20. **Beth-peor**—That is, *house of Peor*. The town probably got its name from having been the chief seat of the worship of the Moabite god *Baal-peor*. Num. xxv, 3–5. It was situated on or beside Mount Peor, and close to the valley where the Israelites encamped immediately before descending into the plain of the Jordan. Deut. iii, 29. It was in this valley—apparently the modern Wady Hesban — Moses was buried, (Deut. xxxiv, 6,) and Mount Pisgah, on which he died, could not have been far distant to the south. The valley of Heshbon has never been fully explored. "Whatever traveller may succeed in doing so will be rewarded by the discovery of the ruins of Beth-peor, and the closest approximation that has yet been made to the place of Moses' sepulchre."—*J. L. Porter*. **Ashdoth-pisgah and Beth-jeshimoth**—See notes on chap. xii, 3.

21. **All the cities of the plain**—That is. all the other minor cities of the southern plain which had not been particularly described. **All the kingdom of Sihon**—These words must not be taken as the entire extent of the territory belonging to Sihon, but must be qualified by the statement of verse

27, that the northern part of his kingdom, which extended even to the Sea of Chinnereth, was allotted to Gad. The words are therefore to be understood of the southern part of his territory, which, lying south of Mount Gilead, and including by far the larger part of the kingdom, with its capital and most important cities, might easily have been called **all the kingdom. Dukes of Sihon**—For their defeat by Moses see Num. xxxi, 1–12. These *dukes* were sheiks of the neighbouring towns, tributary to and dependent upon Sihon.

22. **Balaam...the soothsayer**—A Syrian prophet and diviner whom Balak hired to curse Israel, but whose curses were supernaturally turned to blessings in his mouth. His history and oracles are detailed in Num. xxii–xxiv.

23. **This was the inheritance of ...Reuben** — The tribe of Reuben never did excel. Compare Gen. xlix, 4. They were never noted for mighty deeds, and their indifference in the war with Sisera, when the mighty ones went up to battle and they "abode among the sheepfolds to hear the bleatings of the flocks." is properly satirized in the song of Deborah. Judges v, 16, note. Their territory was overrun by the army of Tiglath-pileser, and they were carried away captive into upper Mesopotamia. 1 Chron. v, 26. Then their depopulated cities and country were repossessed by their ancient owners, the Moabites, and hence it is that we find so many cities of Reuben afterwards in possession of the Moabites.

GAD'S LOT, 24–28.

24. **The tribe of Gad** had their inheritance in the central district of

25 ᵏAnd their coast was Jazer, and all the cities of Gilead, ˡand half the land of the children of Ammon, unto Aroer that *is* before ᵐRabbah; **26** And from Heshbon unto Ramath-mizpeh, and Betonim; and from Mahanaim unto the

k Num. 32. 35.——*l* Comp. Num. 21. 26, 28, 29, with Deut. 2. 19; Judg. 11. 13, 15.——*m* 2 Sam. 11. 1; 12. 26.

eastern Palestine, between Reuben and Manasseh, so that the mountains of Gilead fell largely to them. Mr. Buckingham describes this elevated region as having "its plains covered with a fertile soil, its hills clothed with forests, and at every new turn presenting the most magnificent landscapes that could be imagined. Every new direction of our path opened up to us views which surprised and charmed us by their grandeur and beauty. Deep valleys, filled with murmuring streams and verdant meadows, offered all the luxuriance of cultivation, and herds and flocks gave life and animation to the scene." Mr. E. Smith travelled through Gilead in 1834. and found the ground clothed with luxuriant grass a foot or more in height, and decked with a rich variety of wild flowers.

25. **Jazer**—Written also *Jaazer*. It was an important city, having dependent villages, (Num. xxi, 32,) and giving its name to the surrounding country, "the land of Jazer." Num. xxxii, 1. It was one of the four cities of Gad assigned to the Levites. Chap. xxi, 39. Jeremiah (chap. xlviii, 32) speaks of the "sea of Jazer," which may have been some lake or pool in the vicinity. Burckhardt, Van de Velde, and others, identify it with a ruined town called *Seir* or *Sir*, some twelve miles north of Heshbon. **All the cities of Gilead**—That is, of the southern portion of Gilead, for the northern was given to Manasseh. Ver. 31. **Half the land of the children of Ammon**—The country between the Arnon and the Jabbok. See Judges xi, 13, note. This ancient possession of the children of Lot Israel captured, not of Ammon, but of Sihon, king of the Amorites, who had previously taken it out of the hand of the king of Moab. Num. xxi, 26. Yet it retained the name of its ancient owners. **Aroer that is before Rabbah** —That is, Aroer is **before** or *in front of* Rabbah to one who advances towards Rabbah from the Jordan. This Aroer

is supposed by many to be identical with the ruined site Ayra, which Burckhardt discovered about seven miles southwest of es-Salt, and nearly half way between the Jordan and Rabbah. **Rabbah** was the great city and capital of the Ammonites, and is called in Deut. iii, 11 *Rabbath of the children of Ammon*, and here Og's great iron bedstead was preserved. But as Israel was not to meddle with the children of Ammon, (Deut. ii, 19,) Rabbah was not disturbed, nor included in the territory of Gad. It was afterwards besieged and taken by David. 2 Sam. xii, 29. Its ruins are known under the modern name of *Amman*, about twenty-two miles east of the Jordan.

26. **From Heshbon** — Which belonged to the Reubenites, (ver. 17,) but stood so near the boundary between Reuben and Gad as to be occupied in common by both tribes. Compare verse 17 and chap. xxi, 39, notes. **Ramath-mizpeh**—Probably identical with *Ramoth-gilead* and *Mizpeh of Gilead*, which was allotted to the Levites and appointed one of the cities of refuge. Chap. xx, 8; xxi, 38. Most modern scholars are inclined to locate it at the village of *es-Salt*, thirty miles north of Heshbon. "This is indicated," says Porter, "(1) by its position on the summit of a steep hill; (2) by its old ecclesiastical name, *Saltus Hieraticus*, which appears to point to its original sacerdotal and holy character; (3) by the fact that about two miles to the northwest of es-Salt is the highest peak of the mountain range, still bearing the name *Jebel Jilead;* (4) by the statement of Eusebius that Ramoth-Gilead lay in the fifteenth mile from Philadelphia towards the west, and this *is* the exact distance of es-Salt from Rabbath-Ammon." From its lofty position and sacred character it became a great sanctuary of the eastern tribes. See Judg. x, 17, note. **Betonim**—Probably identical with a ruined village Batneh, marked on the

border of Debir; **27** And in the valley, ⁕Beth-aram, and Beth-nimrah, °and Succoth, and Zaphon, the rest of the kingdom of Sihon king of Heshbon, Jordan and *his* border, *even* unto the edge ᴾ of the sea of Chinnereth on the other side Jordan eastward. **28** This *is* the inheritance of the children of Gad after their families, the cities and their villages.

29 And Moses gave *inheritance* unto the half tribe of Manasseh: and *this* was *the possession* of the half tribe of the children of Manasseh by their families.

n Num. 32. 36.——*o* Gen. 33. 17; 1 Kings 7. 46.——*p* Num. 34. 11.

maps of Menke and Van de Velde about five miles west of es-Salt. **Mahanaim** —The place where Jacob met with the angels of God, and therefore called by a name which signifies a *double host* or *camp.* Gen. xxxii, 2, note. It stood on the border between Gad and Manasseh, (verse 30,) and was assigned to the Levites. Chap. xxi, 38. Here after Saul's death Abner made Ishbosheth king, (2 Sam. ii, 8,) and to this place David fled during the rebellion of Absalom. Its site is yet a matter of uncertainty. Some think it is the modern Mahneh, near Jebel Ajlun; while Porter suggests that it may have stood upon the site now occupied by the ruins of Gerasa. **The border of Debir** is utterly unknown. The Hebrew for

of Debir is לִדְבִר, and the first letter ל, *lamedh,* may be a part of the name, *Lidbir.* Reland thinks it may be the same as *Lodebar,* which, according to 2 Sam. ix, 4, must have been in this same vicinity.

27. **The valley**—The Jordan valley from the border of Reuben northward to the sea of Chinnereth. **Beth-aram** is doubtless the same as *Beth-haran* in Num. xxxii, 36. In Eusebius, Jerome, and the Talmud it is called Bethramtha. It has not been accurately identified, but very probably will be found at the ruins called er-Ram just north of the Wady Heshban. The site of **Beth-nimrah** is still preserved in Nimrin, located, according to Robinson's map, near the mouth of the Wady Shoaib, and about twelve miles north of er-Ram. In Num. xxxii, 3, it is called simply *Nimrah.* From its abundance of water and likeness of name in the Septuagint it seems to meet the requirements of the Bethabara of the New Testament. See note on John i, 28. **Succoth**—An important place east of the Jordan, where Jacob built a house and made booths for his cattle after his meeting with Esau. Gen. xxxiii, 17. Its exact location is unknown. **Zaphon** is mentioned again only at Judges xii, 1, where see note. No modern trace of it has been discovered. **The rest of the kingdom of Sihon**—That is, the portion of it that was left after allotting the southern part to the tribe of Reuben. See note on verse 21. **Sea of Chinnereth**—See note on chap. xi, 2. The subsequent fate of the children of Gad was very like that of the tribe of Reuben. See note on verse 23.

MANASSEH'S (EASTERN) LOT, 29–33.

29. **The half tribe of Manasseh** —The division of a tribe in Israel into two parts is a strange and singular fact. In some respects it seems accidental, in other respects providential. " Machir, Jair, and Nobah, the sons of Manasseh, were no shepherds. They were pure warriors, who had taken the most prominent part in the conquest of those provinces which up to that time had been conquered, and whose deeds are constantly referred to with credit and renown. Num. xxxii, 39; Deut. iii, 13–15. 'Jair the son of Manasseh took all the tract of Argob... sixty great cities.' 'Nobah took Kenath and the daughter towns thereof, and called it after his own name.' Deut. xxxii, 42. 'Because Machir was a man of war, therefore he had Gilead and Bashan.' Chap. xvii, 1. The district which these ancient warriors conquered was the most difficult in the whole country. And had they not remained in these wild and inaccessible districts, but had gone forward and taken their lot with the rest, who shall say what changes might not have occurred in the history of their nation

30 And their coast was from Mahanaim, all Bashan, all the kingdom of Og king of Bashan, and *q* all the towns of Jair, which *are* in Bashan, threescore cities: **31** And half Gilead, and *r* Ashtaroth, and Edrei, cities of the kingdom of Og in Bashan, *were pertaining* unto the children of Machir the son of Manasseh, *even* to the one half of the *s* children of Machir by their families. **32** These *are the countries* which Moses did dis-

q Num. 32. 41; 1 Chron. 2. 23.——*r* Chap. 12. 4.
         s Num. 32. 39, 40.

tribute for inheritance in the plains of Moab, on the other side Jordan, by Jericho, eastward. **33** *t* But unto the tribe of Levi Moses gave not *any* inheritance: the LORD God of Israel *was* their inheritance, *u* as he said unto them.

CHAPTER XIV.

AND these *are the countries* which the children of Israel inherited in the land of Canaan, *a* which Eleazar the

t Verse 14; chap. 18. 7.——*u* Num. 18. 20; Deut.
        10. 9; 18. 1, 2.——*a* Num. 34. 17, 18.

through the presence of such energetic and warlike spirits?"— *Grove*, in Smith's Dict. But perhaps these very warlike spirits were providentially settled in these eastern hills to save western Palestine from the proximity of dangerous foes that might otherwise have settled there.

The country of Bashan, occupied by these Manassites, was, according to Porter, "the richest in all Palestine. It is to this day the granary of a great part of Syria. Its whole surface is dotted with ruined or deserted towns and villages."

30. **All Bashan**—This region, distinguished for its fertility, thrifty herds and flocks, and lofty oaks, extended from Gilead on the south to Mount Hermon on the north, and from the Jordan valley on the west far into the eastern and northeastern desert. See on Deut. iii, 1–14. **All the towns of Jair**—That is, the towns that were taken by Jair, the son of Manasseh, and called by his own name. Num. xxxii, 41. They have the name *Havoth-jair* and *Bashan-havoth-jair*, (Deut. iii, 14,) and Porter affirms the two names are not to be confounded. "The towns of Havoth-jair were situated in Gilead south of the river Hieromax, while those of Bashan-havoth-jair were **in Bashan**, and identical with the sixty great cities of Argob." According to this distinction the **threescore cities** here mentioned constituted *Bashan-havoth-jair.* See 1 Kings iv, 13, note.

31. **Half Gilead** — The northern half, for the southern was assigned to Gad. Ver. 25. **Ashtaroth** — Generally supposed to be identical with the

Ashteroth-karnaim of Gen. xiv, 5. It was doubtless so called from being the seat of worship of the Phenician goddess Ashtoreth, the Greek Astarte. Its ruins are supposed to lie at the modern Tell-Astereh, some fifteen miles east of the Sea of Galilee. **Edrei** was the other chief city of the kingdom of Bashan, and here King Og was defeated and slain. Num. xxi, 33–35. It was a stronghold among the rocks, and its ruins have been found in the modern Edra, thirty miles or more northeast of the Sea of Galilee. J. L. Porter visited the ruins a few years ago and thus wrote: "The situation is most remarkable; without a single spring of living water; without river or stream; without access, except over rocks and through defiles all but impassable; without tree or garden. In selecting the site every thing seems to have been sacrificed to security and strength. The huge masses of shattered masonry could scarcely be distinguished from the rocks that encircled them, and all, ruins and rocks alike, are black as if scathed by lightning." **Unto the children of Machir**—"Because he was a man of war, therefore he had Gilead and Bashan." Chap. xvii 1. **Even to the one half**—The heads of the families of this half are named in 1 Chron. v, 24.]

CHAPTER XIV.

INTRODUCTION TO THE WEST JORDANIC ALLOTMENTS, 1–5.

{1. **These are the countries**— Passing from the eastern side of the Jordan, our historian now traces the boundaries of the tribes on its western

priest, and Joshua the son of Nun, and the heads of the fathers of the tribes of the children of Israel, distributed for inheritance to them. **2** [b]By lot *was* their inheritance, as the LORD commanded by the hand of Moses, for the nine tribes, and *for* the half tribe. **3** [c]For Moses had given the inheritance of two tribes and a half tribe on the other side Jordan: but unto the Levites he gave none inheritance among them. **4** For [d]the children of Joseph were two tribes, Manasseh and Ephraim: therefore they gave no part unto the Levites in the land, save cities to

dwell *in*, with their suburbs for their cattle and for their substance. **5** [e]As the LORD commanded Moses, so the children of Israel did, and they divided the land.

6 Then the children of Judah came unto Joshua in Gilgal: and Caleb the son of Jephunneh the [f]Kenezite said unto him, Thou knowest [g]the thing that the LORD said unto Moses the man of God concerning me and thee [h]in Kadesh-barnea. **7** Forty years old *was* I when Moses the servant of the LORD [i]sent me from Kadesh-barnea to espy out the land; and I brought him word

---

[b] Num. 26. 55; 33. 54; 34. 13.——[c] Chap. 13. 8, 32, 33.——[d] Gen. 48. 5; 1 Chron. 5. 1, 2.——[e] Num. 35. 2; chap. 21. 2.

[f] Num. 32. 12; chap. 15. 17.——[g] Num. 14. 24, 30; Deut. 1. 36, 38.——[h] Num. 13. 26.——[i] Num. 13. 6; 14. 6.

---

side, constituting the main area of the Holy Land. The directions of Moses (Num. xxvi. 53–56) were obeyed in the allotment. Yet God so overruled the lots as to fulfil the predictions of the prophecies of the dying Jacob. Gen. xlix. **Eleazar the priest**—The term *High Priest* had not yet been invented. Eleazar was the third son of Aaron, and came into the high-priesthood by the death of his two sacrilegious brothers, Nadab and Abihu. See notes on Exod. vi, 23; Lev. x, 1; Num. iii, 4; Num. xx. 28. He aided Moses in the census of the people, (Num. xxvi, 3,) assisted at the inauguration of Joshua, and now is the proper person to superintend the sacred lots by which the conquered lands were divided. The original document describing the division we might naturally suppose to be prepared under his superintendence and preserved in the archives of the tabernacle. In the form in which the records here stand in the sacred volume they form a part of the *law*, and they were, we might suppose, preserved with the sacred records in the ark of the covenant. The persons who were to divide western Palestine among the nine tribes and the half tribe of Manasseh were designated by Jehovah before the death of Moses, and their names are given in Num. xxxiv, 17–28.

4. Joseph...two tribes—So making up the twelve tribes without reckoning the tribe of Levi, who were to have no allotment, but were to be

scattered among the tribes as judicial and ecclesiastical advisers and judges among the people. }

CALEB'S INHERITANCE, 6–15.

6. Children of Judah came— Caleb was of the tribe of Judah, and probably by his request the elders of his own tribe accompany him to Gilgal, lest they might suspect that he was using his office of commissioner to carve out a splendid portion for himself. They may have seconded his petition as having an important bearing on the question of their own portion, which would naturally contain the tract of Caleb, their tribesman, so that the granting of his request would virtually establish southern Canaan as their lot. **Caleb** was one of the two spies so famous for their faith in Jehovah, and for their courage and independence in making a very unpopular minority report, for which they narrowly escaped stoning at the hands of the infuriated people. Num. xiv, 6–10. They were spared in the ensuing plague which swept off the faithless ten, and were also excepted when Moses declared that none who were above twenty years old when they came out of Egypt should enter Canaan. Num. xiv, 29, 30. **Kenezite**—That is, a son of Kenaz. He was a pure Hebrew, not an Edomite. **Kadesh-barnea**—Chap. x, 41, note.

{ 7. **Forty years old was I—** When, in the plains of Moab near the banks of the Jordan, Moses numbered Israel, not a man was left of those who

again as *it was* in mine heart. **8** Nevertheless [k]my brethren that went up
with me made the heart of the people
melt: but I wholly [l]followed the LORD
my God. **9** And Moses sware on that
day, saying, [m]Surely the land [n]whereon
thy feet have trodden shall be thine inheritance, and thy children's for ever,
because thou hast wholly followed the
LORD my God. **10** And now, behold,
the LORD hath kept me alive, [o]as he
said, these forty and five years, even
since the LORD spake this word unto
Moses, while *the children of* Israel [1]wan-
dered in the wilderness: and now, lo,
I *am* this day fourscore and five years
old. **11** [p]As yet I *am as* strong this
day as *I was* in the day that Moses sent
me: as my strength *was* then, even so
is my strength now, for war, both [q]to
go out, and to come in. **12** Now therefore give me this mountain, whereof

k Num. 13. 31, 32; Deut. 1. 28.——*l* Num. 14. 24; Deut. 1. 36.——*m* Num. 14. 23, 24; Deut. 1. 36; chap. 1. 3.——*n* Num. 13. 22.——*o* Num. 14. 30.——1 Heb. *walked*.——*p* Deut. 34. 7.——*q* Deut. 31. 2.

had heard the law thundered from Sinai, save these two veterans who now stand face to face, Caleb and Joshua. Num. xxvi, 63. The desert of the sojourn had been the nation's tomb. Joshua had succeeded Moses as leader of the tribes: Caleb now comes forward to claim the patrimony that had been promised by Jehovah to him. **In mine heart**—Heart means here not the affections solely, but the understanding. See note on Rom. x, 10. He made his report a perfect transcript of things as he saw them, uncoloured by cowardice, or faithlessness to Jehovah, or compliance with the people.

8. **My brethren**—Words of tenderness for his long-remembered comrades. **Heart...melt**—In modern sense this would indicate compassion; in the ancient, *fear*. **Wholly followed the Lord my God**—This phrase **wholly followed** is emphatically repeated from Jehovah's own words, (Num. xiv, 24; Deut. i, 36,) here reiterated at verse 9 and at verse 14. This wholeness of his adherence to Jehovah is explained by his and Joshua's loyal speech, given Num. xiv, 6–10. There no treachery of their **brethren** the fellow-spies, no panic of their own, no fury of the people, could disturb the calmness of their witness for God. Then and there the sentence of death in the wilderness, passed upon the entire people, left them untouched. And of that eventful day these two Hebrew princes were now the sole living and speaking mementoes.

9. **Moses sware**—The oath was God's own oath, (Num. xiv, 24; Deut. i, 13,) but declared and accepted by Moses.

10. **Kept me alive**—Not only excepted me from the immediate plague inflicted on the rebellious, and from the death-sentence that laid the nation as corpses in the desert, but from all the decay of years, and the perils of this war of conquest.

11. **Strong this day**—As strong to defend his heritage as he was forty-five years ago to win it. He had kept the ten commandments which his own ears had heard from Jehovah's voice so well, that they had been permanent youth in his blood and bones. **Go out**—To the battle. **Come in**—With the spoils. See Judges i, 20. This was no senile boast of youthful strength, as the three sons of Anak found to their cost. Chap. xv, 14. The old hero never became, like his fellow Joshua, ruler of all Israel, but he had a son-in-law-nephew that did.

12. **Give me this mountain**—Hebron is the highest point of southern Palestine, (see chap. x, 3, note,) higher even than Jerusalem. "The spot on which Caleb had set his heart was the fertile valley of Hebron. Of all the country which the twelve spies, with Caleb and Joshua at their head, had traversed, this is the one scene which remains fixed in the sacred narrative, as if because fixed in the memory of those who made their report. There was one field in the whole land which they might fairly call their own, the field which contained the rocky cave of Machpelah, with the graves of their first ancestors. But it was not even this sacred enclosure which had most powerfully impressed the simple explorers of that childlike age. It was the winding valley whose terraces were covered with the rich verdure and the

the LORD spake in that day; for thou heardest in that day how *the Anakim *were* there, and *that* the cities *were* great *and* fenced: *if so be the LORD *will be* with me, then 'I shall be able to drive them out, as the LORD said. **13** And Joshua "blessed him, 'and gave unto Caleb the son of Jephunneh Hebron for an inheritance. **14** "He-

bron therefore became the inheritance of Caleb the son of Jephunneh the Kenezite unto this day, because that he ˣwholly followed the LORD God of Israel. **15** And ʸthe name of Hebron before *was* Kirjath-arba; *which Arba was* a great man among the Anakim. ᶻAnd the land had rest from war.

---

r Num. 13. 28, 33.——*s* Psa. 18. 32, 34; 60. 12; Rom. 8. 31.——*t* Chap. 15. 14; Judges 10. 2.—— *u* Chap. 22. 6.——*v* Chap. 10. 37; 15. 13; Judges

1. 20; see chap. 21. 11, 12; 1 Chron. 6. 55, 56.—— *w* Chap. 21. 12.——*x* Verses 8, 9.——*y* Gen. 23. 2; chap. 15. 13.——*z* Chap. 11. 23.

---

golden clusters of the Syrian vine, so rarely seen in Egypt, so beautiful a vesture of the bare hills of Palestine. In its rocky hills are still to be seen the ancient winepresses. Thence came the gigantic cluster, (Num. xiii, 24,) the only relic of the Promised Land which was laid at the feet of Moses."—*Stanley.* **Anakim**—The *long-necked;* called also sons of Anak; a race of giants in southern Canaan. See on Num. xiii, 28, 33.

13. **And Joshua blessed him**— Bade him God speed in his warfare, and invoked the help of Jehovah to attend him. **And gave unto Caleb**— Joshua could not resist an appeal from his venerable associate spy, based on facts of which he himself had been cognizant.

15. **Before was Kirjath-arba**— That is, City of Arba. The original name, in Abraham's day, was Hebron. Afterwards Arba, a giant, one of the Anakim, conquered the city and called it the City of Arba. See chap. x. 3, note. **And the land had rest from war**—This is only a repetition of chap. xi, 23, to prepare the way for the account of the peaceful allotment of the land. As Caleb's portion was really " among the children of Judah," the actual conquest of it is recorded under the head of Judah's lot. See chap. xv, 13–19.

CHAPTER XV.

ORIGINAL LOT OF JUDAH, 1–63.

[The tribe of Judah received the first allotment, and a very disproportionate share of the Land of Promise, for its territory embraced nearly the half of western Palestine. This original lot, however, was afterwards diminished by

assigning a part of it to Simeon. Chap. xix, 1. The original borders, districts, and cities of Judah are detailed with great minuteness in this chapter, and to a much greater extent than those of any other tribe. Grove suggests that " this may be due either to the fact that the lists were reduced to their present form at a later period, when the monarchy resided with Judah, and when more care would naturally be bestowed on them than on those of any other tribe; or to the fact that the territory was more important, and more thickly covered with towns and villages, than any other part of Palestine."—*Smith's Bib. Dict.* Many and great were the prophetic blessings pronounced on Judah by his father. Gen. xlix, 8–12. He was to be the pride and glory of his brethren, the mighty conqueror, whose symbol was the lion, and whose preeminence was represented by the sceptre and the ruler's staff, never to depart "until Shiloh come." The same prophetic blessing also characterized his section of the Promised Land. "The elevation of the hills and tablelands of Judah is the true climate of the vine, and at Hebron, according to the Jewish tradition, was its primeval seat. He bound 'his foal unto the vine, and his ass's colt unto the choice vine; he washed his garments in wine, and his clothes in the blood of grapes.' Gen. xlix, 11. A vineyard on a hill of olives, with the 'fence,' and the 'stones gathered out,' and the 'tower in the midst of it,' is the natural figure which, both in the prophetical and evangelical records, represents the kingdom of Judah. Isa. v, 1; Matt. xxi, 33. The vine was the emblem of the nation on the coins of the Maccabees, and in the colossal

CHAPTER XV.

*T*HIS then was the lot of the tribe of the children of Judah by their families; [a] *even* to the border of Edom the [b] wilderness of Zin southward *was* the uttermost part of the south coast. **2** And their south border was from the shore of the salt sea, from the [1] bay that looketh southward: **3** And it went out to the south side [c] to [2] Maaleh-acrabbim, and passed along to Zin, and ascended up on the south side unto Kadesh-barnea, and passed along to Hezron, and went up to Adar, and fetched a compass to Karkaa: **4** *From thence* it passed [d] toward Azmon, and went out unto the river of Egypt; and the goings out of that coast were at the sea: this shall be your south coast. **5** And the east border *was* the salt sea, *even* unto the end of Jordan. And *their* border in the north quarter *was* from the bay of the sea at the uttermost part of Jordan: **6** And the border went up to [e] Beth-hoglah, and passed along by the north of Beth-arabah; and the border went up [f] to the stone of Bohan the son of Reuben: **7** And the border went up toward

---

a Num. 34. 3.——*b* Num. 33. 36.——1 Heb. *tongue.*
         c Num. 34. 4.

2 Or, *The going up to Acrabbim.*——*d* Num. 34. 5.——*e* Chap. 18. 19.——*f* Chap. 18. 17.

---

cluster of golden grapes which overhung the porch of the second temple."
—*Stanley.*

1. **Even to the border of Edom** —The latter part of this verse should be rendered, *to the border of Edom the wilderness of Zin southward from the extremity of Teman.* Teman was a district in the land of Edom, and lay, perhaps, not far southeast of the Dead Sea. Its position, however, is unknown. The sense of the whole verse is: Judah's lot extended into the extreme south, bordering on Edom and the desert of Zin. The Edomites occupied the mountainous region directly south of the Dead Sea, and the wilderness of Zin was the desert tract extending westward from this, in which lay Kadesh. See on Num. xx, 1; xxxiii, 36.

2. **Their south border** seems to have fetched a curve or semicircle from the south end of the Dead Sea, sweeping far round by the wilderness of Zin, and thence northwesterly to the Mediterranean. **Salt sea**—Now commonly called the Dead Sea, and supposed to cover the ancient vale of Siddim and the destroyed cities of Sodom and Gomorrah. See on Gen. xiv, 3; xix, 25. **The bay that looketh southward**—Literally, *the tongue that turneth southward.* The southernmost portion of the Dead Sea somewhat resembles a tongue in shape. Compare Isa. xi, 15.]

3. **It went out to the south side**— Or, *on the south side.* That is, it started out on its southward course. **Maaleh-acrabbim**—The word means *ascent of scorpions,* and was probably the name of a pass in the bald mountain (Halak) eight miles south of the Dead Sea, described in note, chap. xi, 17. It doubtless derived its name from its scorpions, which abound in all this region. **Passed along to Zin**—That is, went along till it joined the edge of the wilderness of Zin, which stretches off to the west and southwest of Mount Hor. **Kadesh-barnea**—The modern Ain Gadis. See chap. x, 41, note. **Hezron, Adar,** and **Karkaa** are now unknown. Compare Num. xxxiv, 1–5.

4. **Azmon** is also unknown. **River of Egypt**—Wady-el-Arish. See note chap. xiii, 3. **At the sea**—The Mediterranean Sea.

5. **East border was the salt sea** —Which formed a boundary line for nearly fifty miles. **End of Jordan**— That is, the mouth of the Jordan; called also in this same verse *the uttermost part of Jordan.* **Bay of the sea** —The northern tongue or extremity of the Dead Sea, at the point where it receives the waters of the Jordan.

6. **Beth-hogla**—The modern Ain Hadjla, a fine spring of beautiful sweet water at the north of the Dead Sea, about two miles west of the Jordan. **Beth-arabah**—*House of solitude:* in the desert of Judah, and apparently not far from Beth-hogla. It is mentioned again in verse 61 and chap. xviii, 22, and in chap. xviii, 18 is called simply Arabah; first allotted to Judah, then relinquished to Benjamin. **Stone of Bohan**—This cannot be located. It was a memorial of a Reubenite warrior slain in the conquest of the land.

Debir from *the valley of Achor, and so **northward**, looking toward Gilgal, that **is** before the going up to Adummim, **which** *is* on the south side of the river: **and** the border passed toward the waters **of** Enshemesh, and the goings out thereof were at [h] Enrogel: **8** And the border

g Chap. 7. 26.——*h* 2 Sam. 17. 17; 1 Kings 1. 9.
i Chap. 18. 16; 2 Kings 23. 10; Jer. 19. 2, 6.

---

7. **Achor**—See chap. vii, 24, note. This **Debir** is not the same with that **named** in x, 38, but another, evidently **not** far from the Valley of Achor. Its **site** is unknown. **Gilgal**—See on chap. **v, 9.** It is called *Geliloth*, chap. xviii, 17. [**Adummim**—Literally, *the ascent of the red* ones, and so called because of the frequent effusion of blood there by **robbers**, (compare Luke x, 30, note,) or **else** from some early tribe of red men (possibly Edomites) who dwelt there. **Keil** thinks the name originated in the **red** colour of the rocks; but Stanley **says** there are no red rocks here, but **the** whole pass is white limestone. **Adummim** was probably at or near the **modern** *ed-Dem*, marked on Menke's **map** about half way between Jerusa-**lem** and Jericho. This is on the **south side** of Wady Kelt, which is doubtless **the river** here referred to.] **En-she-mesh**—The *fountain of the sun*, usually **identified** with the Well of the Apostles, **below** Bethany on the road to Jericho; **but** Dr. Robinson says, "It may very **possibly** have been the fountain near **St. Saba."** **En-rogel**—The *fountain of the fuller*. The Arabic version of **this** verse calls it the *Well of Job*, which **is** its modern name. [An old tradition **and** common opinion has identified it **with** the deep well situated just below **the** junction of the Valley of Hinnom **with** that part of the Valley of Jehosh-**aphat.** It is also called the Well of Ne-**hemiah.** But Dr. Bonar identifies it **with** the Fountain of the Virgin, and **more** recently M. Ganneau maintains **the** same opinion, having discovered a **rock** Zehwele near this fountain, which **he** identifies with the Stone of Zohe-**leth** mentioned 1 Kings i, 9.

8. **Valley of the son of Hin-nom** — A long-standing and almost unanimous opinion of all explorers of the Holy Land identifies this valley

went up [i] by the valley of the son of Hinnom unto the south side of the [k] Jebusite; the same *is* Jerusalem: and the border went up to the top of the mountain that *lieth* before the valley of Hinnom westward, which *is* at the end [l] of the valley of the giants northward:

k Chap. 18. 28; Judges 1. 21; 19. 10.
l Chap. 18. 16.

---

with the deep and narrow ravine that bounds Jerusalem on the west and south. But Capt. Warren, of the Palestine Exploration Company, is convinced that the Hinnom is identical with the Kedron Valley, which is on the east of Jerusalem. In Jer. xix, 2, the valley is said to be "by the entry of the east gate," but there the Hebrew is the *Charsuth*, or Potter's Gate, and the precise meaning is by no means clear. But Robinson (Bib. Res., vol. i, p. 269) says that several Arabic writers of the twelfth century call the Kedron valley *Jehennam*. According to Capt. Warren the border of Judah and Benjamin ran over the southern slope of the mount of Olives, "across from the rock Zoheleth in Siloam to the Virgin's Fount, thence up the Kedron until nearly opposite the south-southeast angle of the noble sanctuary, where it crossed over the hill of Moriah at the southern side of the temple, thence up the Tyropœan Valley to the Jaffa Gate, and so on to Lifta." But this needs confirmation, and ill agrees with what follows. **South side of the Jebusite**—That is, the boundary line ran south of Jerusalem, the city of the Jebusite. The Jebusite citadel, which was taken by David and called the stronghold of Zion, (2 Sam. v, 7,) is commonly supposed to have been on the modern Zion; but Capt. Warren's topography places the boundary on the north side of the modern Zion. **The mountain that lieth before the valley of Hinnom westward**—This most naturally indicates the eminence west of Jerusalem which forms the western side or wall of the upper part of what is now commonly called the Valley of Hinnom. The brow of this hill, according to Robinson, is a rocky ridge. **Which is at the end of the valley of the giants northward**—This is obscure,

9 And the border was drawn from the top of the hill unto [m] the fountain of the water of Nephtoah, and went out to the cities of mount Ephron; and the border was drawn [n] to Baalah, which is [o] Kirjath-jearim: **10** And the border compassed from Baalah westward unto mount Seir, and passed along unto the side of mount Jearim, which is Chesalon, on the north

side, and went down to Beth-shemesh, and passed on to [p] Timnah: **11** And the border went out unto the side of [q] Ekron northward: and the border was drawn to Shicron, and passed along to mount Baalah, and went out unto Jabneel; and the goings out of the border were at the sea. **12** And the west border was [r] to the great sea, and the coast

----

m Chap. 18. 15.——*n* 1 Chron. 13. 6.
o Judges 18. 12.

p Gen. 38. 13; Judges 14. 1.——*q* Chap. 19. 43.
r Verse 47; Num. 34. 6, 7.

What is at the end of the valley? and is this point north of the valley, or the valley north of the point in question? We take the meaning to be, that the mountain (just mentioned) is at the northern end of the Valley of the Giants. **The valley of the giants,** or *of Rephaim,* is usually identified with the upland plain to the southwest of Jerusalem. "This plain," says Robinson. "is broad, and descends gradually towards the southwest until it contracts in that direction into a deeper and narrower valley, called lower down Wady el-Werd, which unites further on with Wady Ahmed, and finds its way to the western plain." So it is sufficiently enclosed with hills to be called a **valley,** (*emek,*) and no other valley or plain so well answers the Scripture notices as this. Here the Philistines encamped when they came to war with David. 2 Sam. v, 18.]

9. **Nephtoah** is identified by Dr. Barclay with Ain Lifta, a spring three miles northwest of Jerusalem, near a village of the same name. **Mount Ephron** is probably the range of hills on the west side of the Wady Beit Hanina, the traditional Valley of the Terebinth. **Baalah, or Kirjath-jearim,** is identified by Dr. Robinson with the modern Kuryet-el-Enab. See chap. ix, 17, note.

10. **Compassed** — That is, encompassed; described a curve. **Mount Seir** must not be confounded with that of Idumea. It is a range running southwest from Kirjath-jearim, between the Wady Aly and the Wady Ghurab. The name still continues in the place called Sairah. **Chesalon** is the modern Kesla, seen by Dr. Robinson on a high point of the lofty ridge south of the Wady Ghurab. [He also recognized **Beth-**

shemesh in the modern Ain-shems, just south of the great Wady Surar. The ruins, which consist of many foundations and remains of ancient walls of hewn stone, are " upon and around the plateau of a low swell or mound between the Surar on the north and a smaller wady on the south." To this place the Ark was brought after its capture by the Philistines. 1 Sam. vi, 9.] **Timnah,** from which Samson fetched his wife, is the modern Tibneh, about two miles west of Beth-shemesh. This Timnah must be distinguished from another place of the same name on the mountains, mentioned at verse 57.

[11. **Unto the side of Ekron northward** — That is, on the north side of Ekron. This was the most northerly of the five great Philistine cities. Compare chap. xiii, 3. It was the last place to which the captured Ark was taken, (1 Sam. v, 10,) and thence it was transported on the new cart to Beth-shemesh. Its site is found in the modern Akir, in a north-westerly direction from Beth-shemesh, and about half way between the latter city and the sea. The site of **Shicron** is unknown. **Mount Baalah** is also uncertain, but probably was the name of a range of hills seen from Ekron on the east of Wady Rubin. **Jabneel** is doubtless the same as *Jabneh,* which Uzziah took from the Philistines. 2 Chron. xxvi, 6. The name and site are still found in Yebna, a village situated on an eminence in the midst of a rich plain, two miles from the sea and three from Ekron. **The goings out...at the sea** — That is, the northern boundary terminated at the Mediterranean Sea.

12. **To the great sea and the coast** — That is, the coast of the Mediterra-

thereof: this is the coast of the children of Judah round about according to their families. **13** [s] And unto Caleb the son of Jephunneh he gave a part among the children of Judah, according to the commandment of the LORD to Joshua, even [t] the city of Arba the father of Anak, which city is Hebron. **14** And Caleb drove thence [u] the three sons of Anak, [v] Sheshai, and Ahiman, and Talmai, the children of Anak. **15** And [w] he went up thence to the inhabitants of Debir: and the name of Debir before was Kirjath-sepher. **16** [x] And Caleb said, He that smiteth Kirjath-sepher, and taketh it, to him will I give Achsah my daughter to wife. **17** And [y] Othniel the [z] son of Kenaz, the brother of Caleb, took it: and he gave him Achsah his daughter to wife. **18** And [a] it came to pass, as

---

[s] Ch. 14. 13.——[t] Ch. 14. 15.——3 Or, *Kirjath-arba*.——[u] Judg. 1. 10, 20.——[v] Num. 13. 22.——[w] Ch. 10. 38; Judg. 1. 11; [x] Judg. 1. 12.——[y] Judg. 1. 13; 3. 9.——[z] Num. 32. 12; chap. 14. 6.——[a] Judg. 1. 14.

---

nean from Jebneel southward formed Judah's western boundary.

The writer, having now given the boundaries of Judah, is about to give a list of the cities within these bounds. But before proceeding to do so he enters a brief account of Caleb's conquest of his portion, which Joshua had allotted him. See chap. xiv, 6–15. As Caleb's possession included the most important city and central seat of the whole tribe of Judah, it is natural that the fact of its conquest should be recorded here.

As verses 13–19 are nearly identical with Judges i, 10–20, some have supposed that this passage in Joshua was copied from that in Judges; and others, on the contrary, maintain that the passage in Judges was taken from this. Keil, however, urges that both passages were drawn from one common source, a document older than either the Book of Joshua or that of Judges.]

13. **Hebron**—See at chap. xiv, 12.

14. **The three sons of Anak**—Joshua had cut off the Anakim from the mountains and destroyed their cities, (chap. xi, 21,) but after his army retired northward these three old chieftains had rallied their scattered adherents and repossessed their cities.

15. **Debir**—See on chap. x, 38.

{ We have now, in 16–19, a glimpse of romance in Hebrew history. It was memorable tradition connected with the capture of Debir, and with the history of one of the princely families of the period.

16. **Caleb said**—The veteran leader finding Debir, perhaps after his previous conquests, a more difficult fortress, arouses his warriors with the promise of a prize. **Smiteth Kirjath-sepher**—

The old name of the city, as quoting the warrior's own words. **My daughter to wife**—Said in the spirit of the Oriental as well as the Roman rule, by which the parent was absolute lord of his children, and of the Oriental custom of marrying parties without regard to previous affection or even acquaintance. Saul thus promised his daughter to the slayer of Goliath. 1 Sam. xvii, 25.

17. **Othniel the son of Kenaz, the brother of Caleb**—The Septuagint, by mistake, here makes Othniel to be the brother of Caleb, thus making him marry his own brother's daughter, his niece: a marriage if not unlawful, yet questionable. But the Septuagint corrects itself at Judges i, 13, where all versions agree that Kenaz was Caleb's brother, and Othniel Kenaz's son. Othniel therefore married his own cousin. **Gave him Achsah**—In being offered as a prize to the warriors it is probable that, in accordance with the spirit of the times, Achsah found a gratification to her feminine pride. The onset of battle was to be made all the more bravely for her beauty, rank, and dower. Of course, all the probabilities of winning lay within the circle of a few well-known heroes, and she would have the assurance of marrying the bravest man of Caleb's princedom. And her best ambition was gratified, since Providence and Othniel's bravery gave her the man of her probable choice—certainly the man who raised her from the rank of daughter of the sheikh to that of wife of the ruler of all the united tribes. Judges iii, 9.

18. **And it came to pass**—We have now full proof that Caleb acted from affection to his daughter and with her

she came *unto him*, that she moved him to ask of her father a field: and [b] she lighted off *her* ass; and Caleb said unto her, What wouldest thou? **19** Who answered, Give me a [c] blessing; for thou hast given me a south land; give me also springs of water. And he gave her the upper springs, and the nether springs. **20** This *is* the inheritance of the tribe of the children of Judah according to their families. **21** And the uttermost cities of the tribe of the chil-dren of Judah toward the coast of Edom southward were Kabzeel, and Eder, and Jagur, **22** And Kinah, and Dimonah, and Adadah, **23** And Kedesh, and Ha-zor, and Ithnan, **24** Ziph, and Telem, and Bealoth, **25** And Hazor, Hadattah, and Kerioth, *and* Hezron, which *is* Hazor, **26** Amam, and Shema, and Moladah, **27** And Hazar-gaddah, and Heshmon, and Beth-palet, **28** And Hazar-shual, and Beer-sheba, and Biz-jothjah, **29** Baalah, and Iim, and

---

[b] See Gen. 24. 64; 1 Sam. 25. 23.

[c] Gen. 33. 11; Deut. 33. 7; 1 Sam. 25. 27:

---

confiding love. **As she came**—In bridal procession, all riding upon asses, from her father's house to the house of her bridegroom, by whom she is escorted to his and her future home. See note on Matt. xxv, 1–6. **She moved him**—Her bridegroom, by the side of whom, probably, she rode in procession. She believes the request of Othniel would be with Caleb even more powerful than her own; but he, perhaps silently, declines. **To ask...a field**—"Underneath the hill on which Debir stood is a deep valley, rich with verdure from a copious rivulet, which, rising at the crest of the glen, falls, with a continuity unusual in the Jude-an hills, down to its lowest depth. On the possession of these upper and lower 'bubblings,' so contiguous to her lover's prize, Achsah had set her heart."—*Stanley*. **Lighted off**— At her bridegroom's door, where she and her father meet each other. **What wouldest thou**— The heart of her father at this melting moment is open to any request, and she seizes the golden chance. }

19. **A blessing**— A special favour, a gift. **Springs of water**—As her por-tion was a field having a southern exposure to blazing suns and sultry winds, she argues the eminent propri-ety of supplementing the gift by add-ing a well-watered adjoining tract. He gave her **the upper springs and the nether,** a tract of hill and dale abounding in water.

The cities of Judah are grouped in four divisions corresponding to the physical geography of Judah's lot: the NEGEB, or south country, verses 21–32; the SHEPHELAH, or valley, 33–47; the MOUNTAIN, 48–60; and the WILDER-NESS, 61, 62. The cities of the Sheph-elah and the Mountain are enumerated by groups. These cities are nearly all unknown. For an elaborate attempt to identify them, see Wilton's *Negeb*, Part III, page 70. In the following notes nothing is said on the names of those places of which no modern trace has been certainly discovered.

26. **Moladah,** afterwards given to Simeon, is the modern *el Milh*, about twenty miles south of Hebron. [This place was identified by Dr. Robin-son. It has two wells about forty feet deep, and the ruins of a for-mer city cover a space around of nearly half a mile square. It was in-habited again after the exile. Neh. xi, 26. The sides of the wells are, accord-ing to Tristram, " of hard marble, pol-ished and deeply fluted all round by the ropes of the water drawers, per-haps for four thousand years. Eight ancient water-troughs stand irregularly around, some oblong, many cup-shaped, and others apparently the scooped pedestals of ancient columns, which have once supported a portico over the well."]

28. **Beer-sheba**—This spot, so much associated with patriarchal history, has been identified with the modern Bir-es-Seba, some thirty miles southwest of Hebron. It afterwards became famous as the southern limit of the Holy Land, in the formula "From Dan to Beer-sheba." For the origin of the name and history see at Gen. xxi, 31; xxvi, 33. Two deep wells are still found there, and a number of smaller ones. The largest well is twelve and a half feet in diameter, and about fifty in depth.

Azem, **30** And Eltolad, and Chesil, and Hormah, **31** And *d* Ziklag, and Madmannah, and Sansannah, **32** And Lebaoth, and Shilhim, and Ain, and Rimmon: all the cities *are* twenty and nine, with their villages. **33** *And* in the valley, *e* Eshtaol, and Zoreah, and Ashnah, **34** And Zanoah, and En-gannim, Tappuah, and Enam, **35** Jarmuth, and Adullam, Socoh, and Azekah, **36** And Sharaim, and Adithaim, and Gederah,

3 and Gederothaim; fourteen cities with their villages: **37** Zenan, and Hadashah, and Migdal-gad, **38** And Dilean, and Mizpeh, *f* and Joktheel, **39** Lachish, and Bozkath, and Eglon, **40** And Cabbon, and Lahmam, and Kithlish, **41** And Gederoth, Beth-dagon, and Naamah, and Makkedah; sixteen cities with their villages: **42** Libnah, and Ether, and Ashan, **43** And Jiphtah, and Ashnah, and Nezib, **44** And Kei-

d 1 Sam. 27. 6.——*e* Num. 13. 23.

3 Or, *or.*——*f* 2 Kings 14. 7.

30. **Hormah**—This is doubtless the same city whose king Joshua smote, and whose original name was *Zephath*. It is located by Robinson and others at the pass *es-Sufah*, far to the south of Hebron; but Palmer, more correctly, identified it with Sebaita some twenty-five miles southwest of Beer-sheba. See note on Judges i, 17.

32. **All the cities are twenty and nine**—This does not agree with the names detailed in the text, which are thirty-six at least. To remove this discrepancy the Rabbins assume that the cities given to Simeon are not counted. But there were twelve or fifteen given to that tribe. Others suggest that several of these places were mere hamlets, and were not counted; or that compound names have been separated, or epithets prefixed been made into names; still others, that one place may have had several names, or that there is an error in the numerical letters for twenty-nine. The Syriac reads thirty-six, an evident change in that version to meet the difficulty. It is more probable that several names were added by a later hand after the country was more thickly peopled, possibly to gratify local pride, and the number twenty-nine was not changed.

33. **In the valley**—Heb., *Shephelah*, the lowland. See on chap. x, 40. These cities are enumerated in four groups. A portion of these in the north was afterwards conceded to Dan. **Eshtaol and Zoreah** afterwards became famous in the tribe of Dan as the scene of Samson's childhood and first daring exploits, (Judges xiii, 25,) and also the place of his burial. Judges xvi, 31. The exact site of Eshtaol is unknown; but Zoreah, or

Zorah, still exists in the modern Surah, just below the summit of a sharp-pointed hill on the north side of the Wady Ghurab. The prospect from the top of this hill is extensive and fine.

34. **Zanoah** is very probably the modern Zanuah, a little to the east of Zorah.

[35. **Jarmuth** was one of the five cities whose kings joined in a league against the Gibeonites, and were defeated in the great battle of Beth-horon. Chap. x, 3. It has been identified with the modern village Yarmuk, about eight miles northeast of Eleutheropolis. It is situated on the crest of a rugged hill, and well named Jarmuth, which means *the lofty.* **Socoh** became afterwards distinguished from being associated with the combat between David and Goliath. 1 Sam. xvii, 1. It was identified by Robinson with the ruins of Shuweikeh, a few miles south of Jarmuth and on the opposite side of the Wady-es-Sumpt.]

36. **Fourteen cities** — Fifteen are enumerated, which discrepancy may be explained as that in verse 32, or by supposing, as is very probable, that the last named city, **Gederothaim,** is an ancient gloss introduced by some confusion of **Gederah** with the *Gederoth* of verse 41.

37–41. This second group of the cities in the Shephelah, sixteen in number, are now nearly all unknown. On **Lachish** and **Eglon,** see chap. x, 3.

42. The third group lay southeast of the second. On **Libnah,** see chap. x, 29.

[43. **Nezib** has been identified by Drs. Robinson and Porter with the ruins of Beit Nusib, about seven miles east of Eleutheropolis, on the way to Hebron. "It is neither in the moun-

lah, and Achzib, and Mareshah; nine cities with their villages: **45** Ekron, with her towns and her villages: **46** From Ekron even unto the sea, all that *lay* [4] near Ashdod, with their villages: **47** Ashdod with her towns and her villages; Gaza with her towns and her villages, unto [g] the river of Egypt, and [h] the great sea, and the border *thereof*.

48 And in the mountains, Shamir, and Jattir, and Socoh, **49** And Dannah, and Kirjath-sannah, which *is* Debir, **50** And Anab, and Eshtemoh, and Anim, **51** [i] And Goshen, and Holon, and Giloh; eleven cities with their villages: **52** Arab, and Dumah, and Eshean, **53** And [5] Janum, and Beth-tappuah, and Aphekah, **54** And Humtah, and

---

4 Heb. *by the place of.*——*g* Verse 4.——*h* Num. 34. 6.——*i* Chap. 10. 41; 11. 16.——5 Or, *Janus.*

---

tains nor in the plain, but in the low hilly country which connects the two. The ruins are of considerable extent. The most important are a massive tower sixty feet square, the masonry of which appears to be of the Jewish type. Near it are the foundations of another great fabric, and the site is strewn with broken columns and large building stones."—*Porter.*]

44. **Keilah** was a walled town not far from Nezib. Its inhabitants were delivered from the oppression of the Philistines by David and his men, who afterwards for a time settled in the town. 1 Sam. xxiii, 1–13. "Eight Roman miles from the ancient Eleutheropolis, on the way to Hebron, is a large ruined tower or castle called *Kela*. It stands on a projecting cliff on the right bank of Wady-el-Feranj. There can be little doubt that this is the long lost Keilah."—*Porter.* [**Achzib** is probably identical with *Chezib*, (Gen. xxxviii, 5,) now Kusaba, fifteen miles southwest of Beit-jibrin. **Mareshah** is supposed by Robinson and Tobler to be the ruins called Marash, one mile and a half south of Beit-jibrin, on a gently-swelling hill leading down from the mountains to the great western plain. The ruins are not extensive, but Robinson thinks they were used in building the neighbouring Eleutheropolis.]

45. The fourth group lay on the Philistine coast, and were then in the possession of the Philistines. **Ekron** —See chap. xiii, note.

47. **Ashdod and Gaza**—See on chaps. xi, 22; x, 41. These cities of the Philistines are thus aggregated, because they were not conquered.

48. **Mountains**—The highlands of Judah were bounded by the lowlands on the west, the wilderness adjacent to

the Dead Sea on the east, the Negeb on the south, and a line touching Jerusalem on the north. At Hebron the land is three thousand feet above the level of the sea. Many fruitful valleys, whose lower declivities are clothed with verdure, wind into the mountain from the lowlands between rugged chalk cliffs. The cities of this district are enumerated in five groups, or, if we accept the text of the Septuagint between verses 59 and 60, we have six groups. **Jattir** Robinson identifies with the ruins of **Attir**, ten miles south of Hebron. **Socoh** must be distinguished from Socoh on the plain. See on verse 35. Robinson recognized it in Shuweikeh, (the diminutive of Shaukeh,) a little northwest of Jattir.

49. **Kirjath-sannah**—The English reader will be assisted in his understanding of many of these names if he remembers that *Kirjath* means *city*. The word following completes the sense, as Kirjath-sannah, city of literature. **Debir**—See on chap. x, 38.

50. **Anab** is still existing northwest of Socoh, without change of name. **Eshtemoh** is probably the modern Semua, "a considerable village, with remains of a wall, built of stones more than ten feet in length."—*Robinson.*

51. **Giloh,** perhaps identical with the modern Rafat, a little south of Eshtemoh, was the birth-place of Ahithophel, and the scene of his suicide. 2 Sam. xv, 12; xvii, 23.

52. This next group of cities was north of the last named, in the vicinity of Hebron. **Dumah**—Robinson passed the ruins of Ed-Daumeh six miles southwest of Hebron, which are probably the remains of this place.

53. **Beth-tappuah,** five miles west of Hebron, is now called Teffuh. It is well peopled, and stands in the midst

Kirjath-arba which *is* Hebron, and
Zior; nine cities with their villages:
55 Maon, Carmel, and Ziph, and Juttah, 56 And Jezreel, and Jokdeam, and

Zanoah, 57 Cain, Gibeah, and Timnah;
ten cities with their villages: 58 Halhul, Beth-zur, and Gedor, 59 And
Maarath, and Bethanoth, and Eltekon;

---

k Chap. 14. 15;   verse 13.

---

of olive groves and vineyards, with
marks of thrift. Portions of an old
wall and fortress are visible among
the houses. **Aphekah** is probably the
same as Aphek. See on chap. xii, 18.

54. **Hebron**—See chap. x, 3, note.

55. The third cluster of mountain
cities lies east of the other two, toward
the desert. **Maon,** modern Main, nine
miles south-southeast of Hebron, is
conspicuously situated on a conical
hill. The summit is crowned with
ruins, foundations of hewn stone, a
square enclosure, and several cisterns.
The view is fine. Many towns of
Judah are in sight. **Carmel,** now
called Kurmul, is a few miles northwest of Maon. Robinson says that
here he found more extensive ruins
than he had yet anywhere seen, unless perhaps at Beth-el. The city was
built in a semicircular amphitheatre
shut in by rocks, in which there is
an artificial reservoir one hundred and
seventeen by seventy-four feet. The
ruins consist chiefly of foundations and
broken walls, scattered in every direction, and thrown together in mournful
confusion and desolation. **Ziph,** modern Zif, five miles southeast of Hebron,
is in ruins. Twice did its treacherous people attempt to betray David,
the youthful outlaw, into the hands of
his persecutor, Saul. 1 Sam. xxiii, 19:
xxvi, 1. **Juttah** is in the vicinity of
Ziph, at the southwest, and is now
called Yutta. Robinson describes it as
having the appearance of a large Mohammedan town, on a low eminence,
with trees around. He agrees with
Reland that this is the city Juda, (Luke
i, 39,) the residence of Zacharias and
Elizabeth, and the birthplace of John
the Baptist. The pronunciation is soft-
ened in the New Testament.

56. **Jezreel** cannot be located. It
was the country of Ahinoam. 1 Sam.
xxv, 43. It must not be confounded
with the city in the plain of Esdraelon.

57. **Gibeah,** meaning *hill,* is identi-

fied by Robinson with Jebah, a village
upon a detached hill in Wady-el-Mu-
surr, ten miles southwest of Jerusalem.
Timnah is a different place from that
near to Adullam, (verses 10 and 35,)
though some have confounded them.

58. **Halhul** still retains its name,
and is found four miles north of Hebron. Here is a ruined mosque, the
reputed sepulchre of the prophet Jonah,
" looking," says Robinson, " much like
the church of a New England village."
Beth-zur, *house of the rock,* is five
miles north of Hebron, and is still
called Beit-zur, the exact Arabic of
the Hebrew name. " Its principal
ruin is the tower, of which only one
side is now standing. There are hewn
stones and fragments of columns scattered about, and many foundations of
buildings."—*Robinson.* The tradition
that Philip baptized the Eunuch here is
improbable, since it is not on the route
from Jerusalem to Gaza. **Gedor** is
identified by Robinson with the modern ruins called Jedur, about eight
miles north of Hebron.

[59. **Bethanoth** is found in the
ruined village Beit-ainun, about three
miles northeast of Hebron. " The
principal ruin is a building eighty-three
feet long and seventy-two broad. The
remains of the town lie on a gentle
slope north of this edifice. The foundations remain, and the streets and
forms of the dwellings can still be
traced."—*Robinson.*]

Between the 59th and 60th verses
the LXX in the Codex Alexandrinus
and Vaticanus insert another group of
eleven cities, namely, *Tekoah, Ephratha*
or *Bethlehem, Phagor, Aitan, Khulan,
Tatam, Thobes, Karem, Galem, Thether,*
and *Manocho.* Whether these cities
have been added by the LXX without
authority, or were really found in the
earliest MSS. of this book, is a question which is not easy to determine.
Hengstenberg maintains the former
opinion and Keil the latter. Some

six cities with their villages: **60** [1] Kirjath-baal which *is* Kirjath-jearim, and Rabbah; two cities with their villages. **61** In the wilderness, Beth-arabah, Middin, and Secacah, **62** And Nibshan, and the city of salt, and En-gedi; six

cities with their villages. **63** As for the Jebusites the inhabitants of Jerusalem, [m] the children of Judah could not drive them out: [n] but the Jebusites dwell with the children of Judah at Jerusalem unto this day.

---

l Chap. 18. 14.——*m* See Judges 1. 8, 21; 2 Sam. 5. 6.——*n* Judges 1 21.

---

find a motive for the erasure of the whole group from the Hebrew text in the desire of the Jews to deny that Jesus sprang from the tribe of Judah.

60. On **Kirjath-baal** see note on chap. ix. 17.

61. **The wilderness**—The wild and rugged territory along the west side of the Dead Sea. Only six cities are mentioned as belonging to this entire district.

62. **En-gedi** is the modern Ain Jidy, on the western shore of the Dead Sea. Here is a rich plain, half a mile square, where are found foundations and heaps of stone. Its vineyards were celebrated by Solomon, its balsam by Josephus, its palms by Pliny.

[63. **The Jebusites**—The hardy and warlike mountaineers who inhabited Jerusalem. They occupied the strongest natural fortress in the country, and it was not until the time of David that they were dispossessed of this their ancient seat. 2 Sam. v, 6–10. **Judah could not drive them out**—Their inability arose from a decay of heroism and perseverance. They failed to meet the condition on which all their successes depended. "Be strong and of good courage." It seems that the united army under Joshua made no direct attempt on Jerusalem after king Adoni-zedek was slain at Makkedah. And when Joshua, by reason of age, ceased to go to war, and the several tribes were left, like Caleb, to subdue and possess their own allotted territory, Judah's courage and faith failed, and the Jebusites continued to dwell among them. They succeeded, however, at one time in capturing and burning the lower city, (Judges i, 8, note,) but the old mountaineers held the high citadel. Benjamin also tried, but ineffectually, to drive them out. Judges i, 21. **Unto this day**—This shows that at the time of the writer David had not yet dislodged the Jebusite from his stronghold, and we must date this book before his day.]

CHAPTER XVI.

Outline of Joseph's Lot, 1–4.

[Chapters XVI and XVII belong together, and describe the allotment made to the house of Joseph, composed of the two powerful tribes of Ephraim and Manasseh. "We are so familiar," says Stanley, "with the supremacy of the tribe of Judah, that we are apt to forget that it was of comparatively recent date. For more than four hundred years—a period equal in length to that which elapsed between the Norman Conquest and the Wars of the Roses—Ephraim, with its two dependent tribes of Manasseh and Benjamin, exercised undisputed preëminence. Joshua, the first conqueror; Gideon, the greatest of the judges, whose brothers were 'as the children of kings,' and whose children all but established hereditary monarchy in their own line; Saul, the first king, belonged to one or the other of these three tribes.

"It was not till the close of the first period of Jewish history that God 'refused the tabernacle of Joseph, and chose not the tribe of Ephraim: but chose the tribe of Judah, even the Mount Zion which he loved.' Psa. lxxviii, 67. That haughty spirit which could brook no equal or superior, which chafed against the rise even of the kindred tribe of Manasseh, in the persons of Gideon and Jephthah, (Judges viii, 1; xii, 1,) and yet more against the growing dominion of Judah in David and Solomon, till it threw off the yoke altogether and established an independent kingdom, would naturally claim, and could not rightly be refused, the choicest portion of the land.

CHAPTER XVI.

AND the lot of the children of Joseph [1] fell from Jordan by Jericho, unto the water of Jericho on the east, to

1 Heb. *went forth.*

Blessed of the Lord be his land; for the precious things of heaven, for the dew, and for the deep that coucheth beneath, and for the precious fruits brought forth by the sun, and for the precious things put forth by the moon, and for the chief things of the ancient mountains, and for the precious things of the lasting hills, and for the precious things of the earth and the fulness thereof, and for the good will of him that dwelt in the bush, let the blessing come upon the head of Joseph.' If Judah was the wild lion that guarded the south, and couched in the fastness of Zion, so Ephraim was to be the more peaceful but not less powerful buffalo, who was to rove the rich vales of Central Palestine, and defend the frontier of the north.

His glory is like the firstling of his bullock, and his horns are like the horns of unicorns, (buffaloes;) with them shall he push the people together to the ends of the earth, and they are the ten thousands of Ephraim, and they are the thousands of Manasseh.' " Deut. xxxiii, 13–17.

1. **Children of Joseph**—That is, Ephraim and the western half of Manasseh. Their lots were first drawn together that these brothers might be contiguous, but there was a subsequent division of their joint territory. **The lot...fell**—Hebrew, *went forth;* that is, from the urn in which the lots were cast. See note on chap. xiii, 6. "It is remarkable that of the whole inheritance assigned to the children of Joseph only the southern boundary is given. But this may be explained partly on the ground that this double tribe had no definite boundary on the north, but merely had a number of cities allotted to them within the line which formed the boundary of Asher and Issachar. (chap. xvii, 10, 11.) and partly from the fact that the Josephites did not expel the Canaanites from the northern part of the territory

the wilderness that goeth up from Jericho throughout mount Beth-el. 2 And goeth out from Beth-el to [a] Luz, and passeth along unto the borders of Archi to

a Chap. 18. 13; Judges 1. 26.

assigned them, but only gradually brought them into subjection and dwelt among them. Hence the limits of their land in this direction were not always the same; and at one time, when they expressed some discontent at the portion allotted to them, Joshua told them that they might enlarge their possessions if they could drive out the Canaanites. Chap. xvii, 12–18."—*Keil.* **From Jordan by Jericho**—Literally, *Jordan of Jericho;* that is, a part of the Jordan directly opposite Jericho, and which might therefore be regarded as belonging especially to Jericho. **The water of Jericho**—This has been commonly understood of the fountain Es Sultan, a mile northwest of Riha, and probably the scene of Elisha's miracle. 2 Kings ii, 19–22. As the border ran on the north side of Jericho, (chap. xviii, 12,) and **on the east of the wilderness,** (for so the Hebrew should here be rendered,) it seems to have turned northward from the **water of Jericho,** and went up so far as to include in Benjamin's territory Zemaraim, the modern Es Sumra, about five miles north of Jericho. Accordingly we understand this border between Ephraim and Benjamin to have commenced at a point of the Jordan directly opposite Jericho, perhaps at the mouth of Wady Nawaimeh, and, running westward, fetched a curve near Jericho and its great fountain, thence, passing northward along the eastern side of the wilderness that stretches east of Beth-el, it went up to Es Sumrah, and then passed westward to Ophni, the modern Jifna, which was also assigned to Benjamin. Chap. xviii, 24.] **The wilderness**—The wild region of country that lies on the east of Beth-el, and is called in chap. xviii, 12, the wilderness of Beth-aven. **Mount Beth-el**—The mountain range on which Beth-el was situated.

2. **From Beth-el to Luz**—Beth-el and Luz were the same city. See note

Ataroth, **3** And goeth down westward to the coast of Japhleti, [b] unto the coast of Beth-horon the nether, and to [c] Gezer: and the goings out thereof are at the sea. **4** [d] So the children of Joseph, Manasseh and Ephraim, took their inheritance.

5 And the border of the children of Ephraim according to their families was

thus: even the border of their inheritance on the east side was [e] Ataroth-addar, [f] unto Beth-horon the upper; **6** And the border went out toward the sea to [g] Michmethah on the north side; and the border went about eastward unto Taanath-shiloh, and passed by it on the east to Janohah; **7** And it went down from Janohah to Ataroth, [h] and to

b Chap. 18. 13; 2 Chron. 8. 5.——*c* 1 Chron. 7. 28; 1 Kings 9. 15.——*d* Chap. 17. 14.

e Chap. 18. 13.——*f* 2 Chron. 8. 5.——*g* Chap. 17. 7. *h* 1 Chron. 7. 28.

on chap. vii, 2. The **Beth-el** of the text is to be understood of the Mount Bethel named in the preceding verse. **Borders of Archi**—Or, *of the Archite.* No trace of this name is found in the vicinity of Beth-el. Perhaps in this name we have the last faint trace of one of the original Canaanitish tribes. **Ataroth** is supposed by Dr. Robinson to be identical with a large village called Atara, on the summit of a hill about six miles northwest of Beth-el; [but this verse and chap. xviii, 13 seem rather to place it between Beth-el and Beth-horon, so that we may rather identify it with the Atara which lies some three miles south of Beth-el. Here Robinson noticed considerable ruins of an ancient town. At Ataroth the border turned westward toward Beth-horon.]

3. On **Japhleti,** or the *Japhletite,* the note on **Archi** (verse 2) will also apply. On **Beth-horon** see at chap. x, 10, and **Gezer,** chap. x, 33. **The sea**—The Mediterranean.

EPHRAIM'S BORDERS, 5–10.

[This outline of Ephraim's borders has evidences of being merely a fragment, and much corrupted at that. All scholars have acknowledged the difficulty of reconciling its different statements, and all attempts at emendation are at best conjectural.

5. **The border...on the east side was Ataroth-addar**—We understand Ataroth-addar to be identical with the Ataroth of verses 2 and 7. At this point the border between Ephraim and Benjamin went northward towards Bethel, and westward towards Beth-horon, so that it was regarded as a prominent point in Ephraim's *eastern* border, where it joined the western border of Benjamin. **Unto Beth-horon**

the upper—Before these words something seems to have fallen out of the text. The words themselves evidently belong to the southern border, for the upper Beth-horon was about five miles directly west of Ataroth.

6. **And the border went out toward the sea** — The Mediterranean. Here the sentence should end, for **to Michmethah** evidently belongs to the northern boundary, and to another sentence. **Toward the sea,** then, completes the account of the boundary in the southwest. We would commence a new sentence with the word **Michmethah,** and render, *Michmethah was on the north side.* Or perhaps it would be better to emend the reading by means of the parallel in chap. xvii, 7, and read, *The border was from Asher to Michmethah on the north.* Michmethah is there said to lie *before Shechem,* but that is indefinite. It is generally supposed to have been northeast of Shechem, but the exact site is unknown. **Went about**—That is, fetched a circuit, or slightly turned its course, **eastward unto Taanath-shiloh.** This is not improbably identical with Ain Tana, about eight miles southeast of Shechem. **Janohah** is still preserved in the village of Yanun, about two miles south of Ain Tana. Van de Velde says that "entire houses and walls of the ancient city are still existing, but covered with immense heaps of earth and rubbish."

7. **From Janohah to Ataroth**—In this verse we have a confusion of the northern and southern borders, resulting doubtless from some transposition in the text. We propose to read, **and it went down from Janohah, and went out at Jordan,** and regard the words **to Ataroth and to Naa-**

Naarath, and came to Jericho, and went out at Jordan. 8 The border went out from Tappuah westward unto the [i] river Kanah; and the goings out thereof were at the sea. This *is* the inheritance of the tribe of the children of Ephraim by their families. 9 And [k] the separate cities for the children of Ephraim *were* among the inheritance of the children of Manasseh, all the cities with their villages. 10 [l] And they drave not out

---

i Chap. 17. 9.——*k* Chap. 17. 9.——*l* Judg. 1. 29; see 1 Kings 9. 16.

---

rath, and came to Jericho, as a fragment transposed from its proper place in the text, and its immediate connexion lost.

8. **From Tappuah westward unto the river Kanah** — This is a completion of the northern boundary westward from the central ridge of Palestine. The site of **Tappuah** is unknown. **The river Kanah** is uncertain. Robinson identifies it with a wady still bearing the name Kanah, which rises south of Shechem and runs southwest. and empties into the Mediterranean four miles north of Joppa. But this is too far south to be a boundary between Ephraim and Manasseh. Compare chap. xvii, 8, 9. It is more probably identical with the Wady Kassab, (stream of reeds,) which falls into the sea nearly west of Shechem.

9. **Separate cities**—That is, cities separated or selected out of Manasseh for the use of Ephraim. Of these only Tappuah is named in chap. xvii, 8, 9. Compare also 1 Chron. vii, 28, 29. It is generally supposed, that when the boundary lines had been drawn, the territory of Ephraim was found not as large proportionally as his numbers and importance demanded. But the relation of Ephraim and Manasseh was such that they might be regarded as having one lot. Compare chap. xvii, 14. Hence they held many cities in common. and hence too, perhaps, the reason why no complete enumeration of the cities of these two brother tribes is anywhere given.]

10. **The Canaanites that dwelt in Gezer**—These held their ancient seat until the days of Solomon. 1 Kings ix, 16. Compare Judges i, 29. **Under**

the Canaanites that dwelt in Gezer: but the Canaanites dwell among the Ephraimites unto this day, and serve under tribute.

CHAPTER XVII.

THERE was also a lot for the tribe of Manasseh; for he *was* the [a] firstborn of Joseph; *to wit*, for [b] Machir the firstborn of Manasseh, the father of Gilead: because he was a man of war,

---

a Gen. 41. 51; 46. 20; 48. 18.——*b* Gen. 50. 23; Num. 26. 29; 32. 39, 40; 1 Chron. 7. 14.

---

tribute—This implies the power to extirpate, but instead of this a fatal compromise was made. Josephus explains the reason: "After this the Israelites grew effeminate as to fighting any more against their enemies, but applied themselves to agriculture, which producing abundance and riches, they indulged in luxury and pleasure, and, contenting themselves with the tributes that were paid them. permitted the Canaanites to live in peace."

CHAPTER XVII.

Manasseh's lot in Western Palestine, 1–13.

1. **Manasseh,** the firstborn of Joseph, and retaining the rights of primogeniture, is put second because of Ephraim's political superiority. Compare note at the beginning of chap. xvi. Thus the prophetic words of their grandfather Jacob are fulfilled: "Ephraim will be greater than Manasseh." Gen. xlviii, 5, 14–19. **Machir** designates not the man but the family. His descendants, Jair and Nobah. conquered Bashan. Num. xxxii. 41. 42. The portion of the half tribe of Manasseh east of the Jordan is here brought in to give a complete view of the settlement of that tribe. See note on chap. xiii, 29. **For he was the firstborn of Manasseh**—And therefore was honourably entitled to a share of the good land promised to the fathers. **The father of Gilead**—Literally. *the father of the Gilead;* that is. the country, as designated by the Hebrew article. He had a son by that name. Num. xxvi. 29. The term **father,** when followed by the name of a country, signifies *lord* or *possessor,* and is

therefore he had [c] Gilead and Bashan.
2 There was also *a lot* for [d] the rest of
the children of Manasseh by their families; [e] for the children of [1] Abiezer, and
for the children of Helek, [f] and for the
children of Asriel, and for the children
of Shechem, [g] and for the children of
Hepher, and for the children of Shemi-
da: these *were* the male children of Manasseh the son of Joseph by their families. **3** But [h] Zelophehad, the son of
Hepher, the son of Gilead, the son of
Machir, the son of Manasseh, had no
sons, but daughters: and these *are* the
names of his daughters, Mahlah, and
Noah, Hoglah, Milcah, and Tirzah.
4 And they came near before [i] Eleazar
the priest, and before Joshua the son of
Nun, and before the princes, saying,
[k] The LORD commanded Moses to give
us an inheritance among our brethren.

Therefore, according to the commandment of the LORD, he gave them an inheritance among the brethren of their
father. **5** And there fell ten portions
to Manasseh, beside the land of Gilead
and Bashan, which *were* on the other
side Jordan; **6** Because the daughters
of Manasseh had an inheritance among
his sons: and the rest of Manasseh's
sons had the land of Gilead. **7** And
the coast of Manasseh was from Asher
to [l] Michmethah, that *lieth* before Shechem; and the border went along on
the right hand unto the inhabitants of
En-tappuah. **8** *Now* Manasseh had the
land of Tappuah: but [m] Tappuah on the
border of Manasseh *belonged* to the children of Ephraim; **9** And the coast descended [n] unto the [2] river Kanah, southward of the river: [o] these cities of
Ephraim *are* among the cities of Manas-

---

[c] Deut. 3. 15.——[d] Num. 26. 29–32.——[e] 1 Chron.
7. 18.——1 Num. 26. 30, *Jeeser*.——[f] Num. 26.
31.——[g] Num. 26. 32.——[h] Num. 26. 33; 27. 1; 36.2.

[i] Chap. 14. 1.——[k] Num. 27. 6. 7.——[l] Chap.
16. 6.——[m] Chap. 16. 8.——[n] Chap. 16. 8.——
2 Or, *brook of reeds*.——[o] Chap. 16. 9.

---

usually applied to the conqueror of
the country. The Machirites had already received their portion east of
Jordan. See chap. xiii, 29–33.

**2. The rest of the children of
Manasseh**—That is, as the next two
verses explain, the descendants of the
five sons named, and also of the five
daughters of Hepher, whose son Zelophehad had no male children. The western lot was thus divided into ten portions, (verse 5,) because there were
claimants through five males and five
females, the latter being descendants of
Hepher. The claim of the latter had
been at one time a matter of doubt, as
the question of woman's rights has
been a matter of dispute in all countries. But Moses had very wisely
carried the question to the Lord for
his decision, who recognized their rights
as inheritors. Num. xxvii, 6, 7.

4. Before Eleazar—As one of the
commission to divide the land. Chap.
xiv, 1.

[5. **Ten portions**—Or, *ten measure-
ments*, alluding to the custom of meas-
uring off land with a line or a chain.
Since each of the five daughters of
Zelophehad obtained a portion, neither
Hepher nor Zelophehad are reckoned.

7. **Coast of Manasseh**—The southern boundary from east to west. "The
author gives the boundary again from

east to west, as in the case of Judah, (chap. xv, 2.ff,) the sons of Joseph-
(xvi. 1,ff,) and Benjamin, xviii, 12.ff.
So the author of the Apocalypse, also,
names the gates of the New Jerusalem, beginning from the east, (Rev.
xxi. 13,) and Ezekiel (xlviii, 1,ff) designates the several tribe divisions in
the like manner from east to west."—
Fay.] **Asher** is here not the portion
of the tribe, which could not constitute a starting point for a line, but a
city, probably the modern Yasir, about
half way between Shechem and Beth-
shean, or about fifteen miles northeast
of the former city. For **Michmethah**
and **river Kanah**, see on chap. xvi,
6–8. **Shechem** is a very ancient city,
called Neapolis, corrupted to Nabulus
and Nablus, in the narrow valley between Mounts Ebal and Gerizim. See
note and cuts at John iv, 5. "The
streets are narrow; the houses high
and in general well built, all of stone,
with domes upon the roofs, as at Jerusalem."—*Robinson*. **En-tappuah** some
understand of a fountain near the city
of Tappuah, (chap. xvi, 8;) others, as
another name of the city itself. The
land of Tappuah mentioned in the
next verse must mean the country in
the neighbourhood of Tappuah.

9. **Cities of Ephraim are among the
cities of Manasseh**—Compare chap.

seh: the coast of Manasseh also *was* on the north side of the river, and the outgoings of it were at the sea: **10** Southward *it was* Ephraim's, and northward *it was* Manasseh's, and the sea is his border; and they met together in Asher on the north, and in Issachar on the east. **11** *p*And Manasseh had in Issachar and in Asher *q*Beth-shean and her towns, and Ibleam and her towns, and the inhabitants of Dor and her towns, and the inhabitants of Endor and her towns, and the inhabitants of Taanach and her towns, and the inhabitants of Megiddo and her towns, *even* three countries. **12** Yet *r*the children of Manasseh could not drive out *the inhabitants of* those cities; but the Canaanites would dwell in that land. **13** Yet it came to pass, when the children of Israel were waxen strong, that they put the Canaanites to *s*tribute: but did not utterly drive them out.

14 *t*And the children of Joseph spake unto Joshua, saying, Why hast thou given me *but* *u*one lot and one portion

p 1 Chron. 7. 29.——*q* 1 Sam. 31. 10; 1 Kings 4. 12. *r* Judges 1. 27, 28.

s Chap. 16. 10.——*t* Chap. 16. 4. *u* Gen. 48. 22.

xvi, 8, note. "The line which separated the possessions of the two brothers ran to the south of the river Kenath, but the cities which were upon the river were assigned partly to Ephraim and partly to Manasseh; those upon the south being assigned to the former, and those upon the north to the latter."—*Masius.* In verse 10 we find Manasseh interlaced with other border tribes.

10. Met together in Asher—Touched upon, bordered on, (literally, *struck.*) Asher on the north, etc.

11. Beth-shean—*House of rest;* the halting place for caravans from Syria or Midian to Egypt. and the emporium for the commerce of these countries. It afterwards was called in the Greek Scythopolis, and is identified with the modern Beisan. at the east end of the plain of Esdraelon, five miles west of the Jordan "The site of the ancient city, as of the modern village, was a splendid one, in this vast area of plain and mountain, in the midst of abundant waters and of exuberant fertility. It must have been a city of temples."—*Robinson.* **Ibleam** was near Megiddo, (2 Kings ix, 27,) but its exact site is unknown. **Dor**—See on chap. xi, 2. **Endor,** the abode of the necromancer consulted by Saul, (1 Sam. xxviii, 7, note,) is now a village of the same name, nearly four miles south of Mount Tabor. For **Taanach** and **Megiddo** see on chap. xii. 21. [It is noticeable that after the mention of **Ibleam and her towns,** in this verse, the **inhabitants** of the next four cities are named as a possession of Manasseh. This sudden transition, and the introduction

of the accusative sign אֶת before **inhabitants,** have greatly perplexed critics. It seems best, with Knobel, to suppose that the idea of possession conveyed by the English version, (*Manasseh had,*) and also by וַיְהִי לְ at the beginning of the verse in the Hebrew, is carried over in the writer's mind, and applied to the inhabitants of these towns as being Manasseh's possession, and rendering a tribute service. **Three countries**—Or, a *triple province,* having a sort of political combination. Others render *three heights,* and understand that the last three cities stood on hills, "a tripolis of mountain cities, in distinction from the places on the plain." —*Fay.*]

12. Could not drive out—See on chap. xv, 63, and xvi, 10.

COMPLAINT OF THE CHILDREN OF JOSEPH, 14–18.

[According to Ewald, this passage is "one of the most remarkable relics of the oldest historical composition. The narration almost stammers, as if it had yet to learn an easy flow. Its prose is as rough and hard as a stone." The event described probably occurred some time after the Josephites had received their portion, and when Joshua was dwelling in Timnath-serah. Chap. xix, 50.]

14. The children of Joseph—Both tribes selfishly combine to bring to bear upon Joshua, a fellow-tribesman, the pressure of their influence to secure an addition to their portion.

to inherit, seeing I *am* ᵛa great people, forasmuch as the LORD hath blessed me hitherto? 15 And Joshua answered them, If thou *be* a great people, *then* get thee up to the wood *country*, and cut down for thyself there in the land of the Perizzites and of the ³giants, if mount Ephraim be too narrow for thee. 16 And the children of Joseph said, The hill is not enough for us: and all the Canaanites that dwell in the land of the valley have ᵂchariots of iron, *both they* who *are* of Beth-shean and her towns, and *they* who *are* ˣ of the valley of Jezreel. 17 And Joshua spake unto the house of Joseph, *even* to Ephraim and to Manasseh, saying, Thou *art* a great people, and hast great power: thou shalt not have one lot *only*: 18 But the mountain shall be thine; for it *is* a

---

ᵛGen. 48. 19; Num. 26. 34, 37.——3 Or, *Rephaim*, Gen. 14. 5; 15. 20.

ᵂ Judges 1. 19; 4. 3.——ˣ Chap. 19. 18; 1 Kings 4. 12.

One lot—The intimation is, that while Joshua professes to treat them as two independent tribes, he has really given them a lot only sufficient for one. **The Lord hath blessed me hitherto**—A reference to their tribal supremacy. See note introductory to chap. xvi.

15. **If thou be a great people**—Here is notable irony, but no "mockery," as Ewald assumes. The great captain could wield cutting sarcasm as well as deadly weapons. It is the best medicine for conceit and self-adulation. Joshua, in his management of this matter, shows great breadth of view and freedom from partisan bias. His own tribe shall receive no more than even-handed justice had allotted. **The wood** is either the region of Mount Gilboa, west of Beth-shean, or that between Shechem and Carmel. [The ancient forests, which thickly covered these mountains and hills, are referred to in 1 Sam. xiv, 25; 2 Sam. xviii, 6. Ewald understands **the wood** metaphorically of the multitude of tall Perizzites and giants, whom these brave Josephites are counselled to cut down.] **And cut down**—Either the forests, or the gigantic foemen who have possession of them, or both. Enlarge your territories for yourselves by your bravery, and thus show that ye are really a great people. **Giants**—*Rephaim.* See on chap. xii, 4. **Mount Ephraim**—This complaint of the Josephites was probably not made immediately after the allotment, but some time later, when the mountainous tract of Ephraim had become commonly designated by the name of this tribe.

16. **The hill is not enough**—And yet they wanted more hill. They did not wish to go into the valleys.

Chariots of iron—Strengthened with iron, and possibly armed with scythes. The timidity and lack of trust in Jehovah evinced by these Josephites is most clearly seen when viewed in the light of the specific command and promise of God: "When thou goest out to battle against thine enemies, and seest *horses and chariots* and a people more than thou, be not afraid of them, for the Lord thy God is with thee." Deut. xx, 1. **Beth-shean**—Verse 11. [**The valley of Jezreel**—That noble and beautiful plain, the richest and most celebrated in Palestine, called in its Greek form Esdraelon, and associated with many of the most famous events of sacred and of common history. It has the form of a triangle, whose base runs fifteen miles southwesterly from the foot of Mount Tabor, and whose southwest side sweeps along the base of Mount Carmel to the Mediterranean Sea. The sons of Joseph were afraid to cope with the inhabitants of this valley, and wanted more territory among the hills. **The valley of Jezreel** was, strictly speaking, the eastern branch of Esdraelon, running towards the Jordan along the Wady Jalud.]

17. **Joshua spake**—The old hero still remains firm, and continues to answer only by yet more stinging irony. **Thou shalt not have one lot only**—Thy unconquered territory even in the mountains shall be another lot, if only thou art a great people enough to take it.

18. **The mountain**—The same as the wood, verse 15, and referring probably to Gilboa. **The outgoings of it**—"The fields and the plains bordering upon the wood."—*Keil.* "The defiles and avenues of approach."—

wood, and thou shalt cut it down : and the outgoings of it shall be thine : for thou shalt drive out the Canaanites, *though* they have iron chariots, *and though* they *be* strong.

---

y Deut. 20. 1.—*a* Chap. 19. 51 ; 21. 2 ; 22. 9 ; Jer.

Bush. "Extremities."—*Fürst.* [**Though they have iron chariots, and though they be strong**—It is altogether better to translate the word כִּי, here twice rendered **though,** by its ordinary meaning. *for.* This particle occurs five times in this verse, and has the same causal meaning every time. Render: *For the mountain is thine ; for it is a forest and thou shalt cut it down, and thine shall be its outgoings ; for thou shalt drive out the Canaanite ; for iron chariots are his ! for strong is he !* The force of Joshua's words is in the irony they contain. The meaning is, *Because* the Canaanite has iron chariots and is so mighty, therefore **thou**—a great people —ought to glory in driving him out. He is a foeman worthy of thy steel.]

CHAPTER XVIII.
The Tabernacle Erected at Shiloh, 1.

The location of the tribes was not yet completed, but it had proceeded so far that it was desirable that the tabernacle should be permanently established in a central place. This could not well be accomplished till Ephraim, in whose borders it was to be located, had received his portion.

1. **Shiloh**—*Rest ;* the first national capital and sanctuary in Palestine. Bethel, "the house of God," from its sacred name and associations, would probably have been selected if it had not been in the hands of the Canaanites. Shiloh, now *Seilun,* remarkable for its seclusion, not for its natural strength or beauty, is situated near the central thoroughfare of Palestine, twenty miles north of Jerusalem and ten south of Nablus. [Tristram describes the modern site as " a mass of shapeless ruins, scarcely distinguishable from the rugged rocks around them, with large hewn stones occasionally marking the site of ancient

CHAPTER XVIII.

AND the whole congregation of the children of Israel assembled together *a* at Shiloh, and *b* set up the

---

7. 12.—*b* Judges 18. 31 ; 1 Sam. 1. 3, 24 ; 4. 3, 4.

---

walls. There is one square ruin, probably a mediæval fortress-church, with a few broken Corinthian columns, the relics of previous grandeur. Straggling valleys, too open to be termed glens, within an amphitheatre of dreary round-topped hills, bare and rocky, without being picturesque, are the only characteristics of this featureless scene." This same writer thus discusses the question why so unattractive a spot as Shiloh should have been chosen as the religious centre of Israel for so many generations : " One reason may probably be found in this very natural unattractiveness, inasmuch as it was a protest against the idolatry of the people of the land, which selected every high hill and every noble grove as the special home of their gods ; here being neither commanding peak nor majestic cedar, neither deep glen nor gushing fountain. Moreover, it was a central point for all Israel, equidistant from north to south, easily accessible to the trans-Jordanic tribes, and in the heart of that hill-country which Joshua first subdued, and which remained to the end of Israel's history the district least exposed to the attacks of Canaanitish or foreign invaders."] Here the remaining seven tribes received their allotments, here the yearly feasts were held, and here the ark remained more than three hundred and fifty years, till taken by the Philistines. 1 Sam. iv, 1–11. The place was afterwards forsaken and accursed of God. Psa. lxxviii, 60 ; Jer. vii, 12–14, and xxvi, 6. **Tabernacle**—This was, according to the rabbinical representation, still a tent, or, rather, a low structure of stones with a tent drawn over it. " Although a city grew round it, and a stone gateway rose in front of it, yet it still retained its name ' *camp* of Shiloh ' and the ' *tent* that God had pitched among men.' "—*Stanley.* Its structure is described in Exod. xxv, xxvi.

tabernacle of the congregation there: and the land was subdued before them.

2 And there remained among the children of Israel seven tribes, which had not yet received their inheritance. **3** And Joshua said unto the children of Israel, ^cHow long *are* ye slack to go to possess the land, which the LORD God of your fathers hath given you? **4** Give out from among you three men for *each* tribe: and I will send them, and they shall rise, and go through the land, and describe it according to the inheritance of them; and they shall come *again* to me. **5** And they shall divide it into seven parts: ^dJudah shall abide in their coast on the south, and ^ethe house of Joseph shall abide in their coasts on the north. **6** Ye shall therefore describe the land *into* seven parts, and bring *the description* hither to me, ^fthat I may cast lots for you here before the LORD our God. **7** ^gBut the Levites have no part among you; for the priesthood of the LORD *is* their inheritance: ^hand Gad, and Reuben, and half the tribe of Manasseh, have received their inheritance beyond Jordan on the east, which

---

c Judges 18. 9; Eccles. 9. 10; Zeph. 3. 16. *d* Chap. 15. 1.——*e* Chap. 16. 1, 4.

f Chap. 14. 2; verse 10.——*g* Chap. 13. 33. *h* Chap. 13. 8.

THE FURTHER SURVEY AND DIVISION OF THE LAND, 2–10.

[We are not to understand that this survey consisted of an exact geographical measurement of the land, nor that it was made with a view to define the precise boundaries of the remaining tribes. It was to gain a fuller information on the topography of the country and the qualities of the different sections. See note on verse 4. Hence the objection of some, that the Canaanites still remaining in the land would not have allowed twenty-one men to pass through and measure their districts, is of no force. These men passed through the land, and took a list of the cities, arranging them into seven groups or parts, (verse 9,) and thus prepared the way for casting lots for them at Shiloh. Whether they were at all molested in taking this survey is not said.]

2. Seven tribes—There seem to have been two causes for this delay in the allotment to these tribes: (1) The fondness for a roving life which these tribes had acquired, and their indisposition to settle down in agricultural pursuits; (2) But chiefly the fact that from the hasty character of the first survey it was found that the lot of Judah, already assigned, was too large, and a new and more accurate survey must be made. With respect to the first cause Bush says: "What a striking picture of the too common apathy and sluggishness of the candidate for the heavenly inheritance! Who does not find that corruptions gather strength by indulgence, and that graces decay for want of exercise? Therefore let us look to ourselves that we lose not the things that we have wrought."

4. Give out—Heb., *appoint.* The commission of twenty-one was fairly constituted; each tribe was equally represented. **[Describe it** — Write down in a book (compare verse 9) a list of the cities, and a description of the different localities. and, as Rosenmüller observes, "what lands were barren, and what were fertile; whether a district were hilly or flat, whether well watered or destitute of springs, and any thing else which served to show the goodness of the soil, and the comparative worth of different localities." **According to the inheritance of them**—That is, with reference to its being divided as an inheritance of the remaining seven tribes.] Josephus says, "Joshua thought the land should be divided by estimation of its goodness, rather than the largeness of its measure." For the adjustment of the lots to the size of the tribes, see on chap. xiii, 6.

5. Judah shall abide—That is, shall maintain the same relative position, but not necessarily the same amount. See chap. xix, 9, where Simeon's portion is taken out of Judah's, to produce equality.

6. Before the Lord—Before the tabernacle at Shiloh, (verse 10,) in which dwelt the Shekinah, the Divine Presence.

7. Levites have no part—See on chap. xiii, 33.

Moses the servant of the LORD gave them. 8 And the men arose, and went away: and Joshua charged them that went to describe the land, saying, [i] Go and walk through the land, and describe it, and come again to me, that I may here cast lots [k] for you before the LORD in Shiloh. 9 And the men went and passed through the land, and described it by cities into [l] seven parts in a book, and came *again* to Joshua to the host at Shiloh. 10 And Joshua cast [m] lots for them in Shiloh before the LORD: and there Joshua divided the land unto the children of Israel according to their divisions.

11 And the lot of the tribe of the children of Benjamin came up according to their families: and the coast of their lot came forth between the children of Judah and the children of Joseph. 12 [n] And their border on the north side was from Jordan; and the border went up to the side of Jericho on the north side, and went up through the mountains westward; and the goings out thereof were at the wilderness of Beth-aven. 13 And the border went over from thence toward Luz, to the side of Luz [o] which *is* Beth-el, southward; and the border descended to Ataroth-addar, near the hill that *lieth* on the south side [p] of the nether Beth-horon. 14 And the border was drawn

---

[i] Gen. 13. 17.——[k] 1 Sam. 14. 41; Acts 1. 24, 26.
[l] Acts 13. 19.——[m] Prov. 18. 18; Ezek. 47. 22.

[n] See chap. 16. 1.——[o] Gen. 28. 19; Judges 1. 23.
[p] Chap. 16. 3.

---

9. [**Seven parts in a book**—The cities and districts were divided into seven parts or groups, and described in a written document. Herodotus (II, 109) thought that land-surveying had its origin in Egypt, and thence passed over into Greece, and in Egypt the Hebrews may have acquired some knowledge of this art; but, as shown above, we need not understand this description of the Israelitish territory as a scientific survey.] **Came again to Joshua**—We have no note of the time occupied by the survey. Josephus says seven months, while the Rabbins say seven years. **To the host** —The Israelitish camp, which assembled **at Shiloh** to witness this allotment of the rest of the land.

BENJAMIN'S LOT, 11–28.

Benjamin's lot lay on the south of the sons of Joseph, so that the descendants of Rachel were all adjoining, and in the very heart of the land. As Benjamin's lot included Mount Moriah, the site of the sacred edifice, we find here a remarkable fulfilment of the prophecy in Deut. xxxiii, 12. "Hemmed in as it was between the two powerful neighbours of Ephraim and Judah, the tribe of Benjamin, nevertheless, retained a character of its own, eminently indomitable and insubordinate. The wolf which nursed the founders of Rome was not more evidently repeated in the martial qualities of the people of Romulus, than the wolf to which Benjamin is compared in his father's blessing, (Gen. xlix, 27.) appears in the eager, restless character of his descendants."—*Stanley*.

11. **Lot...of Benjamin came up** —"The lot comes up when it is drawn out of the urn."—*Masius*.

12. **Their border on the north side** was identical with the south border of Ephraim, (chap. xvi, 1–13,) as far as Lower Beth-horon.

13. [**Went over from thence**—According to our note on chap. xvi, 1, this **border** turned off north of Jericho, and ran up so as to take in Zemaraim, (verse 22;) thence it passed westward to Ophni, (verse 24,) where it curved to the south so as to run down near Beth-el. **To the side of Luz... southward**—Literally, *to the shoulder of Luz*, that is, some eminence in the vicinity. **Southward** here does not mean that the border ran on the south side of Beth-el, but it designates the general course of the border as it passed near Beth-el. **Descended to Ataroth-addar**—That is, the border ran southward by the side of Luz as far as Ataroth.] See notes on chap. xvi, 5, 6. **The nether Beth-horon** still exists in the modern Beit-Ur-el-Tahta, situated on the top of a low ridge, which is separated by a narrow valley from the mountain on which the Upper Beth-horon stands. See note on chap. x, 10. South of this rises an eminence which is doubtless **the hill** here referred to.

thence, and compassed the corner of the sea southward, from the hill that *lieth* before Beth-horon southward; and the goings out thereof were at ^q Kirjath-baal which *is* Kirjath-jearim, a city of the children of Judah: this *was* the west quarter. **15** And the south quarter *was* from the end of Kirjath-jearim, and the border went out on the west, and went out to ^r the well of waters of Nephtoah. **16** And the border came down to the end of the mountain that *lieth* before ^s the valley of the son of Hinnom, *and* which *is* in the valley of the giants on the north, and descended to the valley of Hinnom, to the side of Jebusi on the south, and descended to ^t En-rogel, **17** And was drawn from the north, and went forth to En-shemesh, and went forth toward Geliloth, which

is over against the going up of Adummim, and descended to ^u the stone of Bohan the son of Reuben, **18** And passed along toward the side over against ^{v 1} Arabah northward, and went down unto Arabah: **19** And the border passed along to the side of Beth-hoglah northward: and the outgoings of the border were at the north ² bay of the salt sea at the south end of Jordan: this *was* the south coast. **20** And Jordan was the border of it on the east side. This *was* the inheritance of the children of Benjamin, by the coasts thereof round about, according to their families. **21** Now the cities of the tribe of the children of Benjamin according to their families were Jericho, and Beth-hoglah, and the valley of Keziz, **22** And Beth-arabah, and Zemaraim, and Beth-el,

---

q See chap. 15. 9.——*r* Chap. 15. 9.——*s* Chap. 15. 8.
t Chap. 15. 7.

u Chap. 15. 6.——*v* Chap. 15. 6.——1 Or, *The plain.*——2 Heb. *tongue.*

[14. **Compassed the corner of the sea southward**—Rather, *turned toward the side of the sea southward.* The meaning is simply that from the Lower Beth-horon Benjamin's western border turned southward towards the sea. It did not run *unto* the sea, as some have thought, nor is the reference here to Ephraim's border, which ran off from this point unto the Mediterranean. Dr. Thomson needlessly supposes that the pool of Gibeon is the sea here intended. But in giving these boundaries the word *sea* is so constantly used of the Mediterranean that it is very arbitrary to take it in this single instance in so limited a sense. **The goings out** of Benjamin's western border were not at the sea, but **at Kirjath-baal which is Kirjath-jearim.** On this city see note at chap. ix, 17. It lay almost directly south of Beth-horon, so that we must understand Benjamin's western border to have formed a curve turning from Beth-horon first seaward and then winding gradually round to Kirjath-jearim on the southern border. **This was the west quarter**—Literally, *the side of the sea;* that is, towards the sea.

15. **End of Kirjath-jearim**—The extreme western suburbs of the town. The suburbs of the Levitical cities were a thousand cubits from the outer wall, or nearly half a mile, and the suburbs

of Kirjath-jearim may have extended much further. This will explain the obscure statement that follows: **the border went out on the west,** or *seaward.* That is, the southern border of Benjamin, starting from Kirjath, ran first westward to the extreme suburbs of the city, perhaps a mile or two; then, starting again from the city, it ran eastward, and was identical with the northern border of Judah. See notes on chap. xv, 5–9.

20. **Jordan was the border. .on the east**—But only from the Dead Sea to the mouth of the Wady Kelt, or the Wady Nuwaimeh, opposite Jericho, (chap. xvi, 1, note,) a distance of seven or eight miles. The Benjamites cared little for the plain. They preferred rocky heights and deep ravines, where they naturally became skilled in the use of the sling. See note on Judges xx. 16.]

21. **Cities of. . .Benjamin**—In this list, as in that of the cities of Judah, no note is made on those cities that are now unknown. **Jericho**—Chap. ii, 1. **Beth-hoglah**—Chap. xv, 6.

22. **Beth-arabah** — Chap. xv, 6. [**Zemaraim** — This place is without much doubt identical with the ruins five miles north of Jericho, called es-Sumrah. The name is radically the same, and the site is where we should naturally expect to find the ruins of

23 And Avim, and Parah, and ^wOph-rah, 24 And Chephar-haammonai, and Ophni, and ^xGaba; twelve cities with their villages: 25 Gibeon, and Ramah, and Beeroth, 26 And Mizpeh, and Chephirah, and Mozah, 27 And Rekem, and Irpeel, and Taralah, 28 And Zelah, Eleph, and ^yJebusi which *is* Jerusalem, Gibeath, *and* Kirjath; fourteen cities with their villages. This *is*

w 1 Sam. 13. 17.——*x* Ezra 2. 26; Neh. 7. 30.
y 2 Sam. 21. 14.

this ancient town of Benjamin. **Beth-el**—Chap. vii, 2.

23. **Avim**—This is supposed by Knobel and others to stand for *Ai,* the city near Beth-el which was among the first destroyed by Joshua. See chap. vii, 2, note. **Parah**—"Jerome states that this village still existed in his time, and was situated five miles east of Beth-el. It seems highly probable that we have this old name retained in the wild glen called Wady Farah, which runs down the eastern declivities of Benjamin. It falls into the Wady Suweinit, and in the fork there are the ruins of an ancient village called Farah."—*Porter.* **Ophrah** is identified by Robinson with Taiyibeh, a village five miles northeast of Bethel, occupying a commanding site, and containing ancient ruins.]

24. **Ophni** is doubtless the Gophna of Josephus, (Wars, iii, 3, 5.) and is represented in the modern Jifna, three miles northwest of Beth-el. [**Gaba,** better spelled *Geba,* is not to be confounded with Gibeah of verse 28, (as the English version and some interpreters do at 1 Sam. xiii, 16, where see note.) It still exists under the scarcely altered name *Jeba,* on the top of a steep hill between the Wadies Suweinit and Farah, about six miles southeast by south from Beth-el. This height was held by a Philistine garrison in the time of Saul, (1 Sam. xiii, 3,) but was taken from them by the daring feat of Jonathan. At a later period it was fortified by Asa, (1 Kings xv, 22,) and was inhabited again after the captivity. Ezra ii, 26.

25. **Gibeon**—See chap. ix, 3. **Ramah** is associated with many interesting incidents in the subsequent history

the inheritance of the children of Benjamin according to their families.

CHAPTER XIX.

AND the second lot came forth to Simeon, *even* for the tribe of the children of Simeon according to their families: ^aand their inheritance was within the inheritance of the children of Judah. 2 And ^bthey had in their

z Chap. 15. 8.——*a* Verse 9.
b 1 Chron. 4. 28.

of Israel. It is to be found in the modern er-Ram, six miles north of Jerusalem. It stands on the top of a conical hill, half a mile east of the great northern road from Jerusalem. Broken columns are found in the vicinity, and many large hewn stones, remains of the ancient city, are still to be seen in the walls and foundations of the modern houses. **Beeroth**—See chap. ix, 17.]

26. **Mizpeh**—Probably the modern Neby Samwil. See note on 1 Sam. vii, 5. **Chephirah**—See chap. ix, 17.

28. **Jebusi,** or, *the Jebusite.* See chap. x, 1. **Gibeath,** commonly called *Gibeah,* famous as the birthplace and residence of Saul, the first king of Israel. It was the scene of that atrocious crime which led almost to the annihilation of the tribe of Benjamin. Judges xix, 15, ff. Robinson identifies it with the lofty and commanding hill el Fal, three or four miles north of Jerusalem. **Kirjath** — See chap. ix, 17. "For a short time Benjamin rose to the highest rank in the commonwealth, when this tribe gave birth to the first king. Its ultimate position in the nation was altered by the one great change which affected the polarity of the whole political and geographical organization of the country, but of none more than that of Benjamin, when the fortress of Jebus, hitherto within its territory, was annexed by Judah, and became the capital of the monarchy."—*Stanley.*

CHAPTER XIX.

SIMEON'S LOT, 1–9.

1. **Simeon...within the inheritance of Judah**—As Judah's lot was assigned first, when the Hebrews had

inheritance Beer-sheba or Sheba, and Moladah, **3** And Hazar-shual, and Balah, and Azem, **4** And Eltolad, and Bethul, and [c] Hormah, **5** And Ziklag, and Beth-marcaboth, and Hazar-susah, **6** And Beth-lebaoth, and Sharuhen; thirteen cities and their villages: **7** [d] Ain, [e] Remmond, and Ether, and Ashan; four cities and their villages: **8** And all the villages that *were* round about these cities to Baalath-beer, Ramath of the south. This *is* the inheritance of the tribe of the children of Simeon according to their families. **9** Out of the portion of the children of Judah *was* the inheritance of the children of Simeon: for the part of the children of Judah was too much for them: [f] therefore the children of Simeon had their inheritance within the inheritance of them.

10 And the third lot came up for the children of Zebulun according to their

---

c Judges 1. 17.——d 1 Chron. 4. 32.

e Num. 33. 19, 20.——f Verse 1.

---

larger expectations than they ever realized, it was very natural that they should assign too large a portion to Judah. This error is now discovered and rectified by carving Simeon's lot out of Judah's. Simeon's inheritance, except the first thirteen cities, was not a compact territory, but it consisted chiefly of cities scattered about in Judah. Thus was fulfilled the prophetic declaration of Jacob respecting Simeon and Levi, that they should be "divided in Jacob and scattered in Israel." Gen. xlix, 5–7. "Simeon is the exact counterpart of Reuben. With Reuben he marched through the desert. As Reuben in the east, so Simeon in the west, blends his fortunes with those of the Arab hordes on the frontier, and dwindles away accordingly, and only re-appears in the dubious but characteristic exploits of his descendant Judith."—*Stanley.*

2. **Beer-sheba**—See on chap. xv, 28. **Sheba** is probably a repetition of the copyist, otherwise there would be fourteen cities instead of thirteen, as stated in verse 6.

As the cities of Simeon were taken out of the portion originally assigned to Judah, all whose sites are now known are described in the notes on chap. xv. Some of the names here given do not appear there, some may be different names of the same place, but in the absence of any certain knowledge of them we do best to abstain from mere conjectural comments.

8. **All the villages**—All the surrounding villages and country that were subject to the cities named.

9. **Too much for them**—This may mean that it was more than Judah could subdue and retain, or that it exceeded their necessities, or that it was too large relatively. It reflects great honour upon Judah that they should, without selfish remonstrances and murmurings, submit to this diminution of their lot. The national feeling must have been yet strong in this patriotic tribe, for States are always tenacious of their boundaries.

ZEBULUN'S LOT, 10–16.

10. **Zebulun**—"The four tribes of Zebulun, Issachar, Asher, and Naphtali obtain contiguous portions in the north of Palestine, as they were allied in birth, and as they marched through the desert. They formed, as it were, a state by themselves. A common sanctuary seems to have been intended for them in Mount Tabor."—*Stanley.* As Zebulun preceded his elder brother Issachar in the blessing of the patriarch Jacob and the lawgiver Moses, so he precedes him in the allotment. [Jacob predicted that Zebulun should "dwell at the haven of seas," (Gen. xlix, 13,) and Josephus well explains that his "lot included the land which lay as far as the lake of Gennesaret. and that which belonged to Carmel and the sea." It thus lay between two seas, and had, perhaps, fishermen on the Sea of Galilee, and merchants navigating the Mediterranean along with the Phenicians. Moses also said prophetically of this tribe, "They shall suck of the abundance of the seas and of treasures hid in the sand." Deut. xxx, 19. These prophecies do not necessarily imply that Zebulun's territory would border on these seas.

10. **The border...unto Sarid**—This southern border of Zebulun, like the north border of Ephraim, (chap.

families: and the border of their inheritance was unto Sarid: **11** *And their border went up toward the sea, and Maralah, and reached to Dabbasheth, and reached to the river that *is* [h] before Jokneam; **12** And turned from Sarid eastward toward the sunrising unto the border of Chisloth-tabor, and then goeth out to Daberath, and goeth up to Japhia, **13** And from thence passeth

on along on the east to Gittah-hepher, to Ittah-kazin, and goeth out to Remmon-[1] methoar to Neah; **14** And the border compasseth it on the north side to Hannathon: and the outgoings thereof are in the valley of Jiphthah-el: **15** And Kattath, and Nahallal, and Shimron, and Idalah, and Beth-lehem: twelve cities with their villages. **16** This *is* the inheritance of the chil-

---

g Gen. 49. 13.——*h* Chap. 12. 22.

1 Or, *which is drawn*.

---

xvi, 6,) seems to start from a central point in the line, and go first westward and then eastward. Verse 12. The position of **Sarid** was probably not far from Mount Tabor, but its site is unknown, and therefore the exact line of this border cannot now be traced.

11. **Toward the sea**—The Mediterranean. But apparently not *to* the sea, for Asher reached to Carmel, (verse 26,) and, according to chap. xvii, 10, touched Manasseh on the south. **Maralah** may, perhaps, be found in the little village Mahil, which occupies the top of a hill four miles southwest of Nazareth, and contains the ruins of a temple and other vestiges of antiquity. But this is not certain. **Jokneam**—The modern Tell Kaimon, close to the base of Carmel and on the south bank of the Kishon. See on chap. xii, 22. So **the river** here mentioned must be the ancient Kishon. See on Judges v, 21.]

12. **Chisloth-tabor,** Robinson is inclined to identify with the village of Iksal, near the base of Mount Tabor, on a low, rocky ridge, and containing many excavated sepulchres. On Mount Tabor see note at Judges iv, 6. **Daberath** has been identified with the modern Deburieh, a small village just at the northwestern base of Tabor. **Japhia,** now called Yáfa, is a half hour's ride southwest of Nazareth, and contains about thirty houses. It is the traditional birthplace of St. James.

13. **Gittah-hepher** was the birthplace of the prophet Jonah. 2 Kings xiv, 25. Modern monastic tradition identifies it with el-Meshad, one of the many Moslem tombs of Jonah, about five miles northeast of Nazareth. **Remmon,** Robinson conjectures, is

Rummanneh, seven miles north of Nazareth. **Methoar** is not a proper name, but a participle, which may be rendered as in the margin, *which is drawn*, or, with Gesenius, *which stretches* or *extends*, to Neah. The site of **Neah** is unknown.

[14. **The border...on the north side**—The northern border cannot be accurately traced, for **Hannathon,** the only city named, is unknown, and the identification of **the valley of Jiphthah-el** with the great Wady Abilin, as Robinson proposes. is hardly a settled thing. But regarding the identity as established, all we know of the northern border of Zebulun is, that it terminated on the west in the Wady Abilin. The western border is not given here at all, but is vaguely intimated in verse 27, where a boundary of Asher is described.

15. **Beth-lehem** is the only one of the five cities named in this verse which has been with any certainty identified. Dr. Robinson found it about six miles west of Nazareth, still bearing the name *Beit-lahm*, but only a miserable village, with no traces of antiquity except the name. This verse seems to be only a fragment of the list of cities belonging to Zebulun; a supposition confirmed by the mention of **twelve cities** when only five are named. Even if we suppose that all the border cities named are counted, we meet with as great a difficulty, for then we have at least sixteen cities named. We may appropriately say with Keil: "From all that has been hitherto ascertained, we can merely decide respecting the inheritance of Zebulun that it comprised the western half of the plain of Esdraelon, between Jokneam and Tabor, and extended to the mountains of Galilee."]

dren of Zebulun according to their families, these cities with their villages.

17 *And* the fourth lot came out to Issachar, for the children of Issachar according to their families. **18** And their border was toward Jezreel, and Chesulloth, and Shunem, **19** And Haphraim, and Shihon, and Anaharath. **20** And Rabbith, and Kishion, and Abez, **21** And Remeth, and En-gannnim, and En-haddah, and Beth-pazzez; **22** And the coast reacheth to Tabor, and Shahazimah, and Beth-shemesh; and the outgoings of their border were at Jordan: sixteen cities with their villages. **23** This *is* the inheritance of the tribe of the children of Issachar according to their families, the cities and their villages.

24 And the fifth lot came out for the

ISSACHAR'S LOT, 17–23.

The territory of this tribe was bounded on the north by Zebulun, on the east by the Jordan, and on the south and west by Manasseh. It took in a large portion of the most beautiful and desirable parts of the great plain of Esdraelon. For the sake of securing themselves in so desirable a portion as the fertile plain of Esdraelon the children of Issachar became humbly subservient to the Canaanites of the adjacent fortified towns, and to the proud country of Phenicia on the near seacoast. They assumed a position of almost slavish servitude to them, becoming their common carriers, mule-drivers, and servants of all work, thereby fulfilling the prophecy of the dying Jacob: " Issachar is a strong ass couching down between two burdens: and he saw that rest was good, and the land that it was pleasant, and bowed his shoulder to bear, and became a servant to tribute." Gen. xlix, 14, 15.

18. **Their border was toward Jezreel**—Or, rather, it encompassed this city. The writer begins to trace the border, but really enumerates the cities included within it. These were all in the eastern part of the plain of Esdraelon. **Jezreel**, a name often applied to the plain of Esdraelon, is here limited to a city standing on a gentle swell which rises out of it. It was the chief residence of King Ahab, and seat of the worship of Baal and Astarte, the cult of the Phenician Jezebel. It was remarkable for its central location, and the great beauty and commanding character of its site. Its modern name is Zerin, containing only a few wretched hovels clustering around an old, ruined tower. **Chesulloth** — Probably the same as *Chisloth-tabor* in verse 12. [**Shunem** was at the modern village of

Solam, which lies at the western base of the Little Hermon, and about three miles north of Jezreel. Here the Philistines encamped before Saul's last battle, (1 Sam. xxviii, 4,) and here was the home of the Shunammite woman whose son Elisha raised to life. 2 Kings iv, 8.

21. **En-gannim** is still found in Jenin, six or seven miles south of Jezreel. " It is now the chief town between Nazareth and Nablus, and contains about two thousand inhabitants, nearly all Moslems. It deals largely in all the products of the country, and with the Bedouins on the east of the Jordan." — *Thomson.* " The most remarkable thing here is the fine flowing public fountain, rising in the hills back of the town, and brought down so as to issue in a noble stream in the midst of the place."—*Robinson.*]

22. **Coast reacheth**—This probably means the northern **coast** or border, where it joined on Zebulun. **Tabor** is here generally supposed to mean not the mountain, but a town on it afterwards given to the Levites. 1 Chron. vi, 77. **Sixteen cities**—This is exactly the number given above, if Tabor be taken as a city.

LOT OF ASHER, 24–31.

[The position of Asher may be generally described as extending along the shore of the Mediterranean from Tantura, on the south of Mount Carmel, to Zidon on the north, and bounded on the east by Zebulun and Naphtali. His territory included the rich plain of Phenicia, and some of the most celebrated cities of antiquity. Truly did Jacob prophesy: " His bread shall be fat, and he shall yield royal dainties," (Gen. xlix, 20;) and Moses: " He shall dip his foot in oil; his shoes shall be iron and brass." Deut. xxxiii, 24, 25.

tribe of the children of Asher according to their families. **25** And their border was Helkath, and Hali, and Beten, and Achshaph, **26** And Alammelech, and Amad, and Mishal; and reacheth to Carmel westward, and to Shihor-libnath; **27** And turneth toward the sunrising to Beth-dagon, and reacheth to Zebulun, and to the valley of Jiph-

thahel toward the north side of Beth-emek, and Neiel, and goeth out to Cabul on the left hand, **28** And Hebron, and Rehob, and Hammon, and Kanah, *even* unto great Zidon; **29** And *then* the coast turneth to Ramah, and to the strong city [2]Tyre; and the coast turneth to Hosah; and the outgoings thereof are at the sea from the coast to

---

i Chap. 11. 8; Judges 1. 31.

2 Heb. *Tzor*, 2 Sam. 5. 11.

The great Phenician plain near Acre was rich in corn and wine and oil, and in the Zidonian metallic manufactories probably many Asherites learned to be skilful workmen in iron and brass. Compare 1 Kings vii, 14. When other tribes were at war with Jabin's hosts Asher dwelt quietly by his harbours. Judges v, 17. Asher never conquered the Phenician territory, but was content to dwell among the Canaanites and learn their ways. See Judges i, 31, 32. Stanley remarks; "One hame only of the tribe of Asher shines out of the general obscurity— the aged widow who, in the very close of the Jewish history, departed not from the Temple at Jerusalem, but served God with prayers and fastings night and day. (Luke ii, 36, where see notes.) So insignificant was the tribe to which was assigned the fortress which Napoleon called the key of Palestine."]

25. **Achshaph**—See on chap. xi, 1. In this list, as in other extended lists of cities, no note is usually taken of those whose sites are now unknown.

26. [**Carmel**—A range of connected hills, whose average height is fifteen hundred feet, running from the northern hills of Samaria northwesterly, and terminating in a lofty promontory which projects boldly into the Mediterranean just south of the bay of Acre. All travellers agree in giving glowing descriptions of the grandeur, beauty, and excellency of Carmel. "There is not a flower," says Van de Velde, "that I have seen in Galilee, or on the plains along the coast, that I did not find on Carmel." Mr. Carne says: "No mountain in or around Palestine retains its ancient beauty so much as Carmel. Its groves are few but luxuriant. It is no place for crags and precipices, or rocks of the wild goats; but its surface is

covered with a rich and constant verdure."] **Shihor-libnath,** *river of whiteness,* is a matter of great dispute. Every stream, from the Belus southward to the Crocodile River inclusive, has been selected as the river here mentioned. It must have been south of Dor, (Tantura,) which belonged to Asher. Chap. xvii, 11.

27. **Beth-dagon,** *house of Dagon,* must be distinguished from that in chap. xv, 41. It was probably a Philistine colony, and situated somewhere east or northeast of Tantura. **Zebulun** is not a city, but the tribe. On **Jiphthah-el,** see at verse 14. **Cabul** is probably the modern village Kabul, which stands on the top of a rocky ridge eight miles east of Acre.

28. **Kanah**—Not Cana of Galilee, but probably the large village Kanah, five miles southeast of Tyre. **Zidon**—See chap. xi, 8, note. It was never conquered by Asher.

29. **Ramah**—Robinson confidently identifies this place with the modern village Rameh, which stands on an isolated hill about ten miles southeast of Tyre. It has no traces of antiquity except some very ancient sarcophagi. **Tyre,** *a rock,* is a colony of Zidon, and is a few miles south on the seacoast. The old city stood on the main land and was strongly fortified. New Tyre, which was taken by Alexander the Great, was built on a rock in the sea. It is probably Old Tyre that is named in the text, but Keil endeavours to prove that New Tyre was in existence in the days of Joshua, discrediting Josephus, who says that it was built two hundred and forty years before the Temple of Solomon. It was a great commercial emporium, and became the burden of prophecies (see Isa. xxiii; Ezek. xxvi) which have been

k Achzib: **30** Ummah also, and Aphek, and Rehob: twenty and two cities with their villages. **31** This *is* the inheritance of the tribe of the children of Asher according to their families, these cities with their villages.

32 The sixth lot came out to the children of Naphtali, *even* for the children of Naphtali according to their families. **33** And their coast was from Heleph, from Allon to Zaanannim, and Adami, Nekeb, and Jabneel, unto Lakum; and

---

k Gen. 38. 5; Judges 1. 31; Micah 1. 14.

---

remarkably fulfilled. **Achzib**, now called Zib, is on the coast nine miles north of Acre.

30. **Ummah**—Dr. Thomson endeavours to identify it with Alma, in the highlands on the coast. **Aphek**—See on chap. xiii, 4. But that Aphek could hardly have been assigned to Asher, being too far beyond his border. **Twenty and two cities**—It frequently happens that the cities named do not agree with the number given. To adjust this difficulty various assumptions have been made, as noted in chap. xv, 32.

Naphtali's Lot, 32–39.

[The territory of Naphtali was bounded on the east by the Jordan and sea of Galilee, on the south by Zebulun, on the west and north by Asher. The northern limit probably ran into the splendid valley of the Litany, which separates the two great ranges of Lebanon. The excellence of Naphtali's portion is indicated in Moses' song, where he speaks of him as " satisfied with favour, and full with the blessing of the Lord, possessing the west and the south." Deut. xxxiii, 23. The latter part should be rendered, " Possess thou the sea and the sunny clime." " Naphtali possessed," says J. L. Porter, "a greater variety of soil, scenery, and climate than any of the other tribes. Its northern portions are the highlands of Palestine. The sublime ravine of the Leontes separates its mountains from the chain of Lebanon, of which, however, they may be regarded as a prolongation. The scenery is here rich and beautiful. In the centre of this park-like region lie the ruins of the sanctuary of the tribe, the northern city of refuge, Kadesh-Naphtali. The ridge rises gradually towards the south, and culminates at Safed, which has an elevation of nearly three thousand feet.

"The southern section of Naphtali was the garden of Palestine. The little plains along the shore of the Sea of Galilee and the vales that run up into the mountains are of unrivalled fertility. Josephus describes the plain on the shore of the lake as an earthly paradise, where the choicest fruits grew luxuriantly, and where eternal spring reigned. His words were not much exaggerated, for now, though more a wilderness than a paradise, its surpassing richness is apparent."

Jacob spoke of Naphtali as " a hind let loose." Gen. xlix, 21. The tribe had many a noble and fleet warrior, but, like the timid hind, they shrunk from aggressive war, and left several of their cities in the hands of the Canaanites. Judges i, 33. The valiant Barak lacked confidence to venture alone against the hosts of Sisera, (iv, 8,) but when fully roused, like a hind brought to bay, he scorned his soul to death on the high places of the battle-field. Judges v, 18, note.]

From his exposed position on the northern frontier Naphtali was the first to fall into the hands of the Assyrian invaders, (2 Kings xv, 29,) but after the captivity the Israelites largely settled again in this territory. His lot included the scene of the great victory of Joshua over the northern confederacy, and also many places where the Greater Joshua, by his mighty miracles and wondrous teachings, confounded his foes and laid the foundation of his everlasting kingdom. This region is Galilee of the Gentiles, whose " people, which sat in darkness, saw great light." Isa. ix, 1; Matt. iv, 16.

33. The cities here mentioned are so far unknown that there is great difficulty in attempting an accurate description of the boundaries of this tribe. The northern and a part of the western boundary seem to have been

the outgoings thereof were at Jordan: **34** And *then* [l] the coast turneth westward to Aznoth-tabor, and goeth out from thence to Hukkok, and reacheth to Zebulun on the south side, and reacheth to Asher on the west side, and to Judah upon Jordan toward the sunris-

ing. **35** And the fenced cities *are* Ziddim, Zer, and Hammath, Rakkath, and Chinnereth, **36** And Adamah, and Ramah, and Hazor, **37** And Kedesh, and Edrei, and En-hazor, **38** And Iron, and Migdal-el, Horem, and Beth-anath, and Beth-shemesh; nineteen cities with

---

l Deuteronony 32. 23.

---

identical, running mainly in a northeasterly direction, and **Heleph**, the starting point, seems to have been some central place on this line, from which the border ran first eastward, but somewhat towards the north, and then seaward. Verse 34. [Van de Velde proposes to identify **Heleph** with Beitlif, an ancient site about twelve miles southeast of Tyre and about the same distance west of Kades. It stands on the edge of a very marked ravine, which may very possibly have formed a part of the border of Naphtali and Asher. **Allon**—As the Hebrew wor1 means an *oak*, some critics very plausibly understand it of some remarkable tree near **Zaanannim**, and render, *From the oak at Zaanannim.* This was probably the same tree by which Heber the Kenite pitched his tent. See Judges iv, 11, note. **Outgoings...at Jordan**—That is, this northwestern boundary terminated at the upper sources of the Jordan.]

34. Turneth westward—Probably in a southwesterly direction. [**Hukkok** is recognised by Robinson and others in the modern Yakuk, a village six or seven miles northwest from the Sea of Galilee. **Zebulun on the south...Asher on the west**—This is merely giving the boundaries in general terms. **And to Judah upon the Jordan**—This is a faulty translation. **And to Judah** belongs to the previous sentence, which describes the western border. Literally, *It touched Asher on the west and at Judah.* Judah was evidently a city on the western border, perhaps at Jehudiyah, marked on Van de Velde's map east of Tyre and a few miles north of Tibnin. The rest of the verse forms a distinct sentence: **Jordan toward the sunrising**—That is, the Jordan formed the eastern boundary.

35. **Hammath**—Not the Hamath of the north, (chap. xiii, 5,) but doubtless the modern Hammam, or warm springs, which send up their hot and sulphurous waters on the western shore of the Sea of Galilee just south of the ruins of the ancient Tiberias.] **Chinnereth**—See chap. xi, 2, note.

36. **Ramah** must be kept distinct from Ramah in Asher. It is identified by Robinson with a large village still called Rameh, which is situated about six miles southwest of Safed on the declivity of a mountain, surrounded by olive groves and overlooking a fertile plain. **Hazor**—See chap. xi, 1, note.

37. **Kedesh**—See on chap. xii, 22. **Edrei**, not the city in Bashan of the same name, (chap. xiii, 31, note,) but another near Kadesh, whose name still lingers, perhaps, in Khureibeh, a few miles west of Lake Merom. **En-hazor** seems to be the modern Ain-Hazur, between Ramah and Hukkok, some ten miles northwest of the Sea of Galilee. One reason why so many places have the same name among the Hebrews is, that the name is descriptive of some characteristic, as high, low, abounding in fountains, etc. Where two places had the same natural features they were apt to receive the same name.

38. **Iron** is probably the modern Yaron, ten miles west of Lake Merom. **Migdal-el**—The modern name Mejdel is the same as the Hebrew Migdal, and the Greek Magdala of the New Testament, chiefly known as the native town of Mary Magdalene. Magdala is a miserable little Moslem village on the western shore of the Sea of Galilee. [But **Migdal-el** seems from the grouping of these cities to have been, not near the Sea of Galilee, but in the north or northwest part of the tribe. Its location cannot at present be decided. **Beth-shemesh** cannot be the same

their villages. **39** This *is* the inheritance of the tribe of the children of Naphtali according to their families, the cities and their villages.

40 *And* the seventh lot came out for the tribe of the children of Dan according to their families. **41** And the coast of their inheritance was Zorah, and Eshtaol, and Ir-shemesh, **42** And ᵐ Shaalabbin, and Aijalon, and Jethlah, **43** And Elon, and Thimnatha, and Ekron, **44** And Eltekeh, and Gibbethon, and Baalath, **45** And Jehud, and Bene-berak, and Gath-rimmon, **46** And Mejarkon, and Rakkon, with the border ³ before ⁴ Japho. **47** And

---

m Judges 1. 35.

3 Or, *over against.*——4 Or, *Joppa*, Acts 9. 36.

---

as that in verse 41 and chap. xv, 10. Some have thought it might be Medjelesh-shems, a few miles northeast of Cesarea Philippi, and a little north of Lake Phiala.] **Nineteen**—Three names are wanting. See on chap. xv, 32.

Dan's Lot, 40–48.

[The territory assigned to Dan was the smallest of all the tribe divisions. But it was not without advantages. Its border on the northeast and south joined respectively on Ephraim, Benjamin, and Judah, the three most powerful tribes of Israel. Its western border was the Mediterranean. The territory thus enclosed embraced the beautiful plain south of Joppa, the cornfield and garden of Southern Palestine. Dr. Robinson thus describes this district, as seen from the tower of Ramleh: "Towards the north and south, as far as the eye could reach, the beautiful plain was spread out like a carpet at our feet, variegated with tracts of brown, from which the crops had just been taken, and with fields still rich with the yellow of ripe corn, or green with the springing millet. Immediately below us the eye rested on the immense olive groves of Ramleh and Lydda, and the picturesque towers, and minarets, and domes, of these large villages. In the plain itself there were not many villages; but the tract of hills, and the mountain side beyond, especially in the northeast, appeared as if studded with them, and, as now seen in the setting sun, they seemed like white villas and hamlets among the dark hills, presenting an appearance of thriftiness and beauty which certainly would not stand a closer examination."

But the children of Dan were unable to hold this beautiful plain, for "the Amorites forced them into the mountain, for they would not suffer them to come down to the valley," (Judg. i, 34,) and they were obliged to receive help from "the hand of the house of Joseph." Verse 35.

Some time after the allotment this tribe enlarged its possessions by the conquest of Laish in the north. Judg. xviii. In this covert but daring movement Dan fulfilled the prophecies of Jacob and of Moses. Gen. xlix, 17; Deut. xiii, 32. Of this tribe was the famous hero Samson, who judged Israel twenty years. By taking Micah's images, and with them establishing a tribe sanctuary at Dan, (Judges xviii, 20. 30,) they seem to have been the first to adopt and establish an illegal worship in Israel, and as the tribe of Dan is not mentioned in Rev. vii, 5–7, among those that were sealed, some of the fathers inclined to believe that from this tribe Antichrist should spring.]

41. Zorah, and Eshtaol—These cities were originally allotted to Judah, (see chap. xv, 33,) and so also were other cities of this list. But the original allotment being found too large for Judah, the southwestern portion was given to Simeon, (ver. 1–9,) and a part of the northwestern to Dan. **Ir-shemesh** is supposed to be the same as Beth-shemesh in chap. xv, 10.

42–45. Aijalon—See chap. x, 12. **Thimnathah** — Perhaps the same as Timnah, chap. xv, 10. **Ekron**—See chap. xiii, 3. The rest of these cities are now unknown.

[**46. Japho**—The ancient Joppa, modern Jaffa, the famous seaport town of Palestine, distinguishable alike in sacred and common history. Hither the Lebanon timber was brought in floats for building Solomon's temple, (2 Chron. ii, 16,) and also for the second

*the coast of the children of Dan went out *too little* for them: therefore the children of Dan went up to fight against Leshem, and took it, and smote it with the edge of the sword, and possessed it, and dwelt therein, and called Leshem, *Dan, after the name of Dan their father. **48** This *is* the inheritance of the tribe of the children of Dan according to their families, these cities with their villages.

49 When they had made an end of dividing the land for inheritance by their coasts, the children of Israel *gave an inheritance to Joshua the son of Nun among them: **50** According to the word of the Lord they gave him the city which he asked, *even* *Timnath-*serah in mount Ephraim: and he built the city, and dwelt therein. **51** *These are* the inheritances, which Eleazar the priest, and Joshua the son of Nun, and the heads of the fathers of the tribes of the children of Israel, divided for an inheritance by lot *in Shiloh before the Lord, at the door of the tabernacle of the congregation. So they made an end of dividing the country.

---

n See Judges 18.——*o* Judges 18. 29.——*p* Ezekiel 45. 7, 8.

q Chap. 24. 30.——*r* 1 Chron. 7. 21.——*s* Num. 34. 17 ; chap. 14. 1.——*t* Chap. 18. 1, 10.

---

temple under Zerubbabel. Ezra iii, 7. Here Jonah embarked when he sought to flee from the presence of Jehovah. Here Peter raised Tabitha, and here was the house of Simon the tanner, where Peter had his vision. See cut of modern town at Acts ix, 42.]

47. **The coast...went out too little**—Here the English version is at fault by inserting **too little**. Masius has given the sense correctly thus: "The Danites emigrated *beyond themselves*, that is, beyond the inheritance in which they were first placed by the divine lot, and set out in search of other possessions." This occurred after the death of Joshua, and is here narrated out of its chronological order, so as to complete the description of Dan's lot. **Therefore...went up to fight**—Rather, *and the children of Dan went up and fought*. **Leshem,** or Laish, is at the extreme north, near the foot of Mount Hermon. A minute account of this expedition and its results is found in Judges xviii, where see notes.

Joshua's Inheritance, 49, 50.

An honourable distinction of Joshua from the whole people and from his tribe is made by conferring on him a separate portion, not by lot, but in accordance with his own choice. It was situated in the territory of Ephraim, the tribe to which he belonged.

50. **The word of the Lord,** as uttered perhaps through the High Priest, or probably to Moses, but which was not recorded in the Mosaic books. The unrecorded promise to Caleb was a similar instance. **Timnath-serah**—That is, the portion that was over and above. [It is called Timnath-heres (*portion of the sun*) in Judges ii, 9, because, as the Jews explain, he made the sun stand still. It was *in Mount Ephraim, on the north side of the hill of Gaash.* See chap. xxiv, 30. This spot is without much doubt at the modern Tibneh, some twelve miles northwest of Beth-el. Here Dr. Eli Smith discovered the ruins of a considerable town. On the south of the town is a hill (probably Gaash) in which are a number of sepulchers which in size and richness will bear comparison with the tombs of the kings at Jerusalem. Here, doubtless, the aged commander passed his last days, and here he died and was buried. Chap. xxiv, 29, 30. "Jerome relates that Paula, when travelling in these parts, marvelled that the distributer of the possessions of the children of Israel should have chosen for himself a situation so rough and mountainous."—*Kitto.*

51. **They made an end of dividing the country**—But after the division and allotment it remained to designate the cities of refuge and the Levitical cities. An account of this is given in the next two chapters.]

CHAPTER XX.

The Six Cities of Refuge, 1–9.

The sentiment of justice impels uncultivated men to the immediate infliction of punishment upon those who give offence to that sentiment by a

CHAPTER XX.

THE LORD also spake unto Joshua, saying, **2** Speak to the children of Israel, saying, *Appoint out for you cities of refuge, whereof I spake unto you by the hand of Moses : **3** That the slayer that killeth *any* person unawares *and* unwittingly may flee thither : and they shall be your refuge from the avenger of blood. **4** And when he that doth flee unto one of those cities shall stand at the entering of *b* the gate of the city, and shall declare his cause in the ears of the elders of that city, they shall take him into the city unto them, and give him a place, that he may dwell

a Exod. 21. 13; Num. 35. 6, 11, 14; Deut. 19. 2, 9.——*b* Ruth 4. 1, 2.

wrong act, especially the act of taking human life. But a man may accidentally and innocently slay his fellow-man. The safeguard of law is therefore needed that vengeance may not hastily wreak itself on the guiltless. In ordinary cases in highly civilized lands there is such a respect for law that the manslayer is screened from summary punishment, and is entrusted to the courts for trial. But where the veneration for law is not strong, (especially as was the case among the Hebrews, who had so recently been in the house of bondage,) where might and not right is the law, the slayer of a brother man would not be safe in the hands of his outraged and excited neighbours. Hence cities of refuge at convenient distances were appointed. In the wilderness, and up to this time in Canaan, the tabernacle of the Lord seems, from Exod. xxi, 14, to have answered for a place of refuge for the man guilty of homicide; but in the time of Moses commandment was given by God to appoint such cities of refuge in the Land of Canaan. See notes on Num. xxxv, 9–34.

3. Unawares and unwittingly— The design of the city of refuge was not to screen criminals, but to afford an opportunity to all accused of so grave a charge to show the absence of a guilty intent. In order to do this the guilty must be temporarily received as well as the innocent. **Avenger of blood**—The next of kin, or the *Goël*, as he is styled in the Hebrew, and still called in the East. In Gen. ix, 5, Jehovah says, "Your blood in return for the life-blood which you have shed will I require." He here expresses his estimate of the sacredness of human life. The avenger of blood is his agent for searching out and punishing murder.

In the absence of magistrates and tribunals, one man in each family was required to act as a sheriff for the redress of his kindred and the protection of the body politic. In ancient Greece the land was regarded as defiled and accursed of the gods so long as a murderer dwelt therein unpunished.

4. Gate of the city—The tribunal of justice, the forum, was at the city gate. The refugee was not kept out of the city till his innocence was proved, but he was permitted to enter, and to relate his cause, and to receive the protection of the city, for this is the meaning of the clause, **they shall take him into the city unto them.** He must at the earliest possible moment be recognized as a fugitive, or the purpose of his flight may be defeated. This recognition he is entitled to have till his case can be examined by the local authorities. The Rabbins relate how every possible facility was to be afforded to the refugee. "The roads to these cities were to be kept in good repair; no hillock was left, no river nor stream was allowed over which there was not a bridge; the road was to be at least thirty-two cubits broad, (three rods,) and every kind of obstruction was to be removed that might hurt the foot or hinder the speed of the fugitive. At every turning or branching of roads posts were erected bearing the words, REFUGE! REFUGE! to guide the fugitive in his flight; so benign and considerate was the provision made for the benefit of the accidental slayer of his fellow-man."—*Bush.* Infinitely greater pains has God taken to lead *guilty* souls to the refuge of the atoning blood of Jesus Christ. He has opened this refuge, built a highway to it from every human soul, sent his Spirit to

among them. **5** [c]And if the avenger of blood pursue after him, then they shall not deliver the slayer up into his hand; because he smote his neighbour unwittingly, and hated him not beforetime. **6** And he shall dwell in that city, [d]until he stand before the congregation for judgment, *and* until the death of the high priest that shall be in those days: then shall the slayer return, and come unto his own city, and unto his own house, unto the city from whence he fled. **7** And they [1]appointed [e]Kedesh in Galilee in mount Naphtali, and [f]Shechem in mount Ephraim, and [g]Kir-

jath-arba which *is* Hebron in [h]the mountain of Judah. **8** And on the other side Jordan by Jericho eastward, they assigned [i]Bezer in the wilderness upon the plain out of the tribe of Reuben, and [k]Ramoth in Gilead out of the tribe of Gad, and [l]Golan in Bashan out of the tribe of Manasseh. **9** [m]These were the cities appointed for all the children of Israel, and for the stranger that sojourneth among them, that whosoever killeth *any* person at unawares might flee thither, and not die by the hand of the avenger of blood, [n]until he stood before the congregation.

---

c Num. 35. 12.——d Num, 35. 12, 25.——1 Heb. *sanctified.*——e Chap. 21. 32; 1 Chron. 6. 76.—— f Chap. 21. 21; 2 Chron. 10. 1.——g Chap. 14. 15: 21. 11, 13.——h Luke 1. 39.——i Deut. 4. 43; chap. 21. 36; 1 Chron. 6. 78.——k Chap. 21. 38; 1 Kings 22.3.——l Ch. 21. 27.——m Num. 35. 15.——n Ver.6.

---

enlighten every eye, and his heralds to cry in every ear, "This is the way; walk ye therein." This way is not for the innocent but for the guilty.

6. Until he stand before the congregation—The local authorities shall summon him and the *Goël* to appear before them for a judicial inquest and verdict. The congregation or jury was to hear both sides, and to decide whether the deed proceeded from malice or was accidental. If he was condemned he was to be executed; but if he was acquitted he was not set at liberty, but was sent back to live in the refuge till the death of the High Priest. Here we see the superiority of this system of protection over the pagan asylum of the altar, in the temple of some god, which shielded the guilty and the innocent alike. **Until the death of the high priest**—This does not mean that the death of the High Priest takes place at the same time with the summons to trial. The only occasions on which an innocent manslayer may leave the refuge are, 1st, temporarily, for a trial where the manslaying occurred; and 2d, permanently, at the death of the High Priest. Why should he be released when the High Priest dies? Probably because he was anointed as the representative and mediator of the people, who alone was able to offer annual expiation for the whole people. His death, therefore, may be regarded as an atonement prefiguring the death of our heavenly High Priest, who through the eternal Spirit offered

himself without spot unto God. Heb. ix, 14, 15.

7. Appointed—Heb., *They sanctified;* set apart to a sacred use, so that all the fugitives were impressed with the thought that when within these cities they were surrounded by the munitions of Jehovah's especial mercy. None but Levitical cities were chosen. Since the object of the refuge was distinctly religious, to preserve the land from blood-guiltiness, it was not proper that a secular city should be chosen. They were very carefully distributed throughout the whole land. The two and a half tribes east of the Jordan had as many as the western tribes, because they were scattered over a territory nearly as large. **Kedesh**—See on chap. xii, 22. **Shechem**—See on chap. xvii, 7. **Hebron**—Chap. x, 3, note.

8. By Jericho—Literally, *Beyond Jordan, Jericho eastward.* The sense is, the side of Jordan opposite from Jericho. These eastern cities were appointed by Moses. See at Deut. iv, 41–43. On **Ramoth,** see chap. xiii, 26, note. The sites of the other two cities are now unknown.

9. And for the stranger—A foreshadowing of the provision for the salvation of the Gentiles through Christ. **And not die by the hand of the avenger of blood.**—There was one important condition which must be constantly fulfilled—the fugitive must not venture beyond the borders of his refuge (Num. xxxv, 27) until the death of the High Priest. Thus must the par-

CHAPTER XXI.

THEN came near the heads of the fathers of the Levites unto [a] Eleazar the priest, and unto Joshua the son of Nun, and unto the heads of the fathers of the tribes of the children of Israel; 2 And they spake unto them at [b] Shiloh in the land of Canaan, saying, [c] The Lord commanded by the hand of Moses to give us cities to dwell in, with the suburbs thereof for our cattle. 3 And the children of Israel gave unto the Levites out of their inheritance, at the commandment of the Lord, these cities and their suburbs. 4 And the lot came out for the families of the Kohathites: and

---

a Chap. 14. 1; 17. 4.   *b* Chap. 18. 1.——*c* Num. 35. 2.

---

doned sinner by faith abide beneath the shelter of the atoning blood, or be irretrievably lost. Heb. vi, 6. These safeguards against interminable and bloody feuds are in striking contrast with the blood-revenge still existing in the East under Mohammedan law. "Two villages have disputed about a stray goat; there was first tremendous shouting, especially among the women, urging on their husbands and brothers to fight; then in a moment of excitement weapons were used, and blood was shed; and blood calls for blood. Thus every member of the family to the remotest degree is kept in constant dread. He stalks about, armed, at all hours and in all places—with his goats on the mountain-side, with his donkey on the road, with his plough in the field; in seed-time and harvest, summer and winter, heat and cold. Imagination makes the 'avenger of blood' follow him like a shadow, ever watchful for an unguarded moment to fall upon him. Many a family has this blood-revenge compelled to flee from house and home, and seek refuge among strangers: many a village it has left desolate, for none will live where the sentence of death hangs constantly over them. In the Koran this fearful law is commended: 'O true believers, the law of retaliation is ordained to you for the slain; the free shall die for the free.'"—Dr. Porter's "*Syria and Palestine.*"

CHAPTER XXI.

DESIGNATION OF THE LEVITICAL CITIES, 1–42.

1. **Heads of the fathers**—The most venerable and influential of the three Levitical families. These applied to the same commissioners for the cities promised by Moses, (Num. xxxv, 1–5.) It is not enough that God makes special promises and provisions. The very persons to whom these promises are made will fail to receive them unless they exert themselves to secure them. Prayer is the key to God's treasury.

2. **With the suburbs thereof**—The area of these suburbs is laid down in Num. xxxv, 4, 5, but so obscurely that great diversity of computation has arisen among expositors. The suburbs were to reach a thousand cubits from the wall of the city on each of the four sides, and yet the measure on each side of the city was to be two thousand cubits. This Keil explains, as in the following diagram, by picturing the city and its suburbs in squares, with the city in the midst, and understanding the two thousand cubits as the length of each outer side of the suburbs, apart from the walls of the cities, which latter, of course, might vary in size. Or we may understand with Maimonides that the two thousand cubits were added to the one thousand as " fields of the suburbs," (Lev. xxv, 34,) and lay outside the suburbs proper.

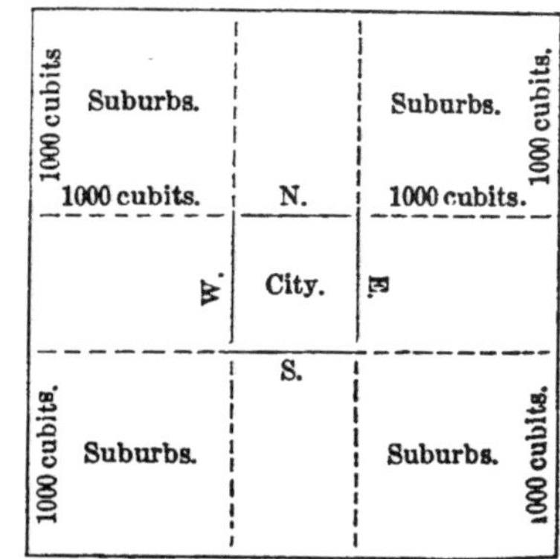

4. **Kohathites**—The first of the families of the Levites among whom the

d the children of Aaron the priest, *which were* of the Levites, *e* had by lot out of the tribe of Judah, and out of the tribe of Simeon, and out of the tribe of Benjamin, thirteen cities. **5** And *f* the rest of the children of Kohath *had* by lot out of the families of the tribe of Ephraim, and out of the tribe of Dan, and out of the half tribe of Manasseh, ten cities. **6** And *g* the children of Gershon *had* by lot out of the families of the tribe of Issachar, and out of the tribe of Asher, and out of the tribe of Naphtali, and out of the half tribe of Manasseh in Bashan, thirteen cities. **7** *h* The children of Merari by their families *had* out of the tribe of Reuben, and out of the tribe of Gad, and out of the tribe of Zebulun, twelve cities. **8** *i* And the children of Israel gave by lot unto the Levites these cities with their suburbs, *k* as the LORD commanded by the hand of Moses. **9** And they gave out of the tribe of the children of Judah, and out of the tribe of the children of Simeon, these cities which are *here* [1] mentioned by name, **10** [1] Which the children of Aaron, *being* of the families of the Kohathites, *who were* of the children of Levi, had: for theirs was the first lot. **11** *m* And they gave them [2] the city of Arba the father of *n* Anak, which *city is* Hebron, *o* in the hill *country* of Judah, with the suburbs thereof round about it. **12** But *p* the fields of the city, and the villages thereof, gave they to Caleb the son of Jephunneh for his possession. **13** Thus *q* they gave to the children of Aaron the priest *r* Hebron with her suburbs, *to be* a city of refuge for the slayer, *s* and Libnah with her suburbs, **14** And *t* Jattir with her suburbs, *u* and Eshtemoa with her suburbs, **15** And *v* Holon with her suburbs, *w* and Debir with her suburbs, **16** And *x* Ain with her suburbs, *y* and Juttah with her suburbs, *and* *z* Beth-shemesh with her suburbs; nine cities out of those two tribes. **17** And out of the tribe of

---

d Verses 8, 19.——*e* See chap. 24. 33.——*f* Verse 20, &c.——*g* Verse 27, &c.——*h* Verse 34, &c.—— *i* Verse 3.——*k* Num. 35. 2.——1 Heb. *called.*—— *l* Verse 4.——*m* 1 Chron. 6. 55.——2 Or, *Kirjath-arba*, Gen. 23. 2.——*n* Chap. 15. 13, 14.——*o* Chap. 20. 7; Luke 1. 39.

p Chap. 14. 14; 1 Chron. 6. 56.——*q* 1 Chron. 6. 57, &c.——*r* Chap. 15. 54; 20. 7.——*s* Chap. 15. 42. ——*t* Chap.15. 48.——*u* Chap. 15. 50.——*v* 1 Chron. 6. 58, *Hilen*, chap. 15. 51.——*w* Chap. 15. 49.—— *x* 1 Chron. 6. 59, *Ashan*, chap. 15. 42.——*y* Chap. 15. 55.——*z* Chap. 15. 10.

---

family of Aaron were exclusively appointed to the priesthood. These by virtue of their office had the precedence in the assignment of the lots, and received **thirteen cities** in contiguous territory; the rest of the Kohathites *ten cities*, (ver. 5,) in tribes also adjoining. There was a divine prescience displayed in so locating the priests that in the future great schism of the State under Rehoboam the seceding tribes found themselves destitute of the divinely-appointed priesthood.

6. **Gershon**—The second division.

7. **Merari**—The third division of the Levites. The three families take their names from the sons of Levi. See the genealogy at Exod. vi, 16–19; also Num iii, 17–39, and 1 Chron. vi.

11. **Hebron**—See on chap. x, 3, and chap. xiv, 12. We here meet the difficulty of a double proprietorship. We have seen in chap. xiv, 13, that Joshua gave Hebron to Caleb as a reward for his fidelity, but now we find that the same city is bestowed upon the priests. Our solution of this difficulty is, that the Levites did not have exclusive ownership of these cities. From Num. iii, 39, we learn that the census of the Levites was about twenty-two thousand males of a month old and upward. This would give less than five hundred males, adult and children, to each of the forty-eight cities. As Hebron and Shechem and several others were large and important, the inference is, that the Levites had ample inheritance in these cities sufficient to give a sacred character to them. We have an intimation of this in verse 12. For the Hebrews who tilled the fields of Caleb's sons must have resided in Hebron for protection. Again, in the law requiring the alienated house and pasture land of the Levite to revert to him in the year of jubilee, there is implied that others than Levites lived with them. Lev. xxv, 32–34.

13. **Libnah**—See on chap. x, 29. In the following list no comment is made on those cities that are now unknown.

14-17. **Jattir**—Chap. xv, 48. **Eshtemoah**—Chap. xv, 50. **Debir**—Chap. x, 38. **Juttah**—Chap. xv, 55. **Beth-shemesh**—Chap. xv, 10. **Gibeon** — Chap. ix, 3. **Geba** — Chap. xviii, 24.

Benjamin, [a] Gibeon with her suburbs, [b] Geba with her suburbs, **18** Anathoth with her suburbs, and [c] Almon with her suburbs; four cities. **19** All the cities of the children of Aaron, the priests, *were* thirteen cities with their suburbs. **20** [d] And the families of the children of Kohath, the Levites which remained of the children of Kohath, even they had the cities of their lot out of the tribe of Ephraim. **21** For they gave them [e] Shechem with her suburbs in mount Ephraim, *to be* a city of refuge for the slayer; and Gezer with her suburbs, **22** And Kibzaim with her suburbs, and Beth-horon with her suburbs; four cities. **23** And out of the tribe of Dan, Eltekeh with her suburbs, Gibbethon with her suburbs, **24** Aijalon with her suburbs, Gath-rimmon with her suburbs; four cities. **25** And out of the half tribe of Manasseh, Tanach with her suburbs, and Gath-rimmon with her suburbs; two cities. **26** All the cities *were* ten with their suburbs for the families of the children of Kohath that remained. **27** [f] And unto the children of Gershon, of the families of the Levites, out of the *other* half tribe of Manasseh *they gave* [g] Golan in Bashan with her suburbs, *to be* a city of refuge for the slayer, and Beeshterah with her suburbs; two cities. **28** And out of the tribe of Issachar, Kishon with her suburbs, Dabareh with her suburbs, **29** Jarmuth with her suburbs, En-gannim with her suburbs; four cities. **30** And out of the

tribe of Asher, Mishal with her suburbs, Abdon with her suburbs, **31** Helkath with her suburbs, and Rehob with her suburbs; four cities. **32** And out of the tribe of Naphtali, [h] Kedesh in Galilee with her suburbs, *to be* a city of refuge for the slayer; and Hammoth-dor with her suburbs, and Kartan with her suburbs; three cities. **33** All the cities of the Gershonites according to their families *were* thirteen cities with their suburbs. **34** [i] And unto the families of the children of Merari, the rest of the Levites, out of the tribe of Zebulun, Jokneam with her suburbs, and Kartah with her suburbs, **35** Dimnah with her suburbs, Nahalal with her suburbs: four cities. **36** And out of the tribe of Reuben, [k] Bezer with her suburbs, and Jahazah with her suburbs, **37** Kedemoth with her suburbs, and Mephaath with her suburbs; four cities. **38** And out of the tribe of Gad, [l] Ramoth in Gilead with her suburbs, *to be* a city of refuge for the slayer; and Mahanaim with her suburbs, **39** Heshbon with her suburbs, Jazer with her suburbs; four cities in all. **40** So all the cities for the children of Merari by their families, which were remaining of the families of the Levites, were *by* their lot twelve cities. **41** [m] All the cities of the Levites within the possession of the children of Israel *were* forty and eight cities with their suburbs. **42** These cities were every one with their suburbs round about them: thus *were* all these cities.

---

a Chap. 18. 25.——*b* Chap. 18. 24, *Gaba.*—— *c* 1 Chron. 6. 60, *Alemeth.*——*d* Verse 5; 1 Chron. 6. 66.——*e* Chap. 20. 7; Gen. 37. 12, 13; Acts 7. 16.

f Verse 6; 1 Chron. 6. 71.——*g* Chap. 20. 8.—— *h* Chap. 20. 8.——*i* Verse 7; see 1 Chron. 6. 77. ——*k* Chap. 20. 8.——*l* Chap. 20. 9.——*m* Num. 35. 7.

---

18. **Anathoth** was the place to which King Solomon banished Abiathar, (1 Kings ii. 26,) and the birthplace of Jeremiah. Jer. i, 1. It is represented by the modern village Anata, four miles northeast of Jerusalem. It is now a small village, but contains remains of the walls and foundations of the ancient city.

21–24. **Shechem**—Chap. xvii, 7. **Gezer**—Chap. x, 33. **Beth-horon**— Chap. x, 10. **Aijalon**—Chap. x, 12. **Tanach**—Chap. xii, 21.

27. **Beeshterah** seems to be a contraction of Beth-Ashterah — *house of Astoreth*—the residence of Og. See chap. ix, 10.

28–39. **Dabareh**—Chap. xix, 12. **En-gannim**—Chap. xix, 21. **Kedesh**

—Chap. xii, 22. **Jokneam**—Chap. xii, 22. **Ramoth**—Chap. xiii, 26. **Heshbon**—Chap. xiii, 17, 26. **Jazer**—Chap. xiii, 25.

42. To this verse the LXX add the following, partly taken from chap. xix, 49, 50, and partly legendary: " And Joshua finished dividing the land in their borders, and the children of Israel gave a portion to Joshua according to the commandment of the Lord; they gave him the city which he asked for, Timnath-serah gave they him in Mount Ephraim, and Joshua fortified the city and dwelt in it. And Joshua took the stone knives with which he circumcised the children of Israel who were born during the journey in the wilderness, and he deposited them in Timnath-serah."

43 And the LORD gave unto Israel
[n]all the land which he sware to give
unto their fathers; and they possessed
it, and dwelt therein. **44** [o]And the
LORD gave them rest round about, according to all that he sware unto their
fathers: and [p]there stood not a man of
all their enemies before them; the LORD
delivered all their enemies into their
hand. **45** [q]There failed not aught of
any good thing which the LORD had
spoken unto the house of Israel; all
came to pass.

CHAPTER XXII.

THEN Joshua called the Reubenites,
and the Gadites, and the half tribe
of Manasseh, **2** And said unto them,
Ye have kept [a]all that Moses the servant
of the LORD commanded you, [b]and have

n Gen. 13. 15; 15. 18; 26. 3; 28. 4, 13. *o* Chap. 11. 23; 22. 4.
p Deut. 7. 24.——*q* Chap. 23. 14.——*a* Num. 32. 20; Deut. 3. 18.——*b* Chap. 1. 16, 17.

THE DIVINE PROMISES FULFILLED, 43–45.

As the wicked are prone to forget the divine threatenings, so the people of God are inclined to neglect the divine promises. Hence the necessity of calling special attention to them, that their fulfilment may exert a salutary influence upon us.

44. **There stood not a man**—The many were humbled and rendered tributary, and all their enemies would have been expelled if the Hebrews had had faith in Jehovah, their unfailing ally. [Some rationalistic critics affirm that this passage is contradicted by other statements of the ancient history which affirm that Israel's enemies were not all subdued, and considerable portions of the land were never in possession of the Israelites. But they forget that the promise to the fathers was accompanied also with the express statement that the Canaanites should be gradually exterminated. See note on next verse. This passage affirms a thorough subjugation of all Canaan, and a division of it for a possession among the Israelites, but not, as some would assume, an extermination of all its original inhabitants. Even Ewald admits, as unquestionable, "that this first irruption into Canaan under Joshua was decisive for all future time, and that the Canaanites were never able in succeeding ages to rally permanently from the losses and disasters which they then underwent." In another place the same rationalistic critic affirms: "There can be no doubt that Joshua, during the first years of the entrance into Canaan, subdued the country on every side, and received the submission of all the Canaanites whose lives were spared. It is very possible that in the first terror of surprise the Philistines, and even the men of Zidon and the rest of the Phenicians, may have paid homage, although these last could never again be subdued."]

45. **There failed not aught of any good**—So far as Jehovah was concerned, for he had expressly said, "I will not drive them out from before thee in one year, lest the land become desolate, and the beast of the field multiply against thee. By little and little I will drive them out from before thee, until thou be increased, and inherit the land." Exod. xxiii, 29, 30. Comp. Deut. vii, 22. Israel's subsequent failure to possess all the land was, as the history itself shows, largely owing to their cowardice. Tribal jealousies also had much to do with their failure.

CHAPTER XXII.

THE TRANS-JORDANIC TRIBES DISMISSED, 1–9.

We have seen (chap. i, 12–15) that Joshua required these tribes to fulfil the condition on which they were permitted to receive their portions before the conquest of Canaan, namely, that they should assist in that conquest, (Num. xxxii, 20,) and we have noted the cheerfulness with which they left their families and possessions (chap. i, 16) and became the vanguard of the invading host, forty thousand strong. Chap. iv, 12, 13. Through all the long war of subjugation they have served faithfully, till at last the land is substantially conquered and actually allotted, and henceforth each tribe is to clear its own inheritance without the aid of the federal army, which is now disbanded with the high encomiums of their chief.

obeyed my voice in all that I commanded you: **3** Ye have not left your brethren these many days unto this day, but
have kept the charge of the commandment of the LORD your God. **4** And
now the LORD your God hath given rest
unto your brethren, as he promised
them: therefore now return ye, and get
you unto your tents, *and* unto the land
of your possession, c which Moses the
servant of the LORD gave you on the
other side Jordan. **5** But d take diligent
heed to do the commandment and the
law, which Moses the servant of the
LORD charged you, e to love the LORD
your God, and to walk in all his ways,
and to keep his commandments, and

to cleave unto him, and to serve him
with all your heart and with all your
soul. **6** So Joshua f blessed them, and
sent them away: and they went unto
their tents. **7** Now to the *one* half of
the tribe of Manasseh Moses had given
possession in Bashan: g but unto the
other half thereof gave Joshua among
their brethren on this side Jordan westward. And when Joshua sent them
away also unto their tents, then he
blessed them, **8** And he spake unto
them, saying, h Return with much riches
unto your tents, and with very much
cattle, with silver, and with gold, and
with brass, and with iron, and with very
much raiment: i divide the spoil of your

---

c Num. 32. 33; Deut. 29. 8; chap. 13. 8.——
d Deut. 6. 6, 17; 11. 22.——e Deut. 10. 12.——
f Gen. 47. 7; Exod. 39. 43; chap. 14. 13; 2 Sam.

6. 18; Luke 24. 50.——g Chap. 17. 5.——h Deut.
8. 9; Prov. 3. 10.——i Num. 31. 27; 1 Sam.
30. 24.

**3. Ye have not left your breth-
ren**—Ye have not permanently abandoned them during seven years of war.
It is not to be supposed that in the
long intervals between the military
campaigns they had not been permitted
to visit on furloughs their families only
a few miles distant beyond the Jordan.
Such frequent permissions to visit their
homes had kept them from murmuring
at the long delay in the division of Canaan. For the provision made for the
protection of their homes, and the
maintenance of their families during
their absence, see chap. i, 14, note.

4. Get you unto your tents—The
word **tents** here, as often elsewhere,
(Judges vii, 8; 1 Sam. iv, 10; xiii, 2;
2 Sam. xviii. 17,) is used for *houses*, or
homes. Its use probably arose from
Israel's dwelling so long in tents.

5. And the law—The Torah. In
note on chap. i, 8, we have shown that
the Torah was already called a book.
We have in this verse grounds for in-
ferring that there was more than one
copy. The Eastern tribes could not
have been commanded to take diligent
heed to obey the Torah if they were
now to be excluded from its constant
perusal. **With all your heart and
with all your soul**—The words **heart**
and **soul** indicate the affectional and
emotional nature, and are used to in-
tensify the exhortation to sincere and
heartfelt obedience unto Jehovah. As
if foreseeing the decay of national feel-

ing which the separation of the deep
trench of the Jordan would tend to
create, Joshua tenderly and earnestly
presses upon the departing tribes the
duty of a faithful study of the law and
a scrupulous obedience to its requirements. He well knew that the Hebrew could be a patriot only as he was
an Israelite indeed; a lover of his nation only as a lover of his nation's
God. With a clear vision did Joshua
see that both individual and national
prosperity must arise from obedience
to the moral law. The redundancy of
the language evinces the intense earnestness of the great leader.

7. Bashan—See chap. ii, 10, note.

8. Much riches—Since the Canaanites were quite advanced in arts, manu-
factures, and agriculture, it is natural
that they should have a large amount
of the precious metals and costly articles embodying wealth. **Much raiment**—Fashions in dress never change
in the East. Hence the people make
permanent investments of their wealth
in dresses. Hence the Saviour's exhortation, "Lay not up for yourselves
treasures upon earth, where the moth
doth corrupt," evidently refers to accu-
mulations of garments. Says a traveller in Palestine, "Not unfrequently one
sees among the inhabitants of a wretched little hamlet, consisting of the merest
hovels, a number of persons dressed in
handsome silks." **Divide the spoil**—
On a previous occasion (Num. xxxi, 27)

enemies with your brethren. **9** And the children of Reuben and the children of Gad and the half tribe of Manasseh returned, and departed from the children of Israel out of Shiloh, which *is* in the land of Canaan, to go unto *k* the country of Gilead, to the land of their possession, whereof they were possessed, according to the word of the Lord by the hand of Moses.

10 And when they came unto the borders of Jordan, that *are* in the land of Canaan, the children of Reuben and the children of Gad and the half tribe of Manasseh built there an altar by Jordan, a great altar to see to. **11** And the children of Israel *l* heard say, Be-

hold, the children of Reuben and the children of Gad and the half tribe of Manasseh have built an altar over against the land of Canaan, in the borders of Jordan, at the passage of the children of Israel. **12** And when the children of Israel heard *of it*, *m* the whole congregation of the children of Israel gathered themselves together at Shiloh, to go up to war against them. **13** And the children of Israel *n* sent unto the children of Reuben, and to the children of Gad, and to the half tribe of Manasseh, into the land of Gilead, *o* Phinehas the son of Eleazar the priest, **14** And with him ten princes, of each *1* chief house a prince throughout all the tribes

k Num. 32.1, 26, 29.——*l* Deut. 13. 12, &c.; Judges 20. 12.——*m* Judges 20.1.——*n* Deut. 13. 14; Judges 20. 12; Prov. 20. 18; Matt. 18. 15.——*o* Exod. 6. 25; Num. 25. 7.——1 Heb. *house of the father*.

Moses commanded that those who did service at home should share equally with those who had perilled their lives in battle, for the obvious reason that guarding the household and raising supplies for the army are just as necessary and as patriotic as hurling javelins and storming hostile cities.

THE ALTAR OF WITNESS AT THE JOR-
DAN, 10–34.

10. By Jordan—Most commentators believe that the altar was on the western bank of the Jordan, because the language of the narrative is, **when they came unto the borders of Jordan, that are in the land of Canaan.** But in the next verse we read that the altar was built "over against the land of Canaan." The purpose of the altar was to answer the taunting insinuation that they were aliens, by exhibiting within their own borders a facsimile of the altar at Shiloh as a proof of their Hebrew nationality and of their conformity to their brethren in religious worship. Josephus says, that the two and a half tribes " crossed the river and built an altar on the bank of the Jordan as a token of their affinity with those on the other side." This altar, constructed by so large a body of men, was probably a vast heap of earth and stones. **A great altar to see to**—Conspicuously located, and huge in its dimensions. That this mound has not been found by any traveller is not strange, when we consider the almost total ne-

glect of Eastern Palestine by all modern explorers ; and, besides, this great altar may long ago have been destroyed.

12. The children of Israel gathered themselves together — The news produced the greatest consternation, and caused an uprising of all the tribes. A separate altar implied the setting up of a new religion, and foreshadowed a secession from the theocratic state. Such a movement, therefore, demanded the most careful investigation, according to the express provision of the law. Deut. xiii. 13, 14. So at a later time all Israel assembled at Mizpeh to investigate the offence of Benjamin. Judges xx. **To go up to war against them**—For the law ordained that if any city went over to idolatry it should be smitten with the edge of the sword, and utterly destroyed. Deut. xiii. 15, 16.

13. Phinehas—Probably his father, Eleazar, was too aged for this service. Phinehas, the grandson of Aaron, had signalized himself while quite a youth by his zeal and energy against licentiousness at Shittim. Num. xxv, 7. Subsequently he was chaplain of the expedition which destroyed the Midianites. Num. xxxi, 6. After his father's death he became the third high priest.

14. Ten princes—Who these princes were is so obscurely told in the rest of the verse that it is difficult to decide as to the precise meaning. The rest of the verse is, literally: *One prince, one prince to the house of a father to all*

of Israel; and [p] each one *was* a head of
the house of their fathers among the
thousands of Israel. **15** And they came
unto the children of Reuben, and to the
children of Gad, and to the half tribe of
Manasseh, unto the land of Gilead, and
they spake with them, saying, **16** Thus
saith the whole congregation of the
LORD, What trespass *is* this that ye have
committed against the God of Israel, to
turn away this day from following the
LORD, in that ye have builded you an
altar, [q] that ye might rebel this day
against the LORD? **17** *Is* the iniquity
[r] of Peor too little for us, from which
we are not cleansed until this day, although there was a plague in the congregation of the LORD, **18** But that ye
must turn away this day from following
the LORD? and it will be, *seeing* ye rebel
to day against the LORD, that to morrow
[s] he will be wroth with the whole congregation of Israel. **19** Notwithstand-
ing, if the land of your possession *be*
unclean, *then* pass ye over unto the land
of the possession of the LORD, [t] wherein
the LORD's tabernacle dwelleth, and take
possession among us: but rebel not
against the LORD, nor rebel against us,
in building you an altar besides the altar
of the LORD our God. **20** [u] Did not
Achan the son of Zerah commit a trespass in the accursed thing, and wrath
fell on all the congregation of Israel?
and that man perished not alone in his
iniquity. **21** Then the children of Reuben and the children of Gad and the
half tribe of Manasseh answered, and

p Num. 1. 4.——*q* Lev. 17. 8, 9; Deut. 12. 12, 14; 1 Sam. 15. 23.——*r* Num. 25. 3, 4; Deut. 4. 3.

s Num. 16. 22.——*t* Chap. 18. 1.——*u* Chap. 7. 1, 5; 1 Cor. 10. 6; Jude 5, 6.

the tribes of Israel, and a chief man of the house of their fathers were they to all the thousands of Israel. It could not be that one was chosen from each chief house in all Israel, for then must more than ten have been chosen. Keil probably explains correctly when he says that this delegation, called in verse 30 *princes of the congregation*, "was composed partly of princes of tribes and partly of heads of families, some tribes being represented in one way and others in the other; and that the latter were sent in cases in which the heads of the tribes were either too old, or otherwise unfitted to take part in the deputation. This supposition is strongly confirmed by the fact that the tribe of Levi was not represented by the chief of the tribe, the high priest Eleazar, but by his son and presumptive successor, Phinehas, who was chosen instead."

16. **What trespass is this**—The erection of the altar is justly regarded as *prima facie* proof of violating the unity of divine worship, inasmuch as sacrifices offered in any other place than at the door of the tabernacle were strictly forbidden. Lev. xvii, 7, 8.

17. **Is the iniquity of Peor too little**—Phinehas had a vivid remembrance of that dreadful outbreak of crime whose curse his active zeal had turned away from the congregation by a bold thrust of his javelin. Num. xxv, 1–13. Hence the naturalness of this historical allusion. **Not cleansed until this day**—Though the divine wrath was turned away, the sad consequences of that crime were still visible. **Although there was a plague**—Rather, *and the plague was in the congregation.*

18. **To-morrow he will be wroth**—The moral universe is pervaded by laws as inflexible as those of the physical world, or, rather, more certain in their consequences; for the physical laws may be suspended for moral ends. **With the whole congregation**—And not with you eastern tribes only. Such are our social and political relations that the crimes of a part are punished on the whole of the nation.

19. **If the land of your possession be unclean**—Not consecrated by the presence of the tabernacle and altar. "If ye think that God has not received your land into the same favour as ours, because he seems to dwell with us, and it is for that reason that ye are about to establish a worship of your own, change your abode and come over to us."—*Masius.*

20. **Achan**—Phinehas now argues that if the sin of an individual brought disasters upon the body politic, much more will that of the eastern tribes. **Perished not alone**—But involved his family and all his possessions in the penal vengeance which came upon himself. See on chap. vii, 24.

said unto the heads of the thousands of Israel, **22** The LORD ᵛGod of gods, the LORD God of gods, he ʷknoweth, and Israel he shall know ; if *it be* in rebellion, or if in transgression against the LORD, (save us not this day,) **23** That we have built us an altar to turn from following the LORD, or if to offer thereon burnt offering or meat offering, or if to offer peace offerings thereon, let the LORD himself ˣrequire *it ;* **24** And if we have not *rather* done it for fear of *this* thing, saying, ²In time to come your children might speak unto our children, saying, What have ye to do with the LORD God of Israel? **25** For the LORD hath made Jordan a border between us and you, ye children of Reuben and children of Gad : ʸye have no part in the LORD : so shall your children make our children cease from fearing the LORD. **26** Therefore we said, Let us now prepare to build us an altar, not for burnt offering, nor for sacrifice : **27** But *that* it *may be* ᶻa witness between us, and you, and our generations after us, that we might ᵃ do the service of the LORD before him with our burnt offerings, and with our sacrifices, and with our peace offerings ; that your children may not say to our children in time to come, Ye have no part in the LORD. **28** Therefore said we, that it shall be, when they should *so* say to us or to our generations in time to come, that we may say *again,* ᵇBehold the pattern of the altar of the LORD, which our fathers made, not for burnt offerings, nor for sacrifices ; but it *is* a witness between us and you. **29** God forbid that we should rebel against the LORD, and turn this day from following the LORD, ᶜto build an altar for burnt offerings, for meat offerings, or for sacrifices, besides the altar of the LORD our God that *is* before his tabernacle. **30** And when Phinehas the priest, and the princes of the congregation and heads of the thousands of Israel which *were* with him, heard the words that the children of Reuben and the children of Gad and the children of Manasseh spake, ³it pleased them. **31** And Phinehas the son of Eleazar the priest said unto the children of Reuben, and to the children of Gad, and to the children of Manasseh, This day we perceive that the LORD *is* ᵈamong us, because ye have not committed this trespass against the LORD : ⁴now ye have delivered the children of Israel out of the hand of the LORD. **32** And Phinehas the son of Eleazar

---

ᵛ Deut. 10. 17.——ʷ 1 Kings 8. 39 ; Job 10. 7 ; 23. 10 ; Psa. 44. 21 ; 139. 1, 2 ; Jer. 12. 3 ; 2 Cor. 11. 11. 31.——ˣ Deut. 18. 19 ; 1 Sam. 20. 16.——2 Heb. *To morrow.*——ʸ 2 Sam. 20. 1 ; 1 Kings 12. 16 ; Ezra 4. 2, 3 ; Acts 8. 21.——ᶻ Gen. 31. 48 ; chap. 24. 27 ; verse 34.——ᵃ Deut. 12. 5, 6, 11, 12. 17. 18, 26, 27.——ᵇ Exod. 25. 40 ; 2 Kings 16. 10 ; Ezek. 43. 10, 11 ; Heb. 8. 5.——ᶜ Deut. 12. 13. 14 ; 2 Kings 18. 22.——3 Heb. *it was good in their eyes.*—— ᵈ Lev. 26. 11, 12 ; 2 Chron. 15. 2.——4 Heb. *then.*

---

22. The Lord God of gods—*El Elohim Jehovah*—This is a most solemn oath. They who twice utter the three names of God declare that they revere him as the mighty, living Being, and are not in rebellion against him. **Save us not this day**—Or, help us not. This implies that they should be left to miserably perish. **Let the Lord himself require it**—That is, Let him punish it. Another strong adjuration is here uttered.

24. For fear—The Hebrew word indicates great and distressing solicitude. The motive of their action was just the opposite of that ascribed to them. It was their intense desire to preserve themselves and their children in the worship of Jehovah that had induced the erection of the memorial altar. **Our children**—The truly pious man will seek to place the safeguards of piety about the path of his offspring.

These eastern tribes had received by far the best portion of the Holy Land, yet they are not satisfied with worldly good. Their broad acres and vast herds are worthless without a portion in the God of Israel.

27. That it may be a witness—Having disavowed that their altar was intended for sacrificial uses, they now plainly declare that it was intended for a memorial that their children were entitled to appear as worshippers before that altar in Shiloh of which this was a facsimile.

31. The Lord is among us—The commission were more than satisfied with the explanation; they were delighted with the loyalty and fidelity of their misjudged brethren. This whole account is highly honourable to both the accusing party and the accused, inasmuch as it shows that both were animated with the high and holy pur-

the priest, and the princes, returned from the children of Reuben, and from the children of Gad, out of the land of Gilead, unto the land of Canaan, to the children of Israel, *e* and brought them word again. **33** And the thing pleased the children of Israel; and the children of Israel *f* blessed God, and did not intend to go up against them in battle, to destroy the land wherein the children of Reuben and Gad dwelt. **34** And the children of Reuben and the children of Gad called the altar *5 Ed :* for it *shall be a* witness between us that the LORD *is* God.

e Prov. 25. 13.——*f* 1 Chron. 29. 20; Neh. 8. 6; Dan. 2. 19; Luke 2. 28.——5 That is, A witness. So chap. 24. 27.

pose of cleaving to the worship of the true God.

33. Did not intend to go up— More literally, *They did not talk of going up.* This is a Hebraism for saying that they abandoned the purpose of civil war, for which they had assembled at Shiloh.

34. Ed ... shall be—These words are not in the original, nor need they be inserted in the translation. We may correctly render: *The children of Gad named the altar that it might be a witness among us that Jehovah is the God.* The lessons which this episode teaches are, first, That appearances do not always imply bad motives; second, That we should watch over each other and cautiously rebuke the first departure from God; third, That apostasy from God awakens in the truly pious great solicitude; and, finally, That a conscience void of offence is a great blessing.

CHAPTER XXIII.

JOSHUA'S ADDRESS TO ISRAEL, 1–16.

[" The closing records of the history of Joshua show us a solemn pause and crisis in the career of Israel. They had now attained that first success which is always a trial of human power and endurance, and which, in their case, was the test of their faithfulness to Jehovah. In Joshua they had a leader equal to the crisis. He lived long after God had given them rest from their enemies, and he was now going the way of all the earth. His last care was to set clearly before the people their true position, and to bind

CHAPTER XXIII.

A ND it came to pass, a long time after that the LORD *a* had given rest unto Israel from all their enemies round about, that Joshua *b* waxed old *and* 1 stricken in age. **2** And Joshua *c* called for all Israel, *and* for their elders, and for their heads, and for their judges, and for their officers, and said unto them, I am old *and* stricken in age: **3** And ye have seen all that the LORD your God hath done unto all these nations because of you; for the *d* LORD your God *is* he that hath fought for

a Chap. 21. 44; 22. 4.——*b* Chap. 13. 1.——1 Heb. *come into days.*——*c* Deut. 31. 28; chap. 24. 1; 1 Chron. 28. 1.——*d* Exod. 14. 14; chap. 10. 14, 42.

them to Jehovah by another solemn covenant."—*Smith's O. T. Hist.*]

1. **A long time**—About fourteen years after the conquest and seven years after the allotment of Canaan, in the one hundred and tenth year of his life, Joshua uttered this speech. **Stricken in age**—Literally, as in the margin, *come into days;* that is, far gone in years.

2. **And for their elders**—The **and** is not in the Hebrew. It should be *for the elders*, the representatives of Israel. This restriction is sometimes not expressed but implied. Hence Bishop Colenso's numerical impossibilities exist nowhere but in his own imagination. All Israel could not stand before the narrow front of the tabernacle, nor could they listen to the feeble words of an infirm old man in any other way than representatively. Probably this assembly was at Timnath-serah, the residence of Joshua; possibly at Shiloh. We have no data for determining the place. As death approaches, the national founder feels a special solicitude for his people. The farewell words of such men have great weight with succeeding generations. The Farewell Address of George Washington to the American people has exerted an incalculable influence upon the nation.

3. **All that the Lord...hath done** —Here is a marked magnifying of the Divine interposition in all the victories of Joshua. True piety always exclaims, " Not unto us, not unto us, but unto thy name be all the praise and glory."

you. **4** Behold, *I have divided unto you by lot these nations that remain, to be an inheritance for your tribes, from Jordan, with all the nations that I have cut off, even unto the great sea [2]westward. **5** And the LORD your God, *he shall expel them from before you, and drive them from out of your sight; and ye shall possess their land, *as the LORD your God hath promised unto you. **6** *Be ye therefore very courageous to keep and to do all that is written in the book of the law of Moses, *that ye turn not aside therefrom *to* the right hand or

to the left; **7** That ye *come not among these nations, these that remain among you; neither *make mention of the name of their gods, nor cause to swear *by them*, neither serve them, nor bow yourselves unto them: **8** [3]But *cleave unto the LORD your God, as ye have done unto this day. **9** [4]For the LORD hath driven out from before you great nations and strong: but *as for* you, *no man hath been able to stand before you unto this day. **10** *One man of you shall chase a thousand: for the LORD your God, he *it is* that fighteth for you,

---

e Chap. 13. 2, 6; 18. 10.——2 Heb. *at the sunset.*
——*f* Exod. 23. 30; 33. 2; 34. 11; Deut. 11. 23; chap. 13. 6.——*g* Num. 33. 53.——*h* Chap. 1. 7.——*i* Deut. 5. 32; 28. 14.——*k* Exod. 23. 33; Deut. 7. 2, 3; Prov. 4. 14; Eph. 5. 11.——*l* Exod. 23. 13; Psa. 16. 4; Jer. 5. 7; Zeph. 1. 5; see Num. 32. 38.

——3 Or, *For if ye will cleave*, &c.——*m* Deut. 10. 20; 11. 22; 13. 4; chapter 22. 5.——4 Or, *Then the LORD will drive.*——*n* Deut. 11. 23.——*o* Chapter 1. 5.——*p* Leviticus 26. 8; Deuteronomy 32. 30; Judges 3. 31; 15. 15; 2 Samuel 23. 8.

---

4. **These nations**——"The nations are mentioned instead of the land which they possessed, because they were given into the hands of the Israelites to be destroyed."——*Keil.* **I have cut off**—After ascribing the conquest to Jehovah, the truth of history requires mention of the human instrumentality. The frequent review of God's mercies is a powerful incentive to gratitude and fidelity to him. It is noticeable how this passage assumes that all the Canaanite nations are cut off and subdued, but not yet exterminated or expelled. This explains the discrepancy often alleged between chap. xi, 23, and chap. xiii, 1.

6. **Very courageous**—This is the same exhortation that God gave to Joshua at the death of Moses. See chap. i, 7, notes.

7. **Neither make mention**—This not only forbids the admiring mention of the names of the pagan gods, but, as we believe, it commands the literal abstinence from uttering their names, as defiling the tongue. As the name of Jehovah was in Jewish estimation too holy to be pronounced, so the names of the Canaanite gods were too vile. **Nor cause to swear by them**—Since swearing by them implied their existence, this also was forbidden. [He who swears and he who administers an oath in the name of a false god virtually recognize and worship the false deity. Thus may a Christian state prostitute itself to idolatry, superstition,

and even utter irreligion, by allowing in its courts of justice a careless, irreverent, or superstitious use of the oath. Better dispense with the civil oath entirely than prostitute the State to either idolatry, superstition, or atheism.] **Neither serve**, by external worship, **nor bow yourselves,** that is, enthrone them over yourselves as authorities to be revered in your hearts. Here is a fourfold prohibition of idolatry, which was rendered necessary by the uncultivated state of the Hebrews, by the strong influence of all the surrounding nations. and especially by that possessed by the idol-worshippers within their own borders whom they had failed to drive out.

8. **Cleave unto the Lord**—*Cling* unto him with a grip which no force can loosen. Fidelity to God always costs strenuous effort. "Strive to enter in at the strait gate." **As ye have done**—As a nation, with individual exceptions.

9. **The Lord hath driven out**—Or, as the margin, *then the Lord will drive.* In this way this sentence becomes the apodosis of the previous verse—*For if ye cleave . . . then the Lord will drive.* **No man hath been able to stand** whom ye have courageously confronted, trusting in God.

10. **One shall chase a thousand**—An enlargement of the promise in Lev. xxvi, 8, and nearly identical with Deut. xxxii, 30, signifying that a few shall vanquish a great multitude. See the

q as he hath promised you. **11** r Take good heed therefore unto s yourselves, that ye love the LORD your God. **12** Else, if ye do in any wise t go back, and cleave unto the remnant of these nations, *even* these that remain among you, and shall t make marriages with them, and go in unto them, and they to you: **13** Know for a certainty that u the LORD your God will no more drive out *any of* these nations from before you; v but they shall be snares and traps unto you, and scourges in your sides, and thorns in your eyes, until ye perish from off this good land which the LORD your God hath given you. **14** And, behold, this day w I *am* going the way of all the earth: and ye know in all your hearts and in all your souls, that x not one thing hath failed of all the good things which the LORD your God spake concerning you; all are come to pass unto you, *and* not one thing hath failed thereof. **15** y Therefore it shall come to pass, *that* as all good things are come upon you, which the LORD your God promised you; so shall the LORD bring upon you z all evil things, until he have destroyed you from off this good land which the LORD your God hath given you. **16** When ye have transgressed the covenant of the LORD your God, which he commanded you, and have gone and served other gods, and bowed yourselves to them; n then shall the anger of the LORD be kindled against you, and ye shall perish quickly from off the good land which he hath given unto you.

CHAPTER XXIV.

AND Joshua gathered all the tribes of Israel to a Shechem, and b called for the elders of Israel, and for their

---

q Exod. 14. 14; 23. 27; Deut. 3. 22.——r Chap. 22. 5.——s Heb. *your souls.*——s Heb. 10. 38, 39; 2 Pet. 2. 20, 21.——t Deut. 7. 3.——u Judges 2. 3. ——v Exod. 23. 33; Num. 33. 55; Deut. 7. 16;

1 Kings 11. 4.——w 1 Kings 2. 2; see Heb. 9. 27. ——x Chap. 21. 43, 45; Luke 21. 33.——y Deut. 28. 63.——z Lev. 26. 16; Deut. 28. 15, 16, &c.—— n 2 Kings 24. 20.——a Gen. 35. 4.——b Chap. 23. 2.

---

night attack of Gideon. Judges vii, 22. Also the acts of David's worthies, one of whom lifted his spear against eight hundred and slew three hundred. 2 Sam. xxiii, 8, 18; 1 Chron. xi, 11.

11. **Take good heed**—This is the condition of the foregoing promise. "Such is the slothfulness of the flesh that it always needs to be stimulated by threats."—*Calvin.* The depravity of men compels a resort to fear when an appeal to hope has been ineffectual.

12. **Make marriages**—This most intimate form of alliance was forbidden in Exod. xxxiv, 12–16, as a precaution against temptation. Thus Christians are forbidden to wed infidels or pagans. 2 Cor. vi, 14. The affections largely determine religious opinions and practice. The heart makes theology.

13. **Snares, traps, scourges, thorns** —This mixing of metaphors vividly portrays the trouble, sudden disaster, wasting captivity, and destruction which idolatry would bring upon their nation. **Until ye perish from off this good land**—The Jews are strangers to that land to-day, so wonderfully has God scattered them, and so marvelously has he preserved their nationality in order that they may be a monument of his truthfulness.

14. **This day I am going**—The expression **this day** is used here, as in Deut. ix, 1, to denote what is about to take place—shortly.

15. **As all good...so all evil things**—The threatenings are as sure as the promises; both alike are grounded on the divine veracity. The sophistry which would explain away the former must destroy the latter. "The pillars of heaven are no firmer than the foundations of hell."—*Whedon.* These words of Joshua are of universal application. They belong to all peoples and to all generations. Before each individual of the human race there lies the path of obedience, ending in the promises, and the path of disobedience, ending in the threatenings of the Almighty. "Knowing therefore the terrors of the Lord, we persuade men."

CHAPTER XXIV.

JOSHUA'S FAREWELL ADDRESS AT SHECHEM, 1–24.

1. **All the tribes**—By their representatives. See chap. xxiii, 2, note. We have no means of determining the date of this transaction. Some suppose that a considerable period had elapsed after the speech recorded in

heads, and for their judges, and for their officers; and they ^cpresented themselves before God. **2** And Joshua said unto all the people, Thus saith the LORD God of Israel, ^dYour fathers dwelt on the other side of the flood in old time, *even* Terah, the father of Abraham, and the father of Nahor: and ^ethey served other gods. **3** And ^fI took your father Abraham from the other side of the

flood, and led him throughout all the land of Canaan, and multiplied his seed, and ^ggave him Isaac. **4** And I gave unto Isaac ^hJacob and Esau: and I gave unto ⁱEsau mount Seir, to possess it; ^kbut Jacob and his children went down into Egypt. **5** ^lI sent Moses also and Aaron, and ^mI plagued Egypt, according to that which I did among them: and afterward I brought you out. And

---

c 1 Samuel 10. 19.——d Genesis 11. 26, 31.——e Genesis 31. 53.——f Genesis 12. 1; Acts 7. 2, 3.——g Genesis 21. 2, 3; Psalm 127. 3.——h Genesis 25. 24–26.——i Genesis 36. 8; Deuteronomy 2. 5.——k Genesis 46. 1, 6; Acts 7. 15.——l Exodus 3. 10.——m Exodus chaps. 7–12.

---

the last chapter, when Joshua, seeing his life was unexpectedly prolonged, resolved on another farewell to his people of a more solemn and formal character. Others hold that there was but one assembly and but one address, begun, perhaps, at Shiloh, and concluded at Shechem, to which place the assembly adjourned for the renewal of the covenant. The Septuagint version has the assembly *at Shiloh;* but there are good reasons for regarding the Hebrew as the correct version. At Shechem Abraham built his first altar in Canaan. Gen. xii, 7. Here Jacob had "sanctified" his family, and exhorted them to "put away the strange gods," (Gen. xxxv, 2–4;) and Joshua, following the command of Moses, had visited the same sanctuary to inscribe the law on a stone monument, and to exact an oath of allegiance to Jehovah with the impressive sanctions of the blessings and the curses. Chap. viii, 30–35. [**Presented themselves before God**—As the expression **before God**, or *before Jehovah,* frequently means before the Ark of the Covenant, many expositors have supposed that the Ark was brought from Shiloh to Shechem at this time. But Hengstenberg and Keil have abundantly shown that the words do not always imply the presence of the Ark. "If *before Jehovah* could *only* refer to the ceremonies at the sanctuary, Jehovah would be present *only* there, *shut up* in his holy place; an absurd idea, destructive of the divine omnipresence, and one which can never be found in the Holy Scriptures."—*Hengstenberg.* Rather does the expression mean that the assembly met as in the presence of God, whose holy name Joshua doubtless invoked. All pres-

ent realized that the eye of Jehovah was upon them.]

2. **On the other side of the flood** —Rather, *the river;* that is, the Euphrates. It was Ur in Chaldea, beyond the Euphrates, whence Abraham was called from an idolatrous family. **Terah,** with Abram his son, removed from Ur westerly to Haran, where he died aged two hundred and five years. Gen. xi, 29–32. That he was a maker of images is a mere legend. [**They served other gods**—"It is not said distinctly of Abraham that he served other gods, on which account we agree with Knobel, who says: Whether, according to our author, Abraham also was originally an idolater, is rather to be denied than affirmed; comp. Gen. xxxi, 53. But dangerous even for him were the idolatrous surroundings; wherefore God took him and caused him to wander through Canaan."—*Fay.* But a love and reverence for the teraphim seemed rooted in the descendants of Terah. See note on verse 14.]

3. **And I took your father Abraham**—There was nothing coercive in this taking. Abraham's experience was like that of modern Christians who follow the Holy Spirit: "He drew me, and I followed on." With this understanding we may adopt Calvin's comment: "It is not said that he sought God of his own accord, but that he was taken by him and led to another place."

4. **Mount Seir** is a rugged ridge extending along the east side of the Valley of Arabah, from the Dead Sea to the Elanitic Gulf. It was afterwards called Edom. Compare marginal references.

5. **Afterward I brought you out** — The nation is contemplated as hav-

I [n] brought your fathers out of Egypt: and [o] ye came unto the sea; [p] and the Egyptians pursued after your fathers with chariots and horsemen unto the Red Sea. 7 And when they [q] cried unto the LORD, [r] he put darkness between you and the Egyptians, [s] and brought the sea upon them, and covered them; and [t] your eyes have seen what I have done in Egypt: and ye dwelt in the wilderness [u] a long season. 8 And I brought you into the land of the Amorites, which dwelt on the other side Jordan; [v] and they fought with you: and I gave them into your hand, that ye might possess their land; and I destroyed them from before you. 9 Then [w] Balak the son of Zippor, king of Moab, arose and warred against Israel, and [x] sent and called Balaam the son of Beor to curse you: 10 [y] But I would not hearken unto Balaam; [z] therefore he

blessed you still: so I delivered you out of his hand. 11 And [a] ye went over Jordan, and came unto Jericho: and [b] the men of Jericho fought against you, the Amorites, and the Perizzites, and the Canaanites, and the Hittites, and the Girgashites, the Hivites, and the Jebusites; and I delivered them into your hand. 12 And [c] I sent the hornet before you, which drave them out from before you, *even* the two kings of the Amorites; *but* [d] not with thy sword, nor with thy bow. 13 And I have given you a land for which ye did not labour, and [e] cities which ye built not, and ye dwell in them; of the vineyards and oliveyards which ye planted not do ye eat. 14 [f] Now therefore fear the LORD, and serve him in [g] sincerity and in truth: and [h] put away the gods which your fathers served on the other side of the flood, and [i] in Egypt; and

---

[n] Exod. 12. 37, 51.——[o] Exod. 14. 2.——[p] Exod. 14. 9.——[q] Exod. 14. 10.——[r] Exod. 14. 20.——[s] Exod. 14. 27, 28.——[t] Deut. 4. 34; 29. 2.——[u] Chap. 5. 6.——[v] Num. 21. 21, 33; Deut. 2. 32; 3. 1.——[w] See Judges 11. 25.——[x] Num. 22. 5; Deut. 23. 4.——[y] Deut. 23. 5.——[z] Num. 23. 11, 20; 24. 10.——[a] Chap. 3. 14, 17; 4. 10–12.

[b] Chap. 6. 1; 10. 1; 11. 1.——[c] Exod. 23. 28; Deut. 7. 20.——[d] Psa. 44. 3, 6.——[e] Deut. 6. 10, 11; chap. 11. 13.——[f] Deut. 10. 12; 1 Sam. 12. 24.——[g] Gen. 17. 1; 20. 5; Deut. 18. 13; Psa. 119. 1; 2 Corinthians 1. 12; Ephesians 6. 24.——[h] Verses 2, 23; Leviticus 17. 7; Ezekiel 20. 18.——[i] Ezekiel 20. 7, 8; 23. 3.

---

ing a continuous life, so that the word **you** does not refer to the Hebrews then alive, as the term *fathers* in the next verse sufficiently indicates.

7. **Ye dwelt in the wilderness**—This was true of the adults of the nation, many of whom were born there. Joshua gives no hint of the painful cause of their long sojourn in the wilderness.

8. **Amorites**—Chap. ii, 10, note. **The other side Jordan,** here means, east of the Jordan.

9. **Balak,** king of the Moabites, wished to injure and destroy Israel, but there is no account of an actual attack by him. Num. xxiii, xxiv; Judges xi, 25.

10. **I delivered you out of his hand**—Balak's hand. He designed to harm by Balaam's curses; but God, in a manner wholly miraculous, and not in harmony with his usual dealings with free agents, interposed, and changed his imprecations to benedictions. This constrained act did not keep Balaam from suffering a violent death while acting with the Midianites against Israel. Num. xxxi, 8.

11. **The men of Jericho**—Heb., *lords* or *property-holders.* **Fought—**

No active warfare is intended, but a standing on the defensive, with closed gates.

12. **And I sent the hornet before you**—The figurative interpretation of the hornet makes it a vivid metaphor for enemies armed with fearful weapons, or for pungent and stinging terrors. But we are inclined to the literal interpretation, which was evidently held by the author of the *Wisdom of Solomon,* (chap. xii, 8,) that a species of wasp, which swarms in warm climates, became an intolerable plague, and drove many of the Canaanites from their land. The ancient historians Pliny, Justin, and Ælian recount instances in which whole tribes have been driven away by frogs, mice, wasps, and other small animals. **Not with thy sword**—Not with weapons only, but with divine help. The purpose of this review of providential interpositions in behalf of the Hebrews is to awaken emotions of gratitude, and to secure perfect holiness and obedience to the divine law. This duty the dying chieftain now proceeds to enforce.

[14. **Put away the gods which your fathers served**—Many expositors hold that these words do not nec-

serve ye the LORD. **15** And if it seem evil unto you to serve the LORD, *k* choose you this day whom ye will serve; whether *l* the gods which your fathers served that *were* on the other side of the flood, or *m* the gods of the Amorites, in whose land ye dwell: *n* but as for me and my house, we will serve the LORD. **16** And the people answered and said, God forbid that we should forsake the LORD, to serve other gods; **17** For the LORD our God, *o* he *it is* that brought us

up and our fathers out of the land of Egypt, from the house of bondage, and which did those great signs in our sight, and preserved us in all the way wherein we went, and among all the people through whom we passed: **18** And the LORD drave out from before us all the people, even the Amorites which dwelt in the land: *therefore* *p* will we also serve the LORD; for he *is* our God. **19** And Joshua said unto the people, *q* Ye cannot serve the LORD: for he *is* a

---

k See Ruth 1. 15; 1 Kings 18. 21; Ezek. 20. 39; John 6. 67.——*l* Verse 14.——*m* Exod. 23. 24, 32,33; 34. 15; Deut. 13. 7; 29. 18; Judges 6. 10.

n Gen. 18. 19.——*o* Exod. 19. 4; Deut. 32. 11, 12; Isa. 46. 4; 63. 7, 14; Amos 2. 9, 10.——*p* Exod. 10. 2; 15. 2; Psa. 116. 16.——*q* Matt. 6. 24.

---

essarily imply the actual possession of idols by the people, but rather a tendency to idolatry, which was ever-too painfully prominent in Israel until after the Babylonish exile. The spirit of the exhortation is, according to this view, well conveyed by Bush: "Keep away, renounce, repudiate, have nothing to do with, idolatry of any sort; being equivalent to a charge to preserve themselves pure from a contagion to which they were peculiarly liable." Subsequent history shows how they failed. But it is scarcely supposable, that if Joshua meant to warn them merely against tendencies to idolatry he would have used the words here employed, and those still stronger ones, in verse 23, *Put away the strange gods which are among you*—the very words used by Jacob when his household gave up their strange gods, and he buried them at Shechem. Gen. xxxv, 2. Better, then, to understand that many of the Hebrews had still in their houses teraphim—the gods which the ancient fathers worshipped beyond the Euphrates. Laban had them in his family, (Gen. xxx, 19,) and Rachel carried them off, and they were probably the strange gods buried at Shechem. Gen. xxxv, 2–4. We again meet with them in the days of the Judges, (Judges xvii, 5, 18, 20,) and in the time of David, and even in his house, (1 Sam. xix, 13:) and also in the time of Josiah, who tried to put them away. 2 Kings xxiii, 24. It is therefore by no means improbable that among many families in Israel these teraphim were zealously kept, and

Joshua, knowing the fact and the danger of it, called this assembly and especially urged this matter, in order to abolish, if possible, this evil.

Though the fathers beyond the Euphrates seem to have worshipped or **served** these teraphim as gods, there is no sure evidence that they were ever worshipped as gods in Israel. But they were images more or less associated with a false worship, and therefore dangerous to the religion of the Hebrews. **In Egypt**—The fathers had carried these teraphim in their families to Egypt, and during all their captivity they had not lost sight of them. Comp. Ezek. xx, 7, 8.]

15. **Choose you this day** — "Joshua releases them from obligation, that, like free men, and of their own accord, they may honestly decide what god they will serve. Liberty of choice is granted to them in order that they might not afterwards plead that they were compelled."—*Keil.* Joshua assumes an important truth—man cannot be godless; if he repudiates the true God, he will fall under the baleful influence of some false religion. He cannot divest himself of his religious nature. Jehovah will not share with any idol the worship of his people; every god must be dethroned before he will reign in their hearts.

19. **Ye cannot serve the Lord**— Joshua utters these discouraging words, based on the waywardness of the people's hearts, to draw out from them the expression of strong purpose to serve Jehovah. Thereby he elicits their energetic **We will,** in verse 21, and

hnly God; he *is* *a jealous God; 'he will not forgive your transgressions nor your sins. **20** "If ye forsake the LORD, and serve strange gods, 'then he will turn and do you hurt, and consume you, after that he hath done you good. **21** And the people said unto Joshua, Nay; but we will serve the LORD. **22** And Joshua said unto the people, Ye *are* witnesses against yourselves that "ye have chosen you the LORD, to serve him. And they said, *We are* witnesses. **23** Now therefore *put away, *said he,* the strange gods which *are* among you, and incline your heart unto the LORD

God of Israel. **24** And the people said unto Joshua, The LORD our God will we serve, and his voice will we obey.

25 So Joshua 'made a covenant with the people that day, and set them a statute and an ordinance 'in Shechem. **26** And Joshua 'wrote these words in the book of the law of God, and took 'a great stone, and 'set it up there 'under an oak, that *was* by the sanctuary of the LORD. **27** And Joshua said unto all the people, Behold, this stone shall be 'a witness unto us; for 'it hath heard all the words of the LORD which he spake unto us: it shall be

---

r Lev. 19. 2; 1 Sam. 6. 20; Psa. 99. 5, 9; Isa. 5. 16.——*s* Ex. 20. 5.——*t* Ex. 23. 21.——*u* 1 Chron. 28. 9; 2 Chron. 15. 2; Ezra 8. 22; Isa. 1. 28; 65. 11, 12; Jer. 17. 13.——*v* Chap. 23. 15; Isa. 63. 10; Acts 7. 42.——*w* Psa. 119. 173.——*x* Verse 14; Gen. 35. 2; Judges 10. 19; 1 Sam. 7. 3.

y See Exodus 15. 25; 2 Kings 11. 17.——*z* Verse 26.——*a* Deuteronomy 31. 24.——*b* See Judges 9.6. ——*c* See Genesis 28. 18; chapter 4. 3.——*d* Genomy 31. 19, 21, 26; chapter 22. 27, 28, 34.——*e* See Genesis 31. 48, 52; Deuteronomy *f* Deuteronomy 32. 1.

---

their self-pledging witness in verse 22. **He is a jealous God**—He demands, like a husband, the undivided affection and service of the people who have avowed their fidelity to him. The word **jealous,** as applied to God, involves evident anthropomorphism. **He will not forgive**—This seems to represent God as implacable, in direct contradiction to that wonderful revelation of his attributes made to Moses in Exod. xxxiv, 7, as "forgiving iniquity, and transgression, and sin." But the same revelation declares that he will by no means clear the guilty. The explanation is, that while God is forgiving to the truly penitent through the blood of sprinkling, he vigorously punishes all incorrigible sinners.

20. Then he will turn—He will alter his attitude toward you. Strictly speaking, God is unchangeable. He is always toward the wicked a consuming fire. When a man changes from righteous to wicked he runs into this consuming fire.

23. The strange gods—*The teraphim.* See note on verse 14. **Incline your heart**—By the free act of your will in the use of the power by God's grace conferred on all.

THE GREAT STONE OF WITNESS, 25–28.

25. A statute and an ordinance —This was the renewal of the law given on Sinai. imposing no new obligations.

26. **Joshua wrote these words**— A description of all that occurred at Shechem in this solemn renewal of the covenant. This was done in order that a written document might be preserved as a witness against the people should they ever transgress the divine law. This chapter contains, probably, the substance of that ancient document. **A great stone**—Which long stood a monumental witness of this solemn transaction. See Judges ix, 6. note. **Sanctuary of the Lord**— The *holy place* first consecrated by Abraham in Canaan. Gen. xii, 7. Here he built an altar and worshipped, by the tree, which was perhaps still standing in the time of Joshua. [Some understand the **sanctuary of the Lord** to mean, here, the tabernacle and ark, which had been brought from Shiloh for this occasion. Others think it refers to the spot where the ark had formerly stood. But the word rendered **sanctuary** may mean any *holy place,* and is not always used of the place where the ark was kept. In Amos vii, 13, it is applied to the place of corrupt worship at Bethel.]

27. **For it hath heard all the words**—By a striking figure the stone is spoken of as hearing. In the same sense, as a witness it would testify against their transgressions whenever their eyes should rest upon it or their thoughts revert to it. How interesting the thought that upon this very

therefore a witness unto you, lest ye deny your God. **28** So *g* Joshua let the people depart, every man unto his inheritance.

29 *h* And it came to pass after these things, that Joshua the son of Nun, the servant of the LORD, died, *being* a hundred and ten years old. **30** And they buried him in the border of his inheritance in *i* Timnath-serah, which *is* in mount Ephraim, on the north side of the hill of Gaash.

31 And *k* Israel served the LORD all the days of Joshua, and all the days of the elders that [1] overlived Joshua, and which had [1] known all the works of the LORD, that he had done for Israel. **32** And *m* the bones of Joseph, which the children of Israel brought up out of Egypt, buried they in Shechem, in a parcel of ground *n* which Jacob bought of the sons of Hamor the father of Shechem for a hundred [2] pieces of silver; and it became the inheritance of the children of Joseph. **33** And Eleazar the son of Aaron died; and they buried him in a hill *that pertained to* *o* Phinehas his son, which was given him in mount Ephraim.

---

g Judg. 2. 6.——*h* Judg. 2. 8.——*i* Chap. 19. 50; Judg. 2. 9.——*k* Judg. 2. 7.——1 Heb. *prolonged their days after Joshua.*

l See Deut. 11. 2; 31. 13.——*m* Gen. 50. 25; Exod. 13. 19.——*n* Gen. 33. 19.——2 Or, *lambs.*——*o* Exod. 6. 25; Judges 20. 28.

---

spot, centuries afterwards, stood THE STONE, THE CORNER STONE, THE TRUE AND FAITHFUL WITNESS. Says Augustine on this passage, "By this stone he certainly signified HIM who was the rock of offence to the unbelieving Jews, and was made the Head of the corner."

JOSHUA'S DEATH AND BURIAL, 29, 30.

[**29. Joshua .... died**— Probably soon after the events just related above. It is noticeable that no mention is made of Israel's weeping for Joshua, as they did for Moses. Comp. Deut. xxxiv, 8. In chapter i, 1, Moses is called *the servant of the Lord;* here that title is given to Joshua. He who was then only *Moses' minister*, attained at length the office of his master, and became, like him, **the servant of the Lord. A hundred and ten years old**—Just the age of Joseph when he died. Gen. l, 26.]

30. **Timnath-serah**— See note on chap. xix, 50. The LXX here add the following legend of the stone knives: "They deposited with him there, in the tomb in which they buried him, the stone knives with which he circumcised the children of Israel in Gilgal, when he had led them out of Egypt according as the Lord commanded. And there they are unto the present day." See also on chap. xxi, 42.

CONCLUDING STATEMENTS, 31–33.

[31. **All the days of the elders that overlived Joshua**—So the holy life and example of a great and good man exerts an influence after he is gone. Though dead he yet speaks, and the surviving generation feels his power.]

32. **The bones of Joseph...buried they**—Since the Hebrew has no pluperfect for the accurate expression of time, this may justly be rendered *they had buried,* in Shechem previous to the death of Joshua, either at the first solemn convocation at that place, (viii, 30–35,) or at the second, the occasion of Joshua's valedictory to the nation. The fact is mentioned here because of its association with the spot of Joshua's last address to Israel. This burial was in obedience to the charge given by Joseph in Gen. l, 25, whose faith grasped the land of promise for his last resting place. Heb. xi, 22. [The traditional site of Joseph's tomb is marked by a little chapel at the southeastern base of Mount Ebal, and a few rods from Jacob's well. "There is nothing remarkable in the appearance of this little whited sepulchre," says Tristram, "yet there seems little reason to question the identity of the spot. It has been preserved from molestation from age to age by the common reverence in which the patriarch is held by Jew, Samaritan, Christian, and Moslem alike, while the fact of his name being the common property of all has prevented any one of them from appropriating and disfiguring by a temple the primitive simplicity of his resting place.

33. **Eleazar .... died** — Probably about the same time, (as Josephus says,) and his death and burial are

mentioned here because of their association both in time and place with those of Joshua. **In a hill**—Rather, *in Gibeah of Phinehas.* Josephus says, "His monument and sepulchre are in the city of Gabatha." Dr. Robinson inclined to locate it at the modern Jibea, about half way between Jerusalem and Shechem. This would be not far from the place of Joshua's death and burial. The presentation of the place to Phinehas was a token of Israel's high regard for him and his father.

Beautifully says Wordsworth here: "Eleazar and Joshua together make a type of the union of the priesthood and government in Christ. The types die, because they are types; but the DIVINE ANTITYPE liveth forever; to whom be all praise, and glory, and dominion, world without end."

JOSEPH'S TOMB.

About the author

I WAS BORN INTO this world in Windham, N. Y., October 5, 1824; into the kingdom of God in Wilbraham Mass., in the spring of 1842. I could never write the day of my spiritual birth, so gradually did the light dawn upon me and so lightly was the seal of my justification impressed upon my consciousness. This was a source of great trial and seasons of doubt in the first years of my Christian life. My early religious experience was variable, and for the most part consisted in

> *Sorrows and sins, and doubts and fears,*
> *A howling wilderness.*

The personality of the Holy Spirit was rather an article of faith than a joyful realization. He had breathed into me life, but not the more abundant life. In a sense I was free; free from the guilt and dominion of sin, but not from strong inward tendencies thereto, which seemed to be a part of my nature. In my early ministry I believed in the possibility of entire sanctification in this life instantaneously wrought. I sought quite earnestly at times, but failed to find anything more than transient uplifts from the dead level. One of these, in 1852, was so marked that it delivered me from doubt of the question of regeneration. These uplifts all came while earnestly struggling after entire sanctification as a distinct blessing. But when I embraced the theory that this work is gradual, and not instantaneous, these blessed uplifts ceased. For, seeing no definite line to be crossed, my faith ceased to put forth its strongest energies. In this condition, a period of fifteen years, I became exceedingly dissatisfied and hungry. God had something better for me. I was led by the study of the promised Paraclete to see that He signified far more than I had realized in the new birth, and that a personal Pentecost was awaiting me. I sought in downright earnestness. Then the Spirit uncovered to my gaze the evil still lurking in my nature; the mixed motives with which I had preached, often preferring the honor which comes from men to that which comes from God.

I was then led to seek the conscious and joyful presence of the Comforter in my heart. I took the promise, "Verily, verily, I say unto you, whatsoever ye shall ask the Father in my name, he will give it you." The "verily" had to me all the strength of an oath. I then wrote my own name in the promise to be sure that I included myself. Then, writing underneath these words, "Today is the day of salvation," I found that my faith had three points to master- - (1) *the Comforter*, (2) *for me*, (3) *now*. Upon the promise I ventured with an act of appropriating faith, claiming the Comforter as my right in the name of Jesus.

I then ran over in my mind the great facts in Christ's life, especially dwelling upon Gethsemane and Calvary, His ascension, priesthood, and all-atoning sacrifice. Suddenly I became conscious of a mysterious power exerting itself upon my sensibilities. My physical sensations, though not of a nervous temperament, in good health, alone, and calm, were indescribable, as if an electric current were passing through my body with painless shocks, melting my whole being into a fiery stream of love. The Son of God stood before my spiritual eye in all His loveliness. This was November 17, 1870, the day most memorable to me. Reputation, friends, family, property, everything disappeared, eclipsed by the brightness of His manifestation. He seemed to say, "I have come to stay." Yet there was no uttered word, no phantasm or image. It was not a trance or vision. The affections were best described as "the love of God shed abroad in the heart by the Holy Ghost." I was more certain that God loved me than I was of the existence of the solid earth and of the shining sun. I intuitively apprehended Christ. This certainty has lost none of its strength and sweetness after the lapse of more than seventeen years. Yea, it has become more real and blissful.

I did not at first realize that this was entire sanctification. The positive part of my experience had eclipsed the negative, the elimination of the sin principle by the cleansing power of the Paraclete. It has always seemed to me that this was the inferior part of the great blessing of the incoming and abiding of the whole Trinity. (John 14:23.)

After seventeen years of life's varied experiences, in sickness and in health, in tests of exceeding severity, there has come up out of the depths of neither my conscious nor unconscious being anything bearing the ugly features of sin, the willful transgression of the known law of God. All this time Satan's fiery darts have been thickly flying, but they have fallen harmless upon the invisible shield of faith in Jesus Christ. As to the future, "I am persuaded that He is able to keep my deposit until that day."

In regard to the process of becoming established in holiness, I find this to be God's open secret — "to walk by the same rule and to mind the same thing" (Philippians 3:16). The rule is, faith in Christ ever increasing in strength; the heart being fertilized with the elements of faith, a knowledge of the Holy Scriptures, the conscience being trained to avoid not merely sinful and doubtful acts, but also those whose moral quality is beyond the reach of all ethical rules, and known to be evil only by their effect in dimming the manifestation of Christ within. The rule of life, I find, must be sufficiently delicate to exclude those acts which bring the least blur over the spiritual eye. (Hebrews 5:14.)

As another indispensable I have found the disposition to confess Christ in His uttermost salvation. The words which the Spirit of inspiration teaches in the Holy scriptures are, after all, the most appropriate vehicle for the expression of the wonderful work of God in perfecting holiness.

I testify that it is possible for believers to be so filled with the Holy Ghost that they can live many years on the earth conscious every day of a fitness for the inheritance of the saints in light, and of no shrinking back, because of a felt need of further inward cleansing, from an instant translation into the society of the holy angels and into the presence of the holy God. I have the evidence that my love is perfected in the fact that I have boldness in view of the Day of Judgment. (1 John 4:17, 18.)

Yet I am conscious of errors, ignorances, infirmities and defects, which, though consistent with perfect loyalty and love to God, need, and by faith receive, every moment, the merit of Christ's death. In other words, the ground of my standing before God is neither perfect rectitude in the past nor a faultless present service, but the divine mercy as administered through Jesus Christ. Hence I daily pray, "Forgive us our debts."

—Daniel Steele,
Boston, March, 1888
(Adapted from *Forty Witnesses*)

<u>Buy your books at 40% off the retail price!</u>
Members of Schmul's Wesleyan Book Club buy these outstanding books at
40% off the retail price!
In addition, buy any book in our warehouse, already on our extensive list of published
titles, at 40% off!
Act now!
Join Schmul's Wesleyan Book Club by calling us toll-free
800-S$_7$P$_7$B$_2$O$_6$O$_6$K$_5$S$_7$
Put a discount Christian bookstore right in your own mailbox.